HARVARD ORIENTAL SERIES
Edited by MICHAEL WITZEL

VOLUME 72

# The Bhaikṣukī Manuscript of the *Candrālaṃkāra*

## Study, Script Tables, and Facsimile Edition

DRAGOMIR DIMITROV

PUBLISHED BY
THE HARVARD ORIENTAL SERIES
THE DEPARTMENT OF SANSKRIT AND INDIAN STUDIES
HARVARD UNIVERSITY

DISTRIBUTED BY
HARVARD UNIVERSITY PRESS
CAMBRIDGE, MASSACHUSETTS
LONDON, ENGLAND

2010

Printed in the United States of America



For information write to Editor, Harvard Oriental Series,
Department of Sanskrit and Indian Studies,
1 Bow Street, Cambridge MA 02138, USA
617-495 3295; email: witzel@fas.harvard.edu

Library of Congress Cataloguing in Publication Data

(Harvard Oriental Series; v. 72)
ISBN 978-0-674-05138-6
I. Dragomir Dimitrov 1973-
II. Title: The Bhaikṣukī Manuscript of the Candrālaṃkāra : Study, Script Tables, and Facsimile Edition
III. Series: Harvard Oriental Series; 72

CIP

*For Diana and Dario*
*in the hope that the magic will never be deciphered*

## CONTENTS


List of Illustrations ix
Abbreviations x
Acknowledgements xi

CHAPTER ONE **Introduction** 1

1.1 The Discovery of the Bhaikṣukī script 3
1.2 The Sindhura Script 6
1.3 Preliminary Analysis of the Candrālaṃkāra Manuscript 9
1.4 Inscriptions in the Bhaikṣukī Script 12
1.5 Manuscripts in the Bhaikṣukī Script 15

1.5.1 The Cambridge portion of the *Candrālaṃkāra* 15
1.5.2 The Kathmandu portion of the *Candrālaṃkāra* 15
1.5.3 The *codex unicus* of the *Candrālaṃkāra* 17
1.5.4 The manuscripts of the *Abhidharmasamuccayakārikā* and the *Maṇicūḍajātaka* 19

CHAPTER TWO **The Candrālaṃkāra and Its Manuscript** 23

2.1 The Candrālaṃkāra 25

2.1.1 A commentary on Ratnamati's *Cāndravyākaraṇapañjikā* 25
2.1.2 The author of the *Candrālaṃkāra* 31
2.1.3 Quotations from the *Candrālaṃkāra* 38
2.1.4 The title of Sāriputta's commentary 40
2.1.5 The last stanza in the *Candrālaṃkāra* manuscript 42
2.1.6 The fate of the *Candrālaṃkāra* manuscript 47

2.2 Further Traces of the Bhaikṣukī Script in Tibet 50
2.3 Letter-Numerals in the Bhaikṣukī Script 53
2.4 The Order of the Folios of the Candrālaṃkāra Manuscript 61

2.4.1 Concordance to the Cambridge microfilm copy 64
2.4.2 Concordance to the Stony Brook microfiche copy 65
2.4.3 The original order of the folios 66

CHAPTER THREE **Script Tables** 71

3.1 Tables of the Bhaikṣukī Script 73

3.1.1 Basic letters 75
3.1.1.1 *Initial vowels* 75
3.1.1.2 *Consonants* 75
3.1.2 Conjunct consonants 76
3.1.2.1 *Conjuncts with a following velar stop* 76
3.1.2.2 *Conjuncts with a following palatal stop* 76
3.1.2.3 *Conjuncts with a following retroflex stop* 77
3.1.2.4 *Conjuncts with a following dental stop* 77
3.1.2.5 *Conjuncts with a following labial stop* 79
3.1.2.6 *Conjuncts with a following nasal* 80
3.1.2.7 *Conjuncts with a following semi-vowel* 81
3.1.2.8 *Conjuncts with a following sibilant* 83
3.1.2.9 *Conjuncts with a fricative -h-* 84
3.1.2.10 *Conjuncts with a geminate* 84
3.1.3 Diacritic vowels 85
3.1.4 Anusvāra, visarga, avagraha, virāma, and other symbols 89
3.1.5 Similar characters 90
3.1.6 Characters in alphabetical order 92

3.2 Palaeographic peculiarities 117

3.2.1 Distinction between *ṛ* and *ra* 117
3.2.2 The geminate *gg* 117
3.2.3 Gemination after *r* 118
3.2.4 Confusion of *ṛ* and *ri* 118
3.2.5 Initial *ī* 118
3.2.6 Differentiation of *b* and *v* 118
3.2.7 Interchange of sibilants 118
3.2.8 Confusion of *kṣ* and *kh* 118
3.2.9 Final consonant 119

3.3 Conclusion 119

APPENDIX: Facsimile Edition of the Candrālaṃkāra Manuscript 121
BIBLIOGRAPHY 181
INDEX 193

## LIST OF ILLUSTRATIONS

### FIGURES

1. Excerpt from fol. $9^{II}a^{3}$ of the Bhaikṣukī manuscript of the *Candrālaṃkāra* [Cambridge University Library, MS Or. 1278] *4*
2. Cecil Bendall (1.7.1856–13.3.1906) [Source: LEUMANN 1909, p. 61] *5*
3. The "Seendoohee Letter" of Brian Houghton Hodgson (1800–1896) [Source: HODGSON 1828, plate 3, after p. 420] *8*
4. Bruno Liebich (7.1.1862–4.7.1939) [Source: An original photograph from 1907 taken in the E. Walsleben photo studio in Breslau, now kept in the Library of the German Oriental Society in Halle] *11*
5. The Bhaikṣukī inscription from Gayā [Source: BANERJI 1933, plate LXVI (c)] *14*
6. Fol. 2b (left part) of the Bhaikṣukī manuscript of the *Maṇicūḍajātaka* [Source: A film kept in the Istituto Italiano per l'Africa e l'Oriente in Rome, Italy] *22*
7. Terracotta panel from the Somapura Mahāvihāra *49*
8. Fol. 119b (left part) of a manuscript of the *Cāndravyākaraṇapañjikā* [Source: A microfilm copy kept in the University Library in Göttingen, Xc 14/69, image xc_14_69_09_B.tif, leaf 6] *60*
9. A brass image of Buddha from Gayā [Source: BANERJI 1933, plate LXVI (c)] *70*

- Reproduction of Rudyard KIPLING's illustration to the story "How the Alphabet was Made" from his *Just so Stories for Little Children* (New York 1902), pp. 140–141. *120*

### MAP

1. Sites of inscriptions and manuscripts in the Bhaikṣukī script, and other places where this script has reportedly been used. *52*

## ABBREVIATIONS

| | |
|---|---|
| AD | *Anno Domini* |
| Cān. | Candragomin's *Cāndravyākaraṇa* |
| CānV. | *Cāndravṛtti* |
| col. | column |
| Dhātup. | *Dhātupāṭha* |
| exp(s). | exposure(s) |
| fol(s). | folio(s) |
| IASWR | Institute for Advanced Studies of World Religions |
| i.o. | instead of |
| MS | manuscript |
| NGMCP | Nepalese-German Manuscript Cataloguing Project |
| NGMPP | Nepal-German Manuscript Preservation Project |
| Pāṇ. | Pāṇini's *Aṣṭādhyāyī* |
| Skt. | Sanskrit |
| Tib. | Tibetan |

# ACKNOWLEDGMENTS

The Bhaikṣukī manuscript of the *Candrālaṃkāra* is in all respects a truly unique codex. It is by far the most extensive specimen among only few other documents written in the peculiar script known in the West under the even more peculiar name of 'Arrow-headed script' or 'Pfeilspitzenschrift', as it is called in German. This script which is usually referred to in India by the name of Bhaikṣukī was used mostly, if not exclusively, by a sect of Buddhist monks, especially in the eleventh and the twelfth centuries. The remarkable manuscript published here contains portions of a grammatical text which until recently was considered to have been irretrievably lost. Already shortly after its completion, this codex set out on a long and precipitous journey which was going to last for many centuries. By some unexpected turns of fate, during the past eight hundred years different locations have come to play a more or less significant role in the history of the *Candrālaṃkāra* manuscript, and people from various parts of the world have become involved in its preservation and study.

It can be hardly surprising then that the present publication dedicated to this intriguing document would not have been possible without the help of many individuals and institutions from across the globe. To all of them I would like to express here my sincere gratitude.

First, I am very grateful to Professor Michael Hahn (Marburg) who gave me the opportunity to work for the ARROW-HEADED SCRIPT PROJECT from March 2007 until February 2008. I also thank Dr Albrecht Hanisch (Kathmandu) for his support in the initial stage of the project when he placed at my disposal his "Vorarbeiten", thus facilitating my own work on the *Candrālaṃkāra* manuscript.

Bhikkhu Pāsādika (Bad Arolsen), who has always been very supportive in my endeavours, was so kind to read a preliminary version of this book. I owe him heartfelt thanks for his corrections, suggestions, and inspiration.

Dr Madhuvajra Vajrācārya (Kathmandu) merits special thanks for allowing me to consult the title list of his father's manuscript collection, and also for his efforts in searching for a portion of the *Candrālaṃkāra* manuscript in his house in Kathmandu.

I am moreover deeply grateful to my friend Hubert de Cleer (Kathmandu) who was able to procure the most reliable and up-to-date information concerning the Kathmandu portion of the manuscript.

I am thankful to Professor Thomas Oberlies (Göttingen) for his keen interest in my research and especially for unselfishly giving me access to manuscript materials which turned out to be very useful in the course of my work.

Dr Mirella Lingorska (Tübingen) was always very helpful and quick in procuring for me books and articles missing in Marburg.

Dr Anne Peters (Göttingen) and Dr Thomas Frasch (Manchester) kindly helped me with my queries concerning some Burmese sources used in this publication.

Dr Craig Jamieson (Cambridge) supported my work at the Cambridge University Library, and Les Goodey LBIPP (Cambridge) prepared with professional precision and care superb images of the *Candrālaṃkāra* portion kept in this library.

I am also indebted to a number of other colleagues and friends whose help I am glad to acknowledge. I may express my gratitude to Dr Diwakar Acharya (Kyoto), Professor Rahul Peter Das (Leipzig), Dr Abhijit Ghosh (Calcutta), Dr Reinhold Grünendahl (Göttingen), Navraj Gurung (Kathmandu), Dr Gergely Hidas (Budapest), Tobias May (Bloomington), Andrew More (Toronto), Professor Mahesh Raj Pant (Kathmandu), Professor Francesco Sferra (Naples), Iain Sinclair (Hamburg), Dr Martin Straube (Marburg), and Dhammananda Thammannawe (Marburg).

Special thanks are due to Professor Jürgen Hanneder (Marburg), the Head of the Department of Indology and Tibetology at the University of Marburg, who promptly secured the necessary additional funds for the purchase of the expensive colour images of the Cambridge portion of the *Candrālaṃkāra* manuscript.

My work would not have come to fruition without the financial assistance of the German Research Foundation (DFG) which funded the ARROW-HEADED SCRIPT PROJECT from its inception in October 2004 until its end in February 2008. I am thus deeply grateful to all individuals at the DFG concerned with this Project.

Last but not least, I would like to express my humble gratitude to Professor Michael Witzel (Harvard) who most graciously enabled the publication of this volume in the *Harvard Oriental Series*.

Parallel to my work on the Bhaikṣukī manuscript I also had the wonderful opportunity to engage myself with the decipherment of the "Runic magic". This book is dedicated to my two close collaborators without whom there would have been no magic at all.

Marburg
December 2009

*Dragomir Dimitrov*

# CHAPTER ONE

## INTRODUCTION

## 1.1 The Discovery of the Bhaikṣukī Script

Preparations for the discovery of the Bhaikṣukī script were made in the early 1880s when at the initiative of Edward Cowell (1826–1903) his pupil Cecil Bendall (1856–1906)[1] took over the task of cataloguing a large number of Nepalese manuscripts collected by Dr Daniel Wright and brought to England from 1873 to 1876. Bendall's work resulted in his well-known *Catalogue of the Buddhist Sanskrit Manuscripts in the University Library, Cambridge*, published in 1883, when he was only 27 years old. Only a year and a half later, the young scholar had the chance to visit Nepal for the first time in his life. Although he was able to stay there for only three weeks, from November 9th to November 28th, 1884, his visit to Nepal proved exceptionally fruitful.

In his detailed account of *A Journey of Literary and Archaelogical Research in Nepal and Northern India, during the winter of 1884–5*, Bendall informs us about one of the most interesting discoveries of his journey, namely an incomplete palm-leaf manuscript written in "a hitherto unnoticed character".[2] He was able to purchase this manuscript consisting of 34 folios. Unfortunately, Bendall has not given any details about the original location of the manuscript and the circumstances under which he acquired it. In 1886, shortly after his return to Europe, at the 7th International Oriental Congress in Vienna he presented his preliminary study of the script and a brief report on the text contained in the manuscript. Bendall considered as the most peculiar characteristic of the

---

[1] In the words of a contemporary of his, Bendall was "an affectionate and loyal pupil, inheriting the gift of kindness with a special gift of setting people to work, even to the point of aggrieved surprise when he did not find them willing to follow his advice. His brain teemed with good suggestions, which burst forth almost simultaneously from his lips." (Ridding 1931, p. 466). For an obituary on Bendall see Rapson 1906, pp. 527–533; see also Leumann 1909, pp. 61–63.

[2] See Bendall 1886a, pp. 22 and 54–55.

script "the small triangle with apex uppermost placed at the top of each letter." On account of this wedge-like top with the point upwards, he suggested that "we might call the character 'point-headed' or 'arrow-headed'."[3]

*ṅgatve ca kathāṃ vipratiṣedha ity āha | itaś caikādeśād ityādi vipratiṣedhaprastāvādādai*

FIGURE 1: Excerpt from fol. $9^{II}a^{3}$ of the Bhaikṣukī manuscript of the *Candrālaṃkāra*

On the basis of BENDALL's analysis, Georg BÜHLER (1837–1898) described the script in his *Indische Palaeographie* (published in 1896) and attributed it to the so-called 'Pfeilspitzentypus'.[4] This script is also sometimes referred to by the Indian name 'Bhaikṣukī' which is mentioned in al-Bīrūnī's *Account of the Religion, Philosophy, Literature, Geography, Chronology, Astronomy, Customs, Laws and Astrology of India about A.D. 1030.* Al-Bīrūnī explicitly notes that the Bhaikṣukī script was "used in Uduṇpûr in Pûrvadeśa" and describes it as "the writing of Buddha".[5] Having acquainted himself with SACHAU's translation of al-Bīrūnī's work only shortly after it had been published, BENDALL was the first to suggest that the script named in this reference from the beginning of the eleventh century and the peculiar script observed by him are possibly identical.[6] The common

[3] BENDALL 1886b, p. 111; cf. WADDELL's "cuneiform headed character" (WADDELL 1892, p. 24).

[4] See BÜHLER 1896, p. 59 and table VI, columns XVIII–XIX.

[5] See SACHAU 1887–88, vol. I, p. 173; SACHAU has added the following comment: "Alberuni writes *Baikshuka*, probably *that of the bhikshu* or beggar-monks, *i.e.* the *śramaṇa* or Buddhistic monks. Is the *Audunpûr* mentioned by Alberuni, identical with the famous Buddhistic monastery *Udaṇḍapuri* in Magadha (?)." (SACHAU 1887–88, vol. II, p. 314). Cf. CHAKRAVARTI 1938, p. 37: "Probably by saying that this script was the writing of Buddha, al-Bīrūnī meant to say that it was usually employed by Buddhist monks – for which reason it came to be known as *Bhaikshukī* or that of the *bhikshus*."

[6] See BENDALL 1890, p. 78: "Should other specimens be found with these characteristics, one would be tempted to conjecture that it is none other than the *bhaikshukî lipi* of Albêrûnî"; cf. BÜHLER 1896, p. 59.

provenance of the written documents in this script and their date, all of them belonging most probably to the eleventh and twelfth centuries, do indeed corraborate BENDALL's cautious suggestion. For this reason, until no counterevidence is found, it seems advisable to call the script in question Bhaikṣukī and desist from using modern names such as 'Arrowheaded script' in English, 'Pfeilspitzenschrift' in German or the Indian equivalent, the 'Śaramātṛkā Lipi'.

FIGURE 2: Cecil Bendall (1.7.1856–13.3.1906)

## 1.2 The Sindhura Script

As Bendall himself indicates in one place, it may well be that Brian Houghton Hodgson (1800–1896), who stayed in Nepal from 1820 to 1843, was the first researcher to supply a specimen of the peculiar script, albeit unknowingly. In his "Notices of the Languages, Literature, and Religion of the Bauddhas of Nepal and Bhot" published in the *Asiatic Researches* as far back as 1828, Hodgson reproduced a Tibetan manuscript of a manual called *Akṣaraviśvamātra* (Tib. *Yi ge sna tshogs kyi phyi mo*) which contains sets of various Indian scripts accompanied by an interlinear Tibetan transliteration.[7] Among these scripts there is one which Hodgson rather bewilderingly called the "Seendoohee Letter" and which in fact appears to be of the same type as the Bhaikṣukī script.[8] Bendall considered the similarity between the two scripts so compelling that "[t]here can be no doubt that the original from which this was transcribed (probably with some unconscious modifications) by Hodgson's pandit must have been closely allied to our „arrow-headed" character". He noted specifically that "[t]he resemblance is very noticeable in many letters, some of them characteristic and peculiar ones [...] The curious and unique form of ç is not exactly reproduced in „Sindhuhi"; but the resemblance is striking enough to confirm a theory of near relationship."[9] As for the misnomer 'Seendoohee' or 'Sindhuhi', it is obviously based on the Tibetan appelation of the script given in the book as 'Sindhu'i yi ge'. Accordingly, the script would have had to be called just 'Sindhu'. It is, however, also possible that the Tibetan name was originally intended to

---

[7] This manuscript consists of eleven folios which Hodgson has reproduced in disorder adding three more folios which apparently belong to another manuscript. The folios appear in the following sequence: 7a, 7b; 3b, 3a; three other folios; 6b, 6a; 4b, 4a; 5b, 5a; 10a, 10b; 11a, 11b; 1b, 1a; 8a, 8b; 9b, 9a; 2a, 2b.

[8] The "Seendoohee" characters appear on fol. 3. The Tibetan letters under the dental series (*ta, tha, da, dha, na*) should of course read ཏ ཐ ད དྷ ན.

[9] Bendall 1895, p. 156.

be read as 'Sindhura', inasmuch as one syllable, namely *ra*, may have been lost through a kind of haplography.

Characters almost identical with those reproduced by HODGSON can also be found in other Tibetan sources. In his *Indian Scripts in Tibet* LOKESH CHANDRA has included a facsimile edition of two script manuals which contain Sindhura characters. The first one is a Peking xylograph of a collection compiled by Lcan luṅ Paṇḍita Ṅag dbaṅ blo bzaṅ bstan pa'i rgyal mtshan (1770–1845).[10] The second source is a manuscript of eleven folios[11] which seems to bear the same title as the manuscript reproduced by HODGSON.[12] In the xylograph the script in question is called 'Sindhu ra'i yi ge', whereas the manuscript contains the form already observed in HODGSON's source.[13]

It will certainly be interesting to find out where and how the name 'Sindhura' originated, whether it has any connection with the place of Sindh, and how the Tibetans came to know about this script. In

[10] The Sindhura characters in this xylograph are reproduced on fol. 10a (see LOKESH CHANDRA 1982, p. 30 [3]).

[11] The complete set of Sindhura characters in this manuscript is written on fol. 4a (see LOKESH CHANDRA 1982, p. 45 [4]).

[12] LOKESH CHANDRA gives the Sanskrit title as *Aksara-viśva-latra*, and cites the Tibetan title (*Yi ge sna tshogs kyi* ...) without the equivalent of the last member of the Sanskrit compound. The correct title reads undoubtedly *Akṣaraviśvamātra* (tib. *Yi ge sna tshogs kyi phyi mo*), even though palaeographically *Akṣaraviśvasānu* (tib. *Yi ge sna tshogs kyi spyi bo*) would have also been a possible reading.

[13] As far as can be judged from the facsimile, the manuscript reads *Sindhu'i yi ge*. This common reading of the manuscript reproduced by HODGSON and the one published by LOKESH CHANDRA is hardly surprising, for the two manuscipts seem in fact to represent just two different copies of one and the same manual. With the exception of the Lantsha and Vartula scripts which are missing in HODGSON's manuscript, the rest are described in the same manner and sequence in both copies. The following scripts appear in HODGSON's manuscript: Dha ri (1b), Kasmī ra (2a), Na ga ra (2b), Sindhu (3a), Rgya mtsha mtha (3b), Ma ga dha (4a), Gau la (4b), Gau ṭa (5a), Masko la (5b), Lha hu ra (6a), Ka ma ta (6b), Bukkaṃ (7a), Kha che (7b), Bal po (8a), Chag la yag gsar (8b), 'Gos lo yigs gsar (9a), 'Phags yul phal pa (9b), and Skyogs lo yig gsar (10a). The last folio contains some Chinese characters and monograms (cf. LOKESH CHANDRA 1982, p. 7).

this context one is reminded of the Sendhapa Śrāvakas who are probably identical with the Hīnayāna Buddhists of the Sāṃmitīya school said to have originally been widely spread in Sindh.[14] Since representatives of the Sāṃmitīya school beyond any doubt used the Bhaikṣukī script in the twelfth century, and the Sindhura characters bear some remarkable similarities with this script, the question arises whether 'Sindhura' and 'Bhaikṣukī' are names of one and the same script. Even if it may seem far-fetched, it can be hypothesized that 'Sindhura' or some similar form of this name was coined by the Sāṃmitīyas themselves who may have been referring to their own place of origin,[15] whereas 'Bhaikṣukī' was a name used by all the others who were pointing out the association of the peculiar script with its users, the Buddhist monks (*bhikṣus*).

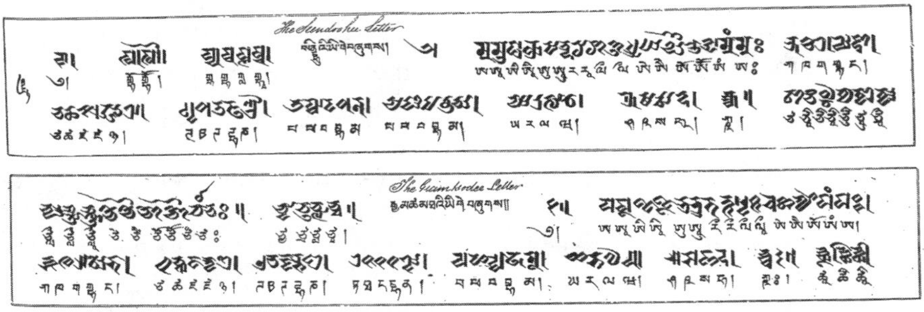

FIGURE 3: The "Seendoohee Letter" of Brian Houghton Hodgson (1800–1896)

---

[14] As SKILLING notes, "[t]he evidence of Hsüan-tsang and I-ching shows that in the 7th century the Sāmmatīyas were predominant in Sindh, and well represented at Mālava and Valabhī. […] If we derive Sendhapa from Saindhava, "belonging to Sindh", the term could refer to the Sāmmatīyas, who might have taken refuge in Magadha when Sindh fell to the Arabs, or simply have been described by the name of their "home country […]" (SKILLING 1997, pp. 106–107).

[15] OL'DENBURG notes *en passant* that it is difficult to say whether 'Sindhura', which he considered the local name ("tuzemnoe nazvanie") of the script, is related to 'Sindhavī' mentioned in an old Jain list of scripts (see OL'DENBURG 1894, p. 51; cf. WEBER 1883, pp. 220, 280 and 400 where the script is called 'Saiṃdhavî'; see SMYTH 1893, pp. 4, 28 and 77, for an English translation of the relevant passages from WEBER's work).

## 1.3 Preliminary Analysis of the Candrālaṃkāra Manuscript

Bendall's preliminary analysis of the manuscript which he had purchased in Nepal disclosed that this codex contains parts of a brief commentary on the *Cāndravyākaraṇa* or, as Kielhorn had suggested to him, a "super-commentary".[16] With the help of two sub-colophons preserved in this incomplete manuscript, the title of the text, namely *Candrālaṃkāra* ("Ornament of the Moon"), could be established. Bendall did not venture to give full account of the contents of the manuscript, however, and supplied only a few brief citations from the *Candrālaṃkāra* where some authors and titles are quoted. Bendall's initial palaeographic examination of the Bhaikṣukī manuscript of the *Candrālaṃkāra* resulted in his pioneer study published in 1886. It included a plate with the basic letters of the alphabet and a selection of *akṣaras*, mainly vocalisations of consonants, and very few conjunct letters (altogether 112 characters).[17]

In 1893 Bruno Liebich (1862–1939), arguably the best expert on the Cāndra school of grammar at that time, was able to spend a few months in London[18] where with the help of his friend, the Tibetologist Heinrich Wenzel (1855–1893), he pursued his studies on Candragomin's grammar and its Tibetan translation.[19] This fruitful collaboration came to an

---

[16] See Bendall 1886b, p. 123: "It would seem then that the work is a 'small commentary' or collection of adversaria on the *Cāndravyākaraṇa*. Professor Kielhorn, who looked through the MS. when I brought it to Vienna expressed an opinion that it was in fact a super-commentary …"

[17] See Bendall 1886b.

[18] This can be inferred from two documents kept now in the University Archive in Wrocław (call no. F 99, pp. 333 and 361). In January 1893 Liebich was awarded a scholarship (1200 mark per month) starting from April 1893. From an official letter sent by Liebich we learn that he applied for a sabbatical in the summer term of 1893.

[19] In the Library of the German Oriental Society in Halle Liebich's English workbooks from this period are preserved which contain a copy of the Tibetan text of the *Cāndravyākaraṇa* in Dbu can script written by Wenzel's hand.

abrupt end after WENZEL's premature death on June 16, 1893.[20] Most likely during his stay in London LIEBICH has had the chance to consult the *Candrālaṃkāra* manuscript which BENDALL kept in his private collection.[21] As a result of this, in 1895 LIEBICH offered a short description of the manuscript in his monograph *Das Cāndra-Vyākaraṇa*:

> Diese Handschrift enthält Buch V und VI des Candra-Alaṅkāra, ist aber am Schlusse unvollständig und weist außerdem im Innern eine Reihe von Lücken auf. Der Candra-Alaṅkāra, von dem sonst nichts bekannt oder erhalten ist, ist ein Commentar zum Cāndrasūtra. Er gehört zur Klasse der sogenannten Ṭīkā's, d. i. Commentare, die nur die schwierigen Stellen erläutern (*vishamapadavyākhyā*), im Gegensatz zu den Pañjikā's, die den Text Wort für Wort erklären (*niḥçeshapadavyākhyā*). Das erste erklärte Sūtra ist V, 1, 1, das letzte VI, 4, 46. Die Zahl der Blätter beträgt jetzt 30. Die Blätter sind von einer späteren Hand numerirt, die Ziffern geben aber nicht die richtige Reihenfolge. Kapitelschlüsse sind nur zwei erhalten; aus ihnen allein erfahren wir den Namen des Commentars, dessen Verfasser unbekannt bleibt.[22]

This brief analysis in German was followed by a brief communication in English which was published one year later in the *Indian Antiquary*:

> *Chandra-Alaṅkâra*, a *Ṭîkâ* of the *Sûtrapâṭha*, by an unknown author. The single existing fragment, referring to the fifth and sixth books, was acquired in Nêpâl by Prof. Bendall, and is now in his own possession. It is written in a very archaic alphabet, the so-called arrow-top character, similar to the South-Indian alphabets and else found in Buddhist votive inscriptions only.[23]

From BENDALL's publications and LIEBICH's brief analysis it is clear that both scholars were very quick to learn reading the newly discovered

---

[20] See LIEBICH 1896b for an obituary on Heinrich WENZEL (1855–1893).

[21] BENDALL was at that time Professor of Sanskrit at the University College, London.

[22] LIEBICH 1895, pp. 40–41.

[23] LIEBICH 1896a, p. 103.

Bhaikṣukī script. However, after LIEBICH had published his analysis of the manuscript in 1895, and one year later BÜHLER had reproduced 73 characters from BENDALL's article in his *Indische Palaeographie*, the *Candrālaṃkāra* manuscript and its script fell into almost complete oblivion. For a long time scholars neglected this extremely valuable manuscript.

FIGURE 4: Bruno Liebich (7.1.1862–4.7.1939)

## 1.4 Inscriptions in the Bhaikṣukī Script

Since the beginning of the twentieth century the rare script was no longer being studied, and only a handful of epigraphists were able to read the few Bhaikṣukī inscriptions discovered in Northern India and Burma. So far only eleven brief inscriptions have been unearthed. They contain altogether thirty-four lines of text, part of which, including the well-known Buddhist formula *ye dhammā*, etc., is common to most of them. The eleven Bhaikṣukī inscriptions are:

1. An inscription from Gayā, Calcutta Museum, inscribed on the base plate of a brass image of Buddha (2½ lines).[24]
2. An inscription from Uren, in the western part of the Monghyr District of Bihar, by the side of the railway line between the Kiul and Kajra stations, about 7 miles from Kiul and 2½ miles from Kajra; inscribed on a sculptured stone base (2 lines).[25]
3. An inscription from Badhauli, about 5 miles southwest of Uren; inscribed on a sculptured stone base (2 lines).[26]
4. A rock-cut inscription from Gurdih, 10 miles southwest of Uren and opposite Husainpur on the Kiul river.[27]

---

[24] Published; see Bendall 1890, pp. 77–78, Bendall 1895, pp. 153–156, and Banerji 1914, pp. 153–156. Cf. Chakravarti 1938, p. 37, note 1: "[...] the image is stated to have belonged to James Robinson, C. E. of Gayā. The same image later on seems to have passed into the possession of Mr. Saurindra Mohan Sinha of Bhāgalpur who presented it to the Museum of the Baṅgīya Sāhitya Parishad, where it is now preserved." John Faithfull Fleet (1847–1917) was the first scholar who examined this inscription (see Fleet 1888, p. 19, note 1). As for the image itself, see Banerji 1933, p. 50 and plate LXVI (c), and Huntington 1984, pp. 148–149.

[25] Published; see Waddell 1892, p. 17 and plate IV, no. 1; Bendall 1895, p. 153 and plate 1, no. 2; Sircar 1958, p. 224, Inscription No. 2.

[26] Published; see Waddell 1892, p. 17 and plate IV, no. 2; Bendall 1895, p. 153 and plate 1, no. 3; Sircar 1958, p. 224, Inscription No. 3.

[27] See Waddell 1892, p. 17, plate IV, no. 4; Bendall 1895, p. 154: "an eye-copy of a longer inscription"; Waddell 1892, p. 17: "the letters of the rock cut wedge-headed inscription when divested of their cuneiform appendages are almost Aśoka-like".

5. An inscription from Kara, about 5 miles northeast from Sirathu and 41 miles from Allahābād; inscribed on a plate (3½ lines).[28]
6. An inscription from Uren, inscribed on a broken Buddhist image at the Śiva-sthāna of the village (1 line, only a few *akṣaras* are visible).[29]
7. An inscription from Uren, inscribed on the base of a mutilated Buddhist image (4 lines).[30]
8. An inscription from Malda, B. R. Sen Museum, West Bengal; inscribed on the pedestal of an image of Avalokiteśvara Lokanātha (4 lines).[31]
9. An inscription from Ghoshīkuṇḍī near Kiul in the Monghyr District of Bihar, Indian Museum, Calcutta; inscribed on the pedestal of an image of Jambhala (9 lines, "may perhaps be assigned to c. 1249 A.D.").[32]
10. An inscription from Kajra, inscribed on the lower part of a sculptured stone slab (2 lines, fragmentary).[33]
11. An inscription on a bronze Buddha image from the Pagoda of Shinma-taung in Burma.[34]

As luck would have it, on his way back from Nepal, in the Calcutta Museum BENDALL himself found a sculpture of Buddha with a short

---

[28] Published; see CHAKRAVARTI 1938, pp. 37–39.

[29] See SIRCAR 1958, p. 222.

[30] Published; see SIRCAR 1958, p. 224, Inscription No. 1 and plate A.

[31] Published; see SIRCAR 1958, pp. 224–226, plate B; cf. SKILLING 1997, p. 112, note 114.

[32] Published; see SIRCAR 1966, pp. 79–84, plate 1; FOUCHER 1900, pp. 123–127 and fig. 20, p. 124; cf. BANERJI 1933, p. 92: "It is really a specimen of the twelth (*sic*) century A.D. (I. M. No. 4571)", see p. 39 and plate LXVI (c).

[33] Published; see SIRCAR 1966, p. 84 and plate 2; NARASIMHASWAMI 1964, p. 64, Sl. No. B 130: "Kājrā.–Lower portion of a broken sculptured slab embedded into a pipal tree near the Railway Station. Prakrit, Bhaikshukī. Fragmentary. Contains parts of the Buddhist formula *Bhagavō āvasō*, etc. and *yē dharmā*, etc."

[34] Published; see SIRCAR 1977, pp. 110–111. SIRCAR's analysis is based on a "photograph of an inscription in four lines which appear to be engraved underneath the bottom-sheet of a small Buddha image found from the ruined Pagoda on a hill." This photograph was sent to SIRCAR by the conservator in charge of the Pagan Branch of the Archaeological Department, Burma. The site of the discovery is apparently an old pagoda which was raised on top of the Shinmadaung hill near Pakhangyi, north of Pakkoku and not far from Pagan (this place in mentioned in LUCE 1969, p. 92).

inscription (no. 1 above) in the same peculiar script as the one he had discovered just a few weeks earlier in Kathmandu. Later BENDALL was able to consult three more inscriptions in the Bhaikṣukī script (nos. 2–4) found by Lawrence Austin WADDELL in 1892. On the grounds of "some remarkable archaisms, and above all several peculiar forms not easy to parallel amongst the alphabets descended from Southern Açoka, which lead one to regard them as survivals of some very early form of writing"[35], he dated these inscriptions "between the $7^{th}$ and $10^{th}$ centuries A.D."[36] The remaining seven inscriptions (nos. 5–11) were discovered later. They were studied by Indian scholars, most notably by Dinesh Chandra SIRCAR (1907–1984) who revised BENDALL's dating and suggested to assign the inscriptions to "a date between the ninth and the twelfth century, preferably to the latter half of this period."[37]

FIGURE 5: The Bhaikṣukī inscription from Gayā

[35] BENDALL 1886, p. 112.

[36] BENDALL 1895, p. 155.

[37] SIRCAR 1958, p. 223. For another overview of the Bhaikṣukī inscriptions see GUPTA 1985, pp. 108–118; the hypothesis about the Bhaikṣukī script being "a mystic script" (GUPTA 1985) or a "secret alphabet used by the Buddhist monks of Magadha", as BANERJI shortly describes it (see BANERJI 1933, p. 92), is in the light of the later discoveries hardly tenable.

## 1.5 MANUSCRIPTS IN THE BHAIKṢUKĪ SCRIPT

It is unfortunate that for a long time scholars limited themselves to the scant epigraphical corpus and neglected altogether the few, though very important manuscript materials in the Bhaikṣukī script which surfaced in the course of time.

### 1.5.1 The Cambridge portion of the *Candrālaṃkāra*

The incomplete manuscript consisting of 34 palm-leaves which BENDALL brought from Nepal to England was the first document in the Bhaikṣukī script to become easily available to the interested public. From a note written by a Cambridge librarian on the box in which the manuscript is placed at present, we learn that this codex was found among BENDALL's papers in December 1934. Thus, BENDALL must have kept the manuscript in his private collection, and it was transferred to its present location in the Cambridge University Library only twenty-eight years after his death.[38] The manuscript has a classmark Or. 1278 and can be consulted in the library's Manuscripts Room. There is an old master microfilm of the manuscript which is, however, incomplete with respect to one folio. Upon my request, on February 29, 2008 this precious codex was digitized by the Imaging Services staff at the Cambridge University Library and a new master microfilm was prepared.

### 1.5.2 The Kathmandu portion of the *Candrālaṃkāra*

On August 17, 1971 another manuscript portion of 23 palm-leaves written in the same script and with an identical ductus as BENDALL's portion was photographed in Kathmandu by the Institute for Advanced Studies of World Religions (IASWR; Stony Brook, USA). However, at that time nobody there was able to analyse the manuscript and read the text. In

[38] Cf. HAHN 2005, pp. 712–711.

the title list prepared by the IASWR it is just noted "Old ms. of unknown title in Khotang (?) script".[39] On the manuscript entry card it is mentioned that the manuscript was found in a "very old Vajrācārya house"; however, no further details are given as to where exactly it was located.[40] Since there are quite many old Vajrācārya houses in Kathmandu, it remained for a long time unclear in whose private collection the manuscript was actually kept. Only recently I was able to confirm that the manuscript was in possession of the prominent Nepalese Dr Mānavajra Vajrācārya. This is evident from the list of his private collection where it is entered under no. 55 in section *Kha* (*Darśanaśāstra*, *Nyāya*, *Mahāyānasūtra*): "?, tāḍapatra, 23 patra, Khoṭāṅga, ā 28 × 7, paṃ. 10, apūrṇa".

Interestingly, two folios of the same manuscript were microfilmed on June 8, 1983 at the initiative of the NEPAL-GERMAN MANUSCRIPT PRESERVATION PROJECT (NGMPP, Reel no.: E 1518/4).[41] The staff of the NGMPP was unaware of the title of the text contained in the manuscript, so on the index card it is only noted as '[Bauddhagrantha]?'. In addition, the name of the manuscript's owner, namely "M. V. Vajrācārya", is also given. It is certain that the two folios belonged to the same part of the manuscript which was already filmed almost twelve years earlier by the IASWR.[42] Furthermore, it is beyond any doubt that both the IASWR and the NGMPP filmed the material in Dr Mānavajra Vajrācārya's private house.[43] This is also substantiated by the fact that, as in the IASWR's

---

[39] See GEORGE 1975, p. 3, no. MBB-I-35.

[40] The following remarks have only been supplied: "I got this text from very old Vajrācārya house. I can't read the script of this text. This book seems very important. So I am trying to read it. If I knew some things about this book I will write again."

[41] The manuscript was entered in the NGMPP's title list as 'Bauddhagrantha' (i.e. "a Buddhist work"). In the database of the NEPALESE-GERMAN MANUSCRIPT CATALOGUING PROJECT (NGMCP) the same codex is registered under the inventory no. 6637 and is currently to be found under the title '[Bauddhagrantha](?)' (see http://134.100.72.204:3000).

[42] The two leaves filmed by the NGMPP are fols. $23^{II}$ and $75^{II}$. They were probably placed at the end in the bundle filmed by the IASWR.

[43] Thus, at least with regard to the two folios HANISCH's conclusion that since 1971 the manuscript "has suffered further fragmentation" is fortunately not correct, for these

catalogue, on the NGMPP's index card the same peculiar "Khotāṅga" script is indicated, which undoubtedly goes back to the information contained in Dr Mānavajra Vajrācārya's own title list.

It is, however, not possible to establish with certainty why only two folios were filmed by the NGMPP. Either 21 folios had disappeared mysteriously between August 1971 and June 1983, possibly soon after they were filmed by the IASWR, or for some strange reason Dr Mānavajra Vajrācārya did not allow the staff of the NGMPP, in particular Aishwaryadhar Sharma and Raju Thapa, to film all the leaves. Unfortunately, the first scenario appears now to be more probable, for during a recent check in his father's manuscript collection Dr Madhuvajra Vajrācārya was able to trace only two folios. The remaining 21 folios are thus either misplaced or no more available in their original location.

### 1.5.3 The *codex unicus* of the *Candrālaṃkāra*

The credit for reviving the interest in the *codex unicus* of the *Candrālaṃkāra* goes to Michael HAHN and Albrecht HANISCH who in 2004 gave a fresh impetus towards the study of this Bhaikṣukī manuscript.[44] The preliminary analysis of the Cambridge and the Kathmandu portions was conducted by HANISCH who confirmed HAHN's initial suggestion that these portions are probably parts of one and the same manuscript.[45] This conclusion was drawn on the basis of the sub-colophons found in both

folios are still in the hereditary house of the Vajrācārya family (see HANISCH 2006, p. 112; the same is repeated in HANISCH 2007, p. 132). The NGMPP's microfilm copy is far better in quality than the IASWR's copy, and it is all the more regrettable that the NGMPP has not had the chance to microfilm the whole material.

[44] At the start, Professor Thomas Oberlies (Göttingen) kindly provided a copy from the IASWR microfiche kept in the library of the Institute of Indian and Tibetan Studies at the University of Göttingen. From a handwritten note it is evident that this fragment was first analysed by a scholar from Göttingen, possibly Professor Gustav Roth, who discovered that the manuscript contains a commentary on the *Cāndravyākaraṇa*.

[45] See HAHN 2005, p. 709, and HANISCH 2006, p. 111. An account of HANISCH's preliminary analysis of the *Candrālaṃkāra* manuscript was published in 2007.

parts and the fact that there is no textual overlapping, as well as on account of the common appearance of the two portions of the manuscript.

Two very similar sub-colophons were found in the Kathmandu portion at the end of the commentary on the first section of the first chapter of the *Cāndravyākaraṇa* (*[Cā]ndre vyākara*$_8$+ + *[ndrāla]ṅkāranāmni ṭipyitake pratha*○*maḥ pādaḥ samāptaḥ*)[46] and in the Cambridge portion at the end of the third section of the sixth chapter (*Cāndre vyākaraṇe Candrālaṅkāranāmni ṭippitake ṣaṣṭhasyādhya:*$_6$*yasya tritīyaḥ* [!] *pādaḥ samāptaḥ*).[47] This clearly indicates that the two portions contain different parts of one and the same treatise.

In addition, by identifying and checking the *pratīkas*, i.e. the abbreviated initial syllables of the grammatical rules from the *Cāndravyākaraṇa* commented on in the text, Hanisch established that there is no obvious textual overlapping. This observation corroborated the assumption that the palm-leaves split between Cambridge and Kathmandu originally belonged together. The very similar appearance of the two portions of the manuscript with regard to their external features and the handwriting[48] further supported this hypothesis.

---

[46] Due to a damage at the left-hand side of the leaf (fol. $31^{I}$b), the first two *akṣaras* (°*ṇe Ca*°) at the beginning of line 9 cannot be seen, and of the following two *akṣaras* (°*ndrāla*°) only few traces can be discerned. The mistake in *ṭipyitake* for **ṭippitake* can be easily explained with the similarity of the two *akṣaras ppi* and *pyi*.

[47] Fol. $61^{II}$b$^{5-6}$. Apart from this, in the Kathmandu fragment two more sub-colophons are preserved: *pañcamasyādhyāya* [!] *dvitīyapādaḥ samāptaḥ* and *pañcamasya tṛtīyapādaḥ samāptaḥ* (fol. $27^{II}$b$^{1-2}$). In the Cambridge fragment the following sub-colophon can also be read: *Candrālaṅkāre pañcamo dhyāyaḥ samāptaḥ* (fol. $36^{II}$a$^{6}$).

[48] The size of the leaves of the Kathmandu fragment is 29.7 × 6.9 cm, as noted on the index card by the NGMPP, or 28 × 7 cm, as noted in Vajrācārya's title list and in the IASWR's catalogue. This corresponds to the size of the Cambridge fragment which I measured when I inspected the manuscript in the University Library in July 2007. The binding hole is to the left of the centre in the middle of a rectangular empty space which divides the text on the leaf from top to bottom in two sections, one on the left side and another one, two times longer, on the right side. The number of lines on each folio varies between 9 and 11.

A closer examination of the text leaves no doubt that the two portions in Cambridge and Kathmandu contain indeed complementary parts of a single manuscript. This is now finally proven by the fact that in seven cases the text from a folio belonging to one of the two portions continues seamlessly on a folio of the other portion. Thus, the commentary on Cān. 1.1.39 starts on a folio from the Kathmandu portion and finishes on a folio from the Cambridge portion. This is also the case with the commentary on Cān. 5.1.59, 5.2.105, and 6.1.61. With regard to the commentary on Cān. 5.1.41 and 5.2.145 we have the reverse situation: the beginning is found in Cambridge and the continuation is available in the Kathmandu portion. Similarly, there are two consecutive folios from the introductory part of the commentary, one of which is in Cambridge, whereas the other folio immediately following it has remained in Kathmandu. In all other cases the seamless transition on the next folio cannot be attested due to missing folios. It can be summarized that we have one incomplete manuscript of the *Candrālaṃkāra* of which altogether 57 folios have been preserved at two different locations.

### 1.5.4 The manuscripts of the *Abhidharmasamuccayakārikā* and the *Maṇicūḍajātaka*

Apart from the *Candrālaṃkāra* manuscript, two more manuscripts in the Bhaikṣukī script are known to exist. During a visit to the Gongkar (Goṅ dkar) monastery in Tibet in 1948, Giuseppe TUCCI (1894–1984) was fortunate to get access to two "Indian manuscripts, written on palm-leaves, from the IX$^{th}$ or X$^{th}$ century: as pristine as if they had been made by the copyist yesterday."[49] TUCCI found out that the manuscripts contain two hitherto unknown works, namely the *Abhidharmasamuccayakārikā* by Saṃghatrāta and the *Maṇicūḍajātaka* by Sarvarakṣita.[50]

---

[49] See SFERRA 2000, pp. 403–404; visit also *http://www.giuseppetucci.isiao.it*.

[50] TUCCI was already at that time obviously in a position to decipher at least the colophons of these manuscripts (cf. HANISCH 2006, p. 113 and note 18). Whether he knew and used the materials on the Bhaikṣukī script published by BENDALL and BÜHLER is not known, but certainly quite possible.

There has been some confusion whether the Italian scholar was able to purchase the originals or he was only allowed to photograph the precious material.[51] From TUCCI's own diary it is clear that he was given the chance to see the manuscripts; however, it is nowhere mentioned that he brought the originals themselves to Rome.[52] We only know for sure that TUCCI managed to take photographs of the valuable material, since the films were available in Rome for some time until they got lost after TUCCI's death. The manuscripts themselves most likely remained in Gongkar, and nothing seems to be known about their present fate.

Only a few scholars became aware of TUCCI's discovery and had access to the film material brought from Tibet. TUCCI himself had been planning to publish an edition of the *Abhidharmasamuccayakārikā* based on the Bhaikṣukī manuscript discovered in Gongkar.[53] However, this publication never appeared. TUCCI's materials on this text could not be found in his archive, and on top of this the film of the manuscript was lost.[54] Besides the short report in TUCCI's diary, all the information we have about the *Abhidharmasamuccayakārikā* manuscript is based on a lecture given by TUCCI in Japan on October 17, 1955.[55] There is also a brief

---

[51] In various publications the impression is given that TUCCI brought the manuscripts to Rome (cf. OKANO 1996, p. 18; HAHN 2005, p. 711; HANISCH 2006, pp. 110–111).

[52] See TUCCI 1956, p. 151 and note 55 on p. 179; cf. SFERRA 2000, pp. 403–404 with a new more precise translation of the relevant passage from TUCCI's original *A Lhasa E Oltre* published in 1950.

[53] See OKANO 1998, p. 15; in the first volumes of the *Serie Orientale Roma* this publication has been mentioned as a work in preparation, allegedly co-authored by Antonio GARGANO. As Professor Sferra kindly informed me in a private communication, GARGANO has actually not been involved with this publication and no related materials are known to have remained in his private library.

[54] SFERRA's recent efforts to trace the film and TUCCI's materials on the *Abhidharmasamuccayakārikā* in Rome have not yielded positive results (see SFERRA 2000, p. 405; in an e-mail sent on August 2, 2007 Professor Sferra confirmed that these materials are still untraceable).

[55] See OKANO 1998, pp. 14–15. TUCCI's lecture was published in Japanese in the *Ôtani Gakuhô* 36-1 (1956), pp. 1–16; OKANO has conveniently summarized the details about the *Abhidharmasamuccayakārikā* contained in this article. According to TUCCI's analysis, Saṃ-

note left by Edward CONZE, who was a good friend of TUCCI and appears to have consulted the photographs of the manuscript or TUCCI's announced edition of the text.[56] From CONZE's note we learn that the manuscript of the *Abhidharmasamuccayakārikā* consisted of 26 or 27 folios.

In 1964 PENSA reported that a critical edition of the *Maṇicūḍajātaka* based on the other Bhaikṣukī manuscript from Gongkar was also being prepared in Rome.[57] Whether TUCCI or some of his students did indeed start working on this is not clear. In any case, for many years scholars knew nothing about the *Maṇicūḍajātaka* manuscript, except for one short description given in TUCCI's lecture from 1955.[58] Although it was obvious that the palm-leaf manuscript comprising 12 folios contains a highly interesting composition by the great Buddhist poet Sarvarakṣita, the work remained unstudied and for a long time the film of the manuscript was considered lost. We had to wait until October 2, 1999 when SFERRA fortunately discovered the much sought-after film while he was "idly searching through a cupboard in the library" of the Istituto Italiano per l'Africa e l'Oriente.[59] This enabled HAHN, who had long been planning to study Sarvarakṣita's *Maṇicūḍajātaka*, to initiate the ARROW-HEADED SCRIPT PROJECT at the University of Marburg (Germany) in October 2004. In the first stage of this project funded by the German Research Council, HANISCH together with HAHN meticulously studied the *Maṇicūḍajātaka* manuscript, edited, analysed, and translated Sarvarakṣita's composition.[60] As already

ghatrāta's treatise consists of 550 stanzas. From OKANO's German translation of the Japanese version of the Sanskrit colophon rendered by TUCCI, it appears that the *Abhidharmasamuccayakārikā* (less probably the manuscript itself) was written in a locality called Nalendra. Whether this is the Nālendra monastery northwest of Lhasa, as OKANO assumes, or rather the Nālandā Mahāvihāra in today's Bihar remains to be clarified (cf. OKANO 1998, p. 16).

[56] See CONZE 1962, p. 281, note 7 ad II 2, I; cf. also *ibid.*, p. 124.

[57] See PENSA 1964, p. 47.

[58] See OKANO 1998, pp. 16–17; cf. now HANISCH 2006, pp. 113–114.

[59] See SFERRA 2000, pp. 404–405.

[60] See HANISCH 2006, pp. 109–161 for a foretaste of the forthcoming edition of the *Maṇicūḍajātaka*.

hinted by TUCCI and now shown by HANISCH, the *Maṇicūḍajātaka* is "a kāvya written in a mixture of Sanskrit and a special kind of Prakrit".[61] Thus, Sarvarakṣita's poetic work is not only very important from a literary point of view, being a newly discovered jewel of Buddhist literature, but it also turns out to be particularly intriguing from a linguistic point of view, for it allows us to get new insights into the Middle Indic dialect used by the Sāṃmitīya Buddhists in the twelfth century.

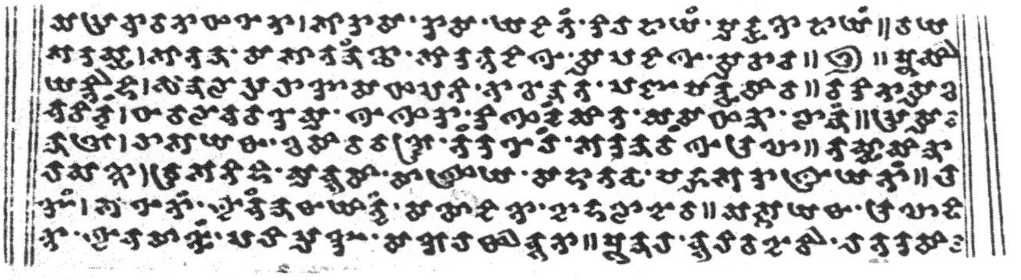

FIGURE 6: Fol. 2b (left part) of the Bhaikṣukī manuscript of the *Maṇicūḍajātaka*

[61] HANISCH 2006, p. 114; HAHN's preliminary remarks on the *Maṇicūḍajātaka* manuscript and its script (cf. HAHN 2005, pp. 712–701) were superseded by HANISCH 2006, pp. 109–161.

# CHAPTER TWO

## The Candrālaṃkāra and Its Manuscript

## 2.1 The Candrālaṃkāra

The main object of study in the second stage of the Arrow-headed Script Project was the Bhaikṣukī manuscript of the *Candrālaṃkāra*. Until recently nothing was known about the *Candrālaṃkāra* besides the initial notes left by Bendall and Liebich, and the preliminary analyses by Hahn and Hanisch. Soon after I had started studying the manuscript in March 2007, I was able to make some new discoveries which shed more light on this grammatical treatise, its author, and the unique manuscript itself.

### 2.1.1 A commentary on Ratnamati's *Cāndravyākaraṇapañjikā*

The first and probably most interesting discovery concerns the proper identification of the text contained in the manuscript. It has eventually become possible to conclude beyond a doubt that the author of the *Candrālaṃkāra* comments on a treatise entitled the *Cāndravyākaraṇapañjikā*. The *Cāndravyākaraṇapañjikā* was composed by Ratnamati and is itself a commentary on Dharmadāsa's *Cāndravṛtti* which is in turn a commentary on the *Cāndravyākaraṇa*, the seminal Sanskrit grammar by the scholar and poet Candragomin (fifth century AD). Thus, the *Candrālaṃkāra* is a sub-sub-commentary in which, as Liebich has already correctly pointed out,[62] only select difficult passages are discussed.

A few years ago, while I was working on the edition of the oldest Sanskrit commentary on Daṇḍin's *Kāvyādarśa* ("Mirror of Poetic Art") composed by Bhikṣu Ratnaśrījñāna from Siṃhala (today's Sri Lanka) in the first half of the tenth century, I came to the conclusion that this commentator and the grammarian Ratnamati are one and the same person.[63] This provoked my interest in Ratnamati's treatise of which I had at my disposal a copy of one incomplete palm-leaf manuscript kept in the

[62] See Liebich 1895, pp. 40–41 (cited above, ch. 1.3).

[63] See Dimitrov 2010, pp. 41–44.

Kaiser Library in Kathmandu.[64] Besides this, I was also acquainted with a short description of another old manuscript found in 1937 by Rāhula SĀṄKṚTYĀYANA in the Źa lu Ri phug in the vicinity of the Źa lu monastery in Tibet. In his report SĀṄKṚTYĀYANA has copied two stanzas from the beginning of Ratnamati's commentary:[65]

*pradhvastāśeṣadoṣāya samastaguṇaśāline* |
*parānugrahadakṣāya Buddhāyāstu namaḥ sadā* ||

Honour forever to Buddha who has destroyed each and every fault, who possesses all virtues, [and] who is accomplished in being compassionate towards others!

*jayati khyātasatkīrtiś Candraḥ sadguṇaratnabhūḥ* |
*vyāptasamastavāṅmayo Vācaspatir ivāparaḥ* ||

All glory to Candra[gomin] who is well known for his good reputation, who is an abode of precious virtues, [and] who is entirely incorporating the ubiquitous speech just like Vācaspati ('the Lord of Speech')!

While analysing one of the unidentified leaves from BENDALL's portion of the Bhaikṣukī manuscript, it soon became clear to me that the author of the *Candrālaṃkāra* is commenting on Ratnamati's salutatory stanzas. Although the pagination at the left-hand margin on the verso side of this leaf can no longer be seen due to damage, it is reasonable to assume that this is the second folio of the entire codex. LIEBICH's observation that the manuscript which he consulted preserves only parts of the commentary on the fifth and sixth chapters of the *Cāndravyākaraṇa* is, therefore, certainly not correct.[66] The Cambridge portion obviously includes one folio

---

[64] See DIMITROV/TAMOT 2007, pp. 25–36.

[65] See SĀṄKṚTYĀYANA 1937, p. 43, note 2 (MS No. XXXIV. I.295).

[66] Cf. LIEBICH 1895, p. 40 (cited above, ch. 1.3). Contrary to HANISCH, I do not think that LIEBICH was of the opinion that "the *CA* [i.e. the *Candrālaṃkāra*] was only a partial commentary on the *CV* [i.e. the *Cāndravyākaraṇa*], viz. on chapters 5 and 6." (HANISCH 2007, p. 129). LIEBICH's observation pertains only to the leaves he consulted, not to the

from the beginning of the *Candrālaṃkāra*[67] and two more folios which contain parts of the commentary on *sūtras* from the first section of the first chapter of the *Cāndravyākaraṇa*.

On the verso side of fol. $2^{I}$ the beginning of the commentary on the second stanza of the *Cāndravyākaraṇapañjikā* is also available. Fortunately, the continuation of the commentary on this stanza could be located on another folio which until recently defied proper identification. It is now clear that, although in a poor state of preservation and quite obliterated, the third folio of the manuscript has also survived the ravages of time. This leaf belongs, however, to the Kathmandu portion of the Bhaikṣukī manuscript. Thus, in both places, Cambridge and Kathmandu, a key to the undisputable identification of the text contained in the Bhaikṣukī manuscript has been preserved.

The analysis of the rest of the text has confirmed the initial observation that the author of the *Candrālaṃkāra* is commenting on Ratnamati's treatise. That he used the *Cāndravyākaraṇapañjikā* is also clear from a number of passages where either Ratnamati is mentioned by name or, as is most often the case, his treatise is referred to briefly by the name of *Ṭīkā*.[68] Although in the preserved portions of the *Candrālaṃ-*

---

work as a whole. In this part of the manuscript there are only two leaves from which it can become immediately clear that they contain parts from the commentary on the first chapter. One of these leaves somehow escaped LIEBICH's attention, whereas the other one he wrongly attributed to the fifth chapter (see below, ch. 2.4).

[67] As far as the absolute beginning of the text is concerned, it can be assumed that only some nine lines or about 400 *akṣaras* written on the verso side of the first folio are missing. The recto side of this folio was most probably left blank.

[68] Cf. e.g. fol. $22^{I}b^{9}$ (... *kaṇḍūr iti Ratnamatiḥ*), fol. $35^{II}b^{2}$ (*lastivādisūtre* [cf. Cān. 1.4.1] | *vyatija jāgarmmahe iti Ratnamatir iḍāgamānityatvāt*), fol. $61^{II}b^{9}$ (*Ratnamatimate tu* ...); fol. $8^{I}a^{1-2}$ (*ata eva sphoṭe py asati śabdavyutpatteḥ karttuṃ śakyatvāt vyutpa*$_{2}$*tter aviṣayaḥ sphoṭo na tu nāsty evety atra nirbbandho mukhyaṣ Ṭīkākṛtā tārkikāṇām iva*), fol. $2^{II}a^{10}$–$2^{II}b^{1}$ (*prakṛtipra*[$2^{II}$b]*tyayavibhāgābhāvād iti Ṭīkāvākyaṃ* ...), fol. $7^{II}a^{5-6}$ (*Ṭīkā°*), fol. $65^{II}b^{10}$ (*Ṭīkā tu pakṣāntareṇa*), fol. $73^{II}b^{9-10}$ (*Ṭīkā tu jalpavyākhyāpakṣe dvitīya iti* ...). When referring to someone else's *Ṭīkā*, the author of the *Candrālaṃkāra* mentions explicitly the commentator's name (e.g. ... *iti Durggaṭīkā* on fol. $11^{II}a^{1, 10}$ with reference to Durgasiṃha's commentary on the *Kātantra*).

*kāra* its direct dependence on Ratnamati's *Cāndravyākaraṇapañjikā* is nowhere stated clearly, it is now obvious that due to the special relationship between the two texts, an edition and a thorough study of Ratnamati's commentary on the *Cāndravṛtti* is a precondition for the comprehensive understanding of the *Candrālaṃkāra*.[69] From the mere fact that such an authority on the Cāndra school of grammar as LIEBICH did not take the opportunity to edit the text when he was first given access to the unique material,[70] it can be surmised that this great scholar was aware of the inadequate conditions for the study of this treatise. Neither was its author known nor were the nature of the text and its relation with other treatises established. It was certainly clear to both BENDALL and LIEBICH that the *Candrālaṃkāra* is a hard nut to crack, and it is quite understandable that they contented themselves with just a short description of it. Even now the soil for an *editio princeps* of the preserved parts of the *Candrālaṃkāra* is not good enough, not only because the *Cāndravyākaraṇapañjikā* itself is not edited yet, but also because some of the grammatical texts most often referred to in the *Candrālaṃkāra* are still largely inaccessible or only insufficiently known.

For the purposes of the present publication it would suffice to offer a transcript of the first two folios of the *Candrālaṃkāra* manuscript.[71]

---

[69] The work on an *editio princeps* of Ratnamati's treatise has been undertaken by the present author with the aim to at least partially fulfil this desideratum.

[70] LIEBICH was probably able to consult the manuscript only briefly during his stay in London, presumably sometime in the period from April till September 1893.

[71] The following typographic symbols have been used here: ⟪ ⟫ double angle brackets indicate an insertion by first hand or second hand; [ ] square brackets denote a reconstruction of partially damaged or illegible *akṣaras*; ( ) round brackets indicate that the reading of the manuscript is uncertain; ⁅ ⁆ square brackets with quill indicate a reconstruction of *akṣaras* which have been lost due to disruption; .. two dots denote an illegible *akṣara* which I have not been able to reconstruct; . one dot indicates a single illegible element of a partially legible akṣara; + a plus symbol indicates an *akṣara* lost due to physical damage; { } braces indicate a deletion by me; ○ denotes the binding hole; ⁝ represents a similar filler symbol in the manuscript. The beginning of a new line is indicated by a line number between subscript angle brackets. Words cited from Ratnamati's commentary appear in bold-face type; quotations of *sūtras* from Candragomin's

## Transcript

**[fol. 2ˡa]** śeṣā hiṃsyā **doṣā** rāgādayo yasya sa ○ **pradhvasta** iti *KARTTARI CĀRAMBHE KTAḤ* (1.2.68) ⟨⟨|⟩⟩ pradhvastavāṁś cāsau āśeṣadoṣaś ceti **pradhva**:⟨2⟩**stāśeṣadoṣaḥ** | itas tataḥ kṣeptuṃ : ○ prārabdhavān ˡ hiṃsyān ˡ rāgādīn ity arthaḥ | yadvā pradhvaṃsitum ārabdho aśeṣa:⟨3⟩doṣo yeneti karmmaṇi kte aśeṣaśa○bdaḥ sāvaśeṣārthaḥ ⟨⟨|⟩⟩ etenotpāditavodhicitta ity uktaṃ | nanv evaṃbhūtaḥ pṛthagja[no]⟨4⟩pi bhavatīti viśinaṣṭi | samasyante : ○ satvasantāne prakṣipyante iti **samastāś** ca te **guṇāś** ca [da]yāmudito pekṣā⟨5⟩kṣamādaya::ḥ | teṣāṃ **śalanaṃ** śālaḥ ○ | *śala gatau* (Dhātup. 1.572)[72] ghañ{a} | jñānaṃ śobhā vā prāptir vāsyāstīti | athavā taiḥ śali(tap)[i](tā) ⟨6⟩ jñātuṃ | śobhitum āptum vā śīlam asye○ti | etena svārthanirapekṣāvyāhataparārthakāritayā ārya tam uktaṃ | a[ta e]⟨7⟩vāha | **parasmai anuggrahas** tena **dakṣo** va:○rddh[i]to bodhisatvatvena lokair jñāto vā | *dakṣa vṛddhau gatau* ceti (Dhātup. 1.446, 1.518)[73] Dhā[tu](pāṭh). .. .. .. .[a]⟨8⟩ta evaitasmād guṇatrayayogād **Bu**:○**ddhaḥ** | budhadhātor dantyauṣṭhavakārapakṣe vaśāditvābhāvād .(ṣa) .. .. + + + + .. .. .. .. ⟨9⟩ jñānaṃ tāṃ jihīte uttarottaram adhiga○cchati pūrvvapūrvvaṃ jahātīti | *JHALO JAŚ* iti (6.3.67) dhasya [da]ḥ (|) .. .. .. .. .. .. .. .. .. .. .. ..

**[fol. 2ˡb]** [kṛ]te Buddhaḥ | athavā *KARTTARI CĀRAMBHE KTAḤ* (1.2.68) | svayaṃ ○ boddhuṃ pravṛttaḥ parañ ca vedayitum iti | yadvā budhyate sa [tair iti b]u[d]dhaḥ | [evaṃ](bhūtā)⟨2⟩ya [na]**amaḥ sade**ti śeṣaḥ ⟨⟨|⟩⟩ bhinnakleśatvena *gṛhī* : ○ *vā navako pi vā vandyo vratadharair* iti (*Gurupañcāśikā* 4bc)[74] vacanāt | dvāv eva vandyau .. + + .. (vṛddha)[ś] (cet)[i] (asarvva)⟨3⟩janaviṣayatvāc cācāryasya tannamaskāra evā○śaṃsyata ity **astu** ity uktaṃ | Bhagavatas tu trailokyagurutvāt svata e[va s]iddha[tvād] . .. .. .. ⟨4⟩[t]enāpi tadviṣayaḥ śiṣyāṇām āśaṃsyate | a○[śr]utatvāt | **siddham ityādi** vākyasya tadarthatvāc ca | bhikṣutvena la[bdhatvān n(ā)]śas(o) nāpi ⟨5⟩ sadā sarvvakālam astv iti vidhau | ā vodheḥ śara○ṇagamane-

---

root text are given in capital letters; other quotations which have been identified are written in italics.

72 Dhātup. 1.572: *śala hula ptḷ pathe gatau* (ed. LIEBICH 1902, p. 18).

73 Dhātup. 1.446: *dakṣa vṛddhau* and Dhātup. 1.518: *kṣaji dakṣa gatau* (ed. LIEBICH 1902, pp. 14, 16).

74 See ed. LÉVI 1929, p. 260; ed. PANDEY 1997, p. 35.

na vidhyabhāvāt ⟨⟨|⟩⟩ ggranthasyādau namo stu pratipannaśāstraketarobhayeṣā:⟨6⟩m ity abhisandhinā *praiṣānujñāyor lloḍ* ity anye SuOgate namaskāram ādbhaḥ[75] ⟨⟨|⟩⟩ nanv ācāryasyānekaggranthakartṛtvāt [k]im iti na Lokānandādau : ⟨7⟩ ṭīkā kriyata iti stūyamānaśālitayā O śāstraṃ stauti **jayatī**tyādi | Candranāmnā praṇītaś **Candraḥ** prabhākaravata upa[ca]⟨8⟩ryamāṇasya dhvanayo bhavanti yathā *yaṣṭī⟨⟨ḥ⟩⟩ praOveśayeti*[76] puṃliṅgaḥ śāstravācī | ata eva pūrvvaśloke nāmānabhidhāne [pi] viś[e]⟨9⟩ṣa[par]iggrahaḥ | athavā sakalalakṣāvabhāsaOkatvāc candayatīti candraḥ | *cadi āhlādane* | *dīptau ce*ti (*Dhātupradīpa* 1.55) Raki[77] | katham avabhāsaya

[fol. 3$^{\text{I}}$a] + + [t]y [ā][ha] | **khyātā** uktāḥ prasiddhā vā satāṃ s(ā)dhuOśabdānāṃ [k]ī[rtti](taṃ) kīrtir ya[tre][ti **khyātasatkīrtt]iḥ** | prasiddham (ā) .. [śa][bda]pra .. + + + + + + + ⟨2⟩ + .. bhūta(m a)nyad apīti viśinaṣṭi | santo [guṇā]Oḥ laghuvi[spaṣṭasampūrṇṇ](aṃ) .. **(sadguṇā)s** ta eva **ratnā:ni** teṣā(ṃ) **[bhū]r** ā[spadam] . .. .. .. .. .. .. (ḥ |) ⟨3⟩ [e]vaṃbhūtam api na loke pracaratīty ato anupāOdeyatvā[d anucitaṃ ggranthaṃ] (karaṇam) [iti ni]rasyann āha | **[vyā]ptaṃ** viśeṣeṇ(ātila) .(o na) [laghutvā]⟨4⟩t ' saṃśayati paryāsavigatena vispaṣṭaOtvā(t{a} āptaṃ) **samastaṃ** pūrṇṇatvāt **vāṅmayaṃ** yena sa tathā | evaṃ [guṇayu]kta[sya vāṅmayaḥ] ⟨5⟩ [p]uṇyaprajñāvadbhiḥ prārthyatvāt | ṭīkāyā O abhāvā(t{a}) [pūrvvam a]pracāro syeti śeṣaḥ | ata evam api ki(m a)sarvva(janaviṣayam i) .. .. (to) ⟨6⟩ (ca) [saṃ]skṛtaprākṛtāpabhraṃsapiśācabhedāO[c caturvvidhayaḥ] .. .. .. iśaḥ | caturvvidhām api bhāṣām a(bhimata)ṃ .. .(rc caturdh)ā .. .. .. (jñeya)⟨7⟩tvāt | sādhutvāsādhutvavicāre ca prapañc[i]Oṣyāmahe | nanv eva(ṃ) [gu]ṇaśāli kim ādhunikajane jñātuṃ śa(kya)ta i(t) . .. (sav)ā .. .. i⟨8⟩ti iṃ kāmaṃ vanati saṃbhajatīti k(v)ip(i) *ÑAMAḤ* O *KITI VAU CE*ty (5.3.17) asya *ŚAU VE*ti (5.4.33) niyamān nivṛtau iṣṭāṃ prāṇinā āpa .. .. .. (paya) .. .. (ro) ⟨9⟩ .ī(t)i (ḍa) iti (ḍaḥ) | [tad u]ktaṃ *yasya dve śīrṣe caOtvāri śṛṅgā[ṇ]i trayaḥ pādāḥ sapta hastāḥ [sa] tridhā [va]ddho [vṛ]ṣa[bh]o rora[vīt]*(īti)[78] |

---

[75] *ādbhaḥ* MS i.o. **āhuḥ* ?

[76] Cf. *Mahābhāṣya* ad Pāṇ. 4.1.48 (II 218.19).

[77] *Raki* MS i.o. **Rakṣitaḥ*. Cf. Cān.-Dhātup. 1.25: *cadi āhlādane*; Pāṇ.-Dhātup. 1.68: *cadi āhlādane dīptau ca*.

[78] Cf. *Ṛgveda* 4.58: *catvā́ri śṛ́ṅgā tráyo asya pā́dā dvé śīrṣé saptá hástāso asya | trídhā baddhó vṛṣabhó roravīti mahó devó mártyām̐ ā́ viveśa* ||; Patañjali quotes *Ṛgveda* 4.58 in his

**[fol. 3ʳb]** sphoṭo dhvaniś ca śiraḥsaṃjñā rūḍhiyogarūḍhiOyaugikāś catvāro 'rthāḥ śṛṅgāṇi kālatrayaṃ caraṇaṃ sapta vibhaktayo hastāḥ [k] + ⟨2⟩c chiraḥsūtpattyā nibandha ity arthaḥ | yadvā tiṅsupau O dvau jātikriyāguṇadravyāṇi catvāri sthānakaraṇaprayatnās trayaḥ prakṛtipratya⟨3⟩yāgamādeśasamāsaliṅgasva[rāḥ] sapta kriOyākārakasambandhaiḥ sambaddhaḥ prāṇinaṃ sambaddhuṃ ˡ śabdayati laghvādiguṇenety arthaḥ | ⟨4⟩ athavā īvnām **aparo** nānyo **V[ā]caspatiḥ** | aOtha teṣāṃ cittam āpūryya[ta] anena āpipartti vāpam iti laghvādiguṇenāśeṣalakṣyapra:⟨5⟩sādhakatvāt | evam upodghātaṃ kṛtvā śāstraOm āha | **si[ddh]am ityādīti** | vyākhyeyasya gadyapadyabhedād viśeṣam āha **śloka** iti | nanu sāva:⟨6⟩śeṣārthavyākhyayā bhavatāṃ śloke pi lāghave(na) O kathaṃ praṇayanaṃ syād ity āha **saṃkhy[e]pavyākhyā** [c]**ātre**ti śāstre śabdārthātmani na kevalaṃ śloke ⟨7⟩ | iti asmā[t]{a} kāraṇāt vākyabhedaṃ kṛtvā **kiñ ciOn mātram** iti | kā cid vivakṣitā mātrā yasya siddham ityādi vākyasya tat tathā | sāvaśeṣārtha⟨8⟩ + (c)ikayā ṭīkayā vibhajyate | kiñ cid [eva] O vā kiñ cin mātra(ṃ) iṣadarthavācino vadhāraṇārthena vā mātraśabdena vibhaktyarthe 'saṃkhya(s)a⟨9⟩ + ([ṣa])ḥ | vibhajyate śloka iti sambandhaḥ | saṃOkṣe[pa]vyākhyāpadāt{a} śrīmanNālandīyāryamahāsaṃgha[p]ā[d]ājñaptā .ā + + r(ṇṇaṃ tatra)

## 2.1.2 The author of the *Candrālaṃkāra*

The established dependence of the *Candrālaṃkāra* on the *Cāndravyākaraṇapañjikā* allows us to set Ratnamati's date as a *terminus post quem* for the author of the *Candrālaṃkāra*. Provided that my identification of the grammarian Ratnamati with the *Kāvyādarśa* commentator Ratnaśrījñāna is correct, it will be possible to conclude that the Bhaikṣukī manuscript must have been written only after the first half of the tenth century.

Since the author of the *Candrālaṃkāra* has made numerous references to the works of other grammarians, including at least two authorities who are most certainly later than Ratnamati, it is possible to come even closer to the date of our text. The scholar most frequently referred

---

*Mahābhāṣya* (I 3.12 ff.), and the same stanza also appears in Rājaśekhara's *Kāvyamīmāṃsā* 1.3 (ed. DALAL/SASTRY 1934, p. 6, l. 15–16; see also *ibid.*, p. 142).

to in the preserved portion of the *Candrālaṃkāra* is Maitreyarakṣita, a Buddhist grammarian from Eastern India (probably from Bengal) who is generally accepted to have flourished around AD 1100.[79] The latest of all grammarians mentioned in the *Candrālaṃkāra* seems to be Puruṣottamadeva, another apparently Buddhist authority associated with the Bengali tradition of Pāṇini's grammar who lived in the twelfth century.[80] From this it is obvious that the *Candrālaṃkāra* cannot have been composed earlier than the beginning of the twelfth century.

We are fortunately in a position to establish with a fair degree of certainty the name of the author of the *Candrālaṃkāra*. In all likelihood this grammatical treatise was written by Sāriputta (Skt. Śāriputra), the author of several works in Pāli, to whom the *Abhidharmārthasaṃgrahaya-sannaya* in Sinhalese is also ascribed.[81] The Mahāthera and Mahāsāmi Sāriputta of Polonnaruva was "one of the chief ornaments of the literary circle in that capital in the reign of Parâkrama Bâhu the Great, in the latter part of the twelfth century A.D.",[82] "[p]erhaps brightest among the constellations that adorned Ceylon's literary firmament during Parākrama-Bāhu's reign",[83] and "famous as *Sāgaramati* or 'Ocean of wisdom' by virtue of his great academic achievements".[84] He was a disciple of Diṁbulāgala Mahākassapa and Anutthera Sumedha, the two most prominent and influential religious leaders during the reign of king Para-

[79] See WIELIŃSKA-SOLTWEDEL 2006, vol. II, pp. 33–38 for a convenient summary of the information concerning Maitreyarakṣita.

[80] Scholars tend to believe that Puruṣottamadeva's most influential work, the *Bhāṣāvṛtti*, was completed still within the first half of the twelfth century (see WIELIŃSKA-SOLTWEDEL 2006, vol. II, pp. 38–51, with bibliographical references). As SHASTRI suggests, Puruṣottamadeva "certainly comes into the picture later than Rakṣita but evidently before Śaraṇa-deva who on his part has quoted the former in his famous Durghaṭa-vṛtti composed in 1173 A.D." (SHASTRI 1972, p. 222).

[81] About Sāriputta and his works see ROHANADEERA 1985, pp. 27–30; VON HINÜBER 2000, pp. 172–173, §§ 372–376; PECENKO 1997, pp. 159–179; CROSBY 2006, pp. 49–59.

[82] RHYS DAVIDS 1884a, p. xii.

[83] MALALASEKERA 1928, p. 190.

[84] WIJESEKERA 1955, p. 93.

kkamabāhu I (1153–1186).[85] Sāriputta is said to have resided at the Jetavana Vihāra at Polonnaruva where he had numerous students among whom Dhammakitti, Buddhanāga, Vācissara, Saṃgharakkhita, and Sumaṅgala are the best known.[86]

Sāriputta was not only a renowned Pāli scholar but also a learned Sanskritist. Following in the steps of his teacher Mahākassapa who composed the *Bālāvabodhana*, a compendium based on the *Cāndravyākaraṇa*,[87] Sāriputta too studied this grammatical tradition. In the concluding part of the Sinhalese paraphrase of the *Abhidhammatthasaṅgaha* it is explicitly mentioned that among other works Sāriputta composed a commentary related to the Cāndra school of grammar. The fifth stanza of the colophon in which this important reference is given reads:

> *Candagomābhidhānena racitā sādhusammatā* |
> *Pañcikā ramaṇīyena 'laṃkārena ca bhūsitā* ||[88]

> … and [Sāriputta also] embellished with a pleasing ornament [i.e. a commentary] the highly esteemed *Pañcikā* composed by [the grammarian] called Candragomin.

It is noteworthy that the *Pañcikā* is ascribed here to Candragomin himself. This ascription should not be taken too literally though, because it may have just been meant in general terms that the commentary belonged to the Cāndra school of grammar. Probably the same *Pañcikā* is referred to in the Pagan inscription dated AD 1442 where a grammatical work entitled *Candrapañcika* is mentioned.[89] Provided that the treatise in

---

85 See PECENKO 1997, pp. 159–160.

86 About Sāriputta's disciples and their works see MALALASEKERA 1928, pp. 196–219.

87 See BECHERT 1987, p. 11.

88 Ed. TISSA/TISSA 1960, p. 283 (the edition reads °*gomā bhi*° i.o. °*gomābhi*°, *ramaṇī yena* i.o. *ramaṇīyena*, and *lamkāreṇa* i.o. *'laṃkārena*).

89 See BODE 1909, p. 107, no. 201; LUCE/TIN HTWAY 1976, p. 239, no. 203. It may be mentioned incidentally that in another older inscription from Pagan dated AD 1223, which also contains a list of texts including some grammatical works donated to a monastery library, neither the *Pañcikā* nor the commentary on it are mentioned (cf. THAN TUN 1998, pp. 37–42).

this collection of texts donated to a monastery in Pagan was indeed identical with Ratnamati's commentary, this evidence could be interpreted as a further proof that in the first half of the second millennium of our era the commentarial literature on the *Cāndravyākaraṇa* was widely spread across a vast area of the Indian subcontinent, from today's Sri Lanka in the south to Nepal and Tibet in the north, and further to Bengal and Burma in the east. The *Cāndravṛtti*, the *Cāndravyākaraṇapañjikā*, and perhaps to a lesser extent even the not so well-recorded *Candrālaṃkāra* belonged to the curriculum of the Buddhist monks who studied Sanskrit grammar as taught by the Cāndra school.

This observation is indirectly confirmed by some references to Sāriputta's commentary on the *Pañcikā* made in various Pāli and Burmese sources.[90] One very old reference is found in the *Dāṭhāvaṃsa*, a chronicle which "covers the story of early Buddhism from the time of Dīpaṅkara onwards, and proceeds to the distribution of the relics after the Buddha's *parinibbāna*".[91] It was completed in the first quarter of the thirteenth century by Dhammakitti, one of Sāriputta's close disciples. In the first stanza of the colophon to this work Dhammakitti refers to his teacher's grammatical composition in the following words:

*yo Candagomiracite varasaddasatthe*
*ṭīkaṃ pasattham akarittha ca Pañcikāya |*
*buddhippabhāvajananiñ ca akā Samanta*
*pāsādikāya Vinayaṭṭhakathāya ṭīkam ||*[92]

He who composed a highly praised commentary on the *Pañcikā* [being itself a sub-commentary] on the excellent grammar written by Candragomin, and [who also] completed an instructive commentary on the *Samantapāsādikā*, the exegetical work on the Vinaya ...

---

[90] Cf. PECENKO 1997, pp. 170–172.

[91] NORMAN 1983, p. 142; see also GEIGER 1930, p. 207; LAW 1932, pp. 284–291; MALALASEKERA 1928, pp. 207–209; VON HINÜBER 2000, p. 95, § 193.

[92] Ed. RHYS DAVIDS 1884b, p. 151; cf. LAW 1925, p. 53.

Although Sāriputta's treatise is not mentioned in the *Saddhammasaṅgaha*, "a mediaeval history of Buddhism composed by Dhammakitti [Mahāsāmi] probably about AD 1400 in Siam",[93] further references to this commentary are found in some chronicles and bibliographic sources of later date. Thus, in Nandapañña's chronicle *Gandhavaṃsa* (written in Burma possibly in the seventeenth century)[94] five works by Sāriputta are noted:

> *Sāriputto nāmācariyo Vinayaṭṭhakathāya Sāratthadīpanī nāma ṭīkaṃ Vinayasaṃgahapakaraṇaṃ Vinayasaṃgahassa ṭīkaṃ Aṅguttaraṭṭhakathāya Sāratthamañjūsaṃ nāma ṭīkaṃ Pañcakañ ceti ime pañca gandhe akāsi.*[95]
>
> The teacher called Sāriputta composed the following five books:
> 1. The *Sāratthadīpanī*, a commentary on the exegetical work on the Vinaya; 2. The *Vinayasaṃgahapakaraṇa*; 3. A commentary on the *Vinayasaṃgaha*; 4. The *Sāratthamañjūsa*, a commentary on the exegetical work on the *Aṅguttara*; and 5. The *Pañcaka*.

In another entry Nandapañña explicitly mentions the *Pañcikā* as the title of a grammatical treatise by Sāriputta:

> *Sakaṭasaddasatthassa Pañcikā nāma ṭīkāgandho attano matiyā Sāriputtācariyena kato.*[96]

---

[93] VON HINÜBER 2000, pp. 2–3, § 4; see also MALALASEKERA 1928, pp. 10, 245–246; NORMAN 1983, pp. 179–180; PECENKO 2002, pp. 63–64. One would have expected a reference to the *Candrālaṃkāra* in the ninth chapter of the *Saddhamasaṅgaha*. However, its absence is in fact not surprising, because, as VON HINÜBER points out, "[t]his seemingly random collection of titles is incomplete, with well known texts such as the Milindapañha [...] missing and in no recognizable order."

[94] See BODE 1909, p. x; LAW 1931–32, pp. 291–295; VON HINÜBER 2000, p. 3, § 4: "[a] later systematic survey of unknown date"; cf. PECENKO 2007, p. 360, note 27. DAS dates this work in the first half of the eighteenth century (see DAS 2000, p. 5).

[95] Ed. MINAYEFF 1886, p. 61. In his translation DAS has not rendered the title of the fifth work, namely *Pañcaka* (cf. DAS 2000, p. 50). As BODE has already assumed, *Pañcaka* is most probably a corrupt spelling of *Pañcikā* (see BODE 1896, p. 66).

[96] Ed. MINAYEFF 1886, p. 71; cf. also BODE 1896, p. 66. BODE has apparently read *sakaṭasaddatthassa* instead of *sakaṭasaddasatthassa*. The translation suggested by DAS is not satisfactory (cf. DAS 2000, p. 61: "The Commentary entitled the Sakaṭasaddasatthassa

The teacher Sāriputta wrote at his own initiative a commentarial work called *Pañcikā* on the *Sakaṭasaddasattha.*

It is worth noting that according to the *Gandhavaṃsa* this commentary was not written at the request of king Parakkamabāhu I, as was the case with most of Sāriputta's other compositions. From this it may be surmised that Sāriputta was not yet at the Jetavana Vihāra when he worked on Sanskrit grammar. Be that as it may, the information contained in the *Gandhavaṃsa* raises some problems, since according to all other sources Sāriputta did not compose the *Pañcikā* itself, but rather a commentary (*ṭīkā*) on it.[97]

Sāriputta's work on grammar is also mentioned by Vimalasāra in his *Sāsanavaṃsadīpa* (completed in AD 1879), which deals with "the history of Buddhism in Ceylon down to the time of the introduction of the Burmese *upasampadā* in A.D. 1802".[98] The Pāli stanza containing this reference reads:

*Pañcikāya tu ṭīkāpi dhīmatā kaviketunā* |
*therena Sāriputtena katā parahitatthinā* ||[99]

Pañcikā was written ..."). The Pāli title *Sakaṭasaddasattha* corresponds to Skt. **Śakaṭaśabdaśāstra*; however, nothing seems to be known about a work by this title.

[97] It may also be somewhat confounding that in a subsequent entry in the *Gandhavaṃsa* the name of Vācissara, a pupil of Sāriputta, is mentioned as the author of a commentary on Moggalāna's *Pañcikā* (see ed. Minayeff 1886, p. 62: *Vācissaro nāmācariyo ... Moggalānabyākaraṇassa Pañcikāya ṭīkā ... akāsi*; cf. also *ibid.*, p. 71). Franke notes that Śrī Rāhula (fifteenth century) was also known under the name of Vācissara and suggests that this *Moggalānabyākaraṇassa Pañcikāya ṭīkā* is probably identical with Śrī Rāhula's *Pañcikāpradīpaya*, a Sinhalese commentary on Moggalāna's *Pañcikā* (see Franke 1902, p. 44). The latter work, which is considered to be lost, is an autocommentary on the *Saddalakkhaṇa*, Moggalāna's seminal Pāli grammar written in the twelfth century.

[98] Norman 1983, p. 182. On the *Sāsanavaṃsadīpa* see Malalasekera 1928, p. 311; Pecenko 2007, p. 363. This work is not to be confused with the *Sāsanavaṃsa* (completed in AD 1861) which is a revised Pāli translation prepared by Paññāsāmī on the basis of a Burmese original composed in AD 1831 (see Lieberman 1976, pp. 137–149). Sāriputta's grammatical treatise is not mentioned in the *Sāsanavaṃsa.*

[99] Ed. Vimalasāra 1929, p. 129, stanza 1203.

The wise Elder Sāriputta, the eminent poet who was seeking the welfare of the others, also composed a commentary on the *Pañcikā*.

Finally, Sāriputta's work is also listed in the Burmese *Piṭakat samuiṅḥ cā tamḥ*, an "annotated list of titles [...] collected in 1888 by Maṅḥ krīḥ Mahāsirijeyasū, the last librarian of the royal Burmese library at Mandalay, which was dispersed when Upper Burma was annexed by the British in 1885".[100] The full record reads as follows:

1124. *Candrikāpañcikāṭīkā.* 11 – *rhaṅ Sāriputrā pru.*
*Sīhuiḷ kyvanḥ Anurādha mruị ne – Sāratthadīpanīṭīkā charā rhaṅ Sāritanūja cī raṅ saññ.*[101]

[Title no.] 1124. The commentary on the *Candrikāpañcikā*. [Author no.] 11, composed by the monk Sāriputrā. This [*Candrikāpañcikāṭīkā*] was written by the monk Sāritanūja, the *Sāratthadīpanīṭīkā* scholar from the city of Anurādha on the island of Siṃhala.

Thus, according to the *Piṭakat samuiṅḥ cā tamḥ* Sāriputta (Sāriputrā or Sāriputtarā in Burmese spelling) was a native Sinhalese from Anurādhapura or, alternatively, he resided there for some time. Anurādhapura was the ancient capital of Siṃhala which in the eleventh century was almost completely deserted, since the capital was moved to Polonnaruva with which place Sāriputta is otherwise usually associated.[102] In the explanatory notes to Sāriputta's other works Ūḥ Yaṃ (Maṅḥ krīḥ Mahāsirijeyasū) mentions two alternative names of our author, namely the synonymous Sāritanūja and his religious title Mahāsāmipāda.[103] In addition, in the *Piṭakat samuiṅḥ cā tamḥ* Sāriputta is said to have been the son of king Buddhadāsa (fourth century AD). However, this information is pro-

100 Von Hinüber 2000, p. 3, § 4; cf. Bechert 1979, pp. xiii and 172.

101 See Yaṃ 1905, p. 139, no. 1124.

102 See Malalasekera 1937–38, s.v. *Anurādhapura*; cf. Frasch 2002 with further bibliographical details.

103 Cf. Yaṃ 1905, p. 30, nos. 202–212, and p. 33, nos. 239–240. About Ūḥ Yaṃ and his bibliographical work see Thaw Kaung 1998, pp. 405–406.

bably drawn from *Cūlavaṃsa* 37.177 and is obviously based on a confusion with a namesake of Sāriputta.[104]

### 2.1.3 Quotations from the *Candrālaṃkāra*

Whether a manuscript of the *Candrālaṃkāra* was still available in Burma in the nineteenth century is difficult to say. Although this cannot be entirely excluded, it is nevertheless more likely that the information about Sāriputta's grammatical treatise given in the Burmese title lists is based upon older bibliographies. In other words, the compiler probably did not consult any actual manuscripts of this work. Since in Sri Lanka, too, not a single copy of Sāriputta's commentary could be located, until recently this work was believed to have been irretrievably lost. The only traces left of it were thought to be three quotations in Śrī Rāhula's *Pañcikāpradīpaya* (completed in AD 1456).[105]

The first quoted passage reads:

---

[104] Cf. Malalasekera 1937–38, s.vv. *Buddhadāsa* and *Sāriputta* 5).

[105] See Bechert 1987, pp. 9–10. Śrī Rāhula has also quoted from Ratnamati's *Cāndravyākaraṇapañjikā*. First, one stanza from the commentary on the initial stanza of the *Cāndravyākaraṇa* has been cited: *me mä kīha, Cāndrapaṃcikākāra ācāryya Ratnamatipādayō* ***śāstram prayojanañ caiva sambandhasyāśrayāv ubhau | taduktyantargatas tasmād bhinno noktaḥ prayojanāt ||*** *yī* (cf. ed. Tennakōn 1962, p. 220 and fol. 0b[4] of Sāṅkṛtyāyana's manuscript of the *Cāndravyākaraṇapañjikā* [leaf 1[4] on image xc_14_69_ 01_B.tif of the duplicate kept in Göttingen). The second quotation is from Ratnamati's commentary on CānV. ad Cān. 2.1.86 (cf. ed. Tennakōn 1962, p. 290; see below). Bechert claims two more quotations from the *Cāndravyākaraṇapañjikā* (see Bechert 1987, p. 8, notes 16–17). The two stanzas quoted by Śrī Rāhula come, however, from another composition by Ratnaśrījñāna, namely from his *Candrakārikā*, a hitherto unpublished work of which only one partly damaged Nepalese palm-leaf manuscript, possibly of the fourteenth century, is known to exist (see Shāstrī 1931, pp. cccxxv and 430–431). The first of these stanzas is the seventh but last in the *Candrakārikā* (see ed. Tennakōn 1962, p. 214: *kīyē mä no, Ratnaśrījñānācāryyayan visin* ***śabdārtharūpāvagamāc ca samyak kavītvavaktṛtvayaśaḥprasiddhiḥ | satkāralābhāv api sambhavetāṃ guṇapriyebhyaḥ phalam aihikan tat ||*** *yī*; cf. fol. 14a[4-5] of the Calcutta MS G 4754, and Shāstrī 1931, p. 431). The other stanza is found on fol. 12b[3-4] of the Calcutta MS of the *Candrakārikā* (see ed. Tennakōn 1962, p. 346: *Ratnaśrījñānācāryyayō* ***na cāpatyādiśabdānām prayogo 'sminn apekṣate | tadacīmātranirdeśād aṇādividhivṛttaye ||*** *yī*).

> ... *ŚrīŚāriputra mahāsvāmipādayan RatnamatiPañcikālaṅkārayehi* ***'yady asabhāyārthā ete vinādayaḥ, evaṃ tarhi vinārthair ity eva vaktavyam, kiṃ bhedopādānenety āha b h e d o p ā d ā n a m ityādi'*** *yī* ...[106]

Since in this passage the author of the *Candrālaṃkāra* has cited the expression *bhedopādānam* from Ratnamati's commentary on CānV. ad Cān. 2.1.86 and clearly refers to its wording,[107] it is quite likely that Śrī Rāhula's quotation originates from the sub-sub-commentary on the same *sūtra*. This cannot be verified, however, because the relevant part of the text is not preserved in the Bhaikṣukī manuscript of the *Candrālaṃkāra*.

The second quotation from the *Candrālaṃkāra* is very brief:

> ... *Sārārthavilasiniyehi 'puthgatthatāyaṃ' yana pāṭhayä RatnamatiPañcikālaṅkārayehi* ***'pṛthagarthatāyām ity asya'*** *yana padayä balā* ...[108]

The text was quoted probably from Sāriputta's sub-sub-commentary ad Cān. 2.2.1.[109] However, this cannot be proven either, because in this case, too, the passage in question is not preserved in the Bhaikṣukī manuscript. To complicate matters, Ratnamati's commentary on this part of the *Cāndravṛtti* is not available in the few fragmentary manuscripts of the *Cāndravyākaraṇapañjikā* known to exist.[110]

---

106 Ed. TENNAKŌN 1962, p. 291.

107 Cf. CānV. ad Cān. 2.1.86: *etābhyāṃ yoge tṛtīyāpañcamyau bhavataḥ | pṛthag Devadattena pṛthag Devadattāt | nānā Devadattena nānā Devadattāt* | (ed. LIEBICH 1918, p. 111) and Ratnamati's explanation, which is fortunately available and more or less readable in the old manuscript of the *Cāndravyākaraṇapañjikā* discovered in Tibet: || *pṛtha[gnānābhyām]* || *tṛtīyā ceti varttate | tatra cakāreṇa pra₄kṛtā pañcamy abhisambadhyate | na dvitīyāpi pūrvavat | yogavibhāgād vinādayaś caite 'sahāye varttante* | *{bhe}bhedopādāOnan tu paryāyānivṛtyarthaṃ* || (fol. 77b[3-4]; leaf 1[3-4] on image xc_14_69_08_B.tif). Both these passages are also quoted by Śrī Rāhula (see ed. TENNAKŌN 1962, p. 290; Ratnamati's text agrees with Śrī Rāhula's reading *tṛtīyā ca bhavati pañcamī ca* in the place of *tṛtīyāpañcamyau bhavataḥ* which is printed in LIEBICH's edition of the *Cāndravṛtti*.

108 Ed. TENNAKŌN 1962, p. 319.

109 Cf. CānV. ad Cān. 2.2.1: *subantaṃ subantena sahaikārthaṃ bhavatīty etad adhikṛtaṃ veditavyam | sa ca pṛthagarthānām ekārthībhāvaḥ samāsa ity ucyate* | (ed. LIEBICH 1918, p. 116).

110 In SĀṄKṚTYĀYANA's manuscript the beginning of the commentary on CānV. 2.2.1 must have been written on fol. 91 which appears to have been missing in 1937.

The third quotation reads thus:

> *me mä kīha. RatnamatiPañcikālaṅkārakāra Śāriputra mahāsvāmipādayō;* '**ci-kīrṣitasya prārambho na parisamāpta** ***ity ekatvenāśritā sarvā sā avivakṣitaparyyavasānā kriyāvartamānaiveti****' yī.*[111]

It has not yet been possible to establish from which part of the *Candrālaṃkāra* the quoted text originates. The expression *cikīrṣitasya prārambho na parisamāpta[ḥ]* seems in any case to be a citation from Ratnamati's commentary.[112]

If it were possible to locate at least one of these quotations in the Bhaikṣukī manuscript of the *Candrālaṃkāra*, this would conclusively prove the hypothesis that the text of this unique manuscript and Sāriputta's commentary quoted by Śrī Rāhula and mentioned in various chronicles are identical. However, even without this final proof there is enough evidence to justify the assumption that Sāriputta's "Ornament of Ratnamati's *Pañjikā*" referred to in the *Pañcikāpradīpaya* and the commentary on Ratnamati's *Cāndravyākaraṇapañjikā* in the Bhaikṣukī manuscript are one and the same work.

### 2.1.4 The title of Sāriputta's commentary

According to the sub-colophons, the title of the work contained in the Bhaikṣukī manuscript is *Candrālaṃkāra* ("Ornament of the Moon"[113]). It is explicitly mentioned only in three sub-colophons, namely at the end of the commentary on the first section of the first chapter (fol. $31^{\mathrm{I}}b^{7-8}$), at the end of the fifth chapter (fol. $36^{\mathrm{II}}a^{6}$), and at the end of the third sec-

---

[111] Ed. TENNAKŌN 1962, p. 376 (there it is written *śārīputra* i.o. *śāriputra* and *vikīrṣitasya* i.o. *cikīrṣitasya*).

[112] The fragmentary Bhaikṣukī manuscript of the *Candrālaṃkāra* does not permit to check the entire commentary for the source of Sāriputta's quotation. A search in the incomplete manuscripts of the *Cāndravyākaraṇapañjikā* also brought no results, possibly because the quoted passage belongs to some part of Ratnamati's work which is either not preserved or not legible in the available materials.

[113] A wordplay with "Ornament of Candra[gomin's Grammar]" is intended here.

tion of the sixth chapter (fol. $61^{II}b^{5-6}$). This title is also confirmed by the concluding stanza of the treatise[114] where the synonymous *Candrālaṃkṛti* (*m.c.* for *Candrālaṃkāra*; the metre employed is Mālinī) is used:

> *(parama)tam anucintyālocya vidvadvariṣṭhaiḥ*
> *saha sahajamanīṣonmeṣaleśāntareṇa* |
> *mama viracitaCa[ndrālaṃ]kṛter jātapuṇyaṃ*
> *pra[bha]va[tu bha]vabhājāṃ satvaraṃ bodhibījaṃ* ||[115]

> May the merit acquired by way of [writing] the *Candrālaṃkṛti*, which I composed after considering different opinions [and] after reviewing [them] with [the help of] the best scholars [and] another little bit of twinkle of [my own] innate intelligence, quickly yield the seed of enlightenment for [all] living beings.

As seen above, in the earliest known reference to Sāriputta's grammatical treatise in the *Abhidharmārthasaṃgrahayasannaya*, the work is described as an *Alaṃkāra* ("Ornament") of a detailed commentary referred to by the name of *Pañcikā*.[116] That Ratnamati's *Cāndravyākaraṇapañjikā* is intended here, becomes clear from the references in Śrī Rāhula's *Pañcikāpradīpaya* where the excerpts from Sāriputta's treatise are said to be from the "Ornament on Ratnamati's *Pañcikā*" (*RatnamatiPañcikālaṅkāra-*

---

[114] Preceding this stanza, on the final folio of the manuscript the second half of one more stanza in the Upajāti metre (– *na kṛtātra śāstre* | *sṛṣṭāpi vṛttiḥ paribhāṣasūtre daḥ sūtritaṃ tasya nibandhaśāstraṃ* ||) and another one in the Vasantatilakā metre (*yad vākyām artharahitaṃ yadi vārtha[m atra] duggranthitaṃ vata mayā dvitayaṃ tathaiva* | *tac cen mataṃ na hṛdi sādhujanasya nūnaṃ śodhyaṃ manīṣibhir anākulanītivijñaiḥ* ||) are preserved in full. Since the penultimate folio is missing, it cannot be decided how many more stanzas the author has added at the end of his treatise.

[115] Line 4: °*vījaṃ* i.o. °*bījaṃ*.

[116] On the word *pañcikā-* and its variant *pañjikā-* cf. GOODALL/ISAACSON 2003, p. xiii, note 2: "It seems to us, however, that *pañcikā* is acceptable and possibly even the original form, derived from the root √*pañc*, 'to diffuse, elaborate' (according to APTE s.v.), and that it is *pañjikā* that is 'deviant'. [...] An exhaustive investigation of the word remains, as far as we are aware, to be undertaken. Our impression is that it is probably one word with two orthographies which some connect with different meanings."

*yehi*). Sāriputta is also called there RatnamatiPañcikālaṅkārakāra, i.e. the author of the "Ornament on Ratnamati's *Pañcikā*".

In the chronicles such as the *Dāṭhāvaṃsa*, the *Gandhavaṃsa*, and the *Sāsanavaṃsadīpa*, this treatise is usually said to be simply a commentary (*ṭīkā*) on the *Pañcikā*. Only in the Burmese *Piṭakat samuiṅḥ cā tamḥ* is it entered under the obviously corrupt title *Candrikāpañcikāṭīkā*.

It can be concluded that *Candrālaṃkāra* was the short title which was given preference in the Bhaikṣukī manuscript. It is likely that this title was also the one used by the author himself. At least since the middle of the fifteenth century, however, a more descriptive form of the title, namely *RatnamatiPañcikālaṃkāra*, has come into use. It was obviously based on the fact that the *Candrālaṃkāra* is a commentary on Ratnamati's *Pañcikā*. Though not attested in any document, one can reconstruct the hypothetical full title of Sāriputta's work as **Cāndravyākaraṇapañjikālaṃkāra* ("Ornament of [Ratnamati's] extensive commentary on Candra[gomin]'s grammar").

### 2.1.5 The last stanza in the *Candrālaṃkāra* manuscript

Since the first folio of the *codex unicus* is not preserved, there is no way to establish what autobiographical information, if any, the beginning of the commentary may have contained. We are fortunate enough, however, to have at our disposal the end of the text, for the final folio has somehow survived the ravages of time. There we find the following stanza in the Vasantatilakā metre, which should be considered in the context of the assumed authorship of the *Candrālaṃkāra*:

*māghāṃśake daśasu Somapurīyaśastra( )*
*vyākhyā( )paṭur vVijayagarbha imām a[kārṣīt]* |
*śrīRāmapālanṛpater abhilikhyamāne*
*dvāviṃśatidvitayavatsararājyakāle* ||[117]

[117] Line 1: °*āṅśake* i.o. °*āṃśake*, °*śastra*° i.o. *°*śāstra*° or *°*śāstā*? Line 2: *vyākhyā paṭur*, *vyākhyāpaṭur* or **vyākhyāṃ paṭur*? Line 4: °*viṅśati*° i.o. °*viṃśati*°, °*vatsambatsara*° i.o. °*vatsara*°.

Unfortunately, this folio is in a bad state of preservation, and the partly corrupt text defies an accurate and indisputable interpretation.[118] It is nonetheless worth analysing the contents of this stanza, for it allows us to get some further insights into the biography of the author and the date of completion of his treatise.

An important question which has first to be dealt with is whether this stanza was composed by Sāriputta himself or it was subsequently added by some unknown copyist. The latter assumption seems to be more plausible. On the one hand, the preceding stanza nicely concludes the treatise and does not necessarily let us expect any further text. On the other hand, the corrupt forms and the contents of the following stanza rather indicate that it came under the pen of a scribe who was not so well-versed in Sanskrit, but who obviously knew the author of the *Candrālaṃkāra* well enough. Only a contemporary fellow co-worker of the author of the treatise would have been in a position to supply the kind of details we find in this stanza.

Noteworthy is the word Somapurīya which seems to refer to the renowned Somapura Mahāvihāra, the great monastery of Somapura located at the site of modern Paharpur in the Rajshahi District of Bangladesh.[119] This foundation was established by the Pāla king Dharmapāla (c. 775–812)[120] and became one of the most influential centres for Buddhist monasticism and scholarship. Prominent professors such as Ratnā-

[118] See HANISCH's "attempt at a first, still very tentative translation": "(This) intelligent commentary on the *Somapurīyaśāstra* (obviously another appellation for the *Cāndravyākaraṇa*) ..., while (this) was written down during the reign of the Venerable King Rāmapāla, which has been filled with victory and lasted for two times 22 years (= in the 44th year of the reign of Rāmapāla?), on the tenth day (of the month) of Māgha." (HANISCH 2007, pp. 149–150, see also *ibid.*, p. 132).

[119] As MAJUMDAR informs, the name of the original place is still preserved in the neighbouring village called Ompur (see MAJUMDAR 1943, p. 115). For a description and a plan of the historical site see MAJUMDAR 1943, pp. 489–493; MAJUMDAR 1971, pp. 613–616; cf. DUTT 1962, pp. 371–376.

[120] Cf. CHIMPA/CHATTOPADHYAYA 1970, p. 266; according to Tāranātha, it was Devapāla at whose initiative this monastery was established.

karaśānti (fl. between 975–1050) and Atiśa Dīpaṃkaraśrījñāna (982–1054) have been associated with this famous Buddhist university. It started declining in the second half of the twelfth century until Somapura was finally abandoned in the thirteenth century.[121]

The first half of the stanza implies that it was Vijayagarbha, a skilful (*paṭuḥ*) scholar (*°*śāstā*) affiliated to the Somapura Mahāvihāra (*Somapurīya°*), who composed (*akārṣīt*) this (*imām*) commentary (**vyākhyām*),[122] i.e. the *Candrālaṃkāra*.[123] The name of Vijayagarbha fits well with the locality, inasmuch as "among the monks of Somapura whose names appear in the inscriptions, lineage-names like '-garbha' and '-mitra' are found."[124] The discrepancy between the author's name mentioned in the stanza and the one established by us is, however, puzzling. It could be avoided, should it be possible to prove that both names are

---

[121] Cf. DUTT 1962, p. 376: "The ruins of the temple and monasteries at Pāhārpur do not bear any evident marks of large-scale destruction. The downfall of the establishment, by desertion or destruction, must have been sometime in the midst of the widespread unrest and displacement of population consequent on the Muslim invasion."

[122] HANISCH's interpretation of **Somapurīyaśāstravyākhyā* as "commentary on the *Somapurīyaśāstra* (obviously another appelation for the *Cāndravyākaraṇa*)" is untenable, for it is hardly possible that **Somapūriyaśāstra* "the treatise from Somapura", if this was at all meant in the stanza, refers to Candragomin's grammar. At the time when this treatise was composed, the Buddhist monastery of Somapura did not yet exist and the town of Somapura sprung up probably much later. There is evidence that in the fifth century the locality was known under the name Vaṭagohāli and a Jaina establishment was present there. Even after the early ninth century when the Somapura Mahāvihāra was established, nothing seems to suggest such a close connection between the *Cāndravyākaraṇa* and Somapura which would have justified the proposed interpretation.

[123] According to an alternative interpretation, Vijayagarbha who was a scholar (*°*śāstā*) from Somapura (*Somapurīya°*) and an expert in [writing] commentaries (*vyākhyāpaṭuḥ*) composed (*akārṣīt*) this (*imām*) [sc. *Candrālaṃkṛti*].

[124] DUTT 1962, p. 376; cf. DIKSHIT 1938, p. 74: "It is interesting to see that all the donors, of whom the first one is mentioned as a *Bhikshu*, have names ending in *garbha*, viz., Ajayagarbha, Śrīgarbha and Daśabalagarbha. It is possible that these indicate one continuity or succession of monks who were at Somapura Vihāra." Atiśa himself was known in his early years under the name of Candragarbha, whereas his two brothers were called Padmagarbha and Śrīgarbha (see CHATTOPADHYAYA 1967, pp. 56–66, cf. also *ibid.*, pp. 30–36).

referring to one and the same person. A plausible explanation in this line might be that upon his arrival at Somapura the foreign monk Sāriputta from the land of Siṃhala was given the additional ordination name Vijayagarbha which was more preferable in the local milieu.[125] It can hardly be ascribed to a coincidence that in the *Candrālaṃkāra* there is an explicit reference to the monk community of the Nālandā Mahāvihāra. This seems to indicate that our author was in one way or another associated with this Buddhist monastic centre, and most likely spent some time in Northern India.[126]

In the second half of the stanza, the forty-fourth (two [times] twenty two) year of the reign of king Rāmapāla is mentioned. This Pāla king ruled in the ancient land of Varendrī which included parts of today's Malda District of West Bengal and the Dinajpur, Bogra and Rajshahi Districts of Bangladesh. The Tibetan polymath Tāranātha (1575–1634) claims that Rāmapāla ruled for about forty-six years,[127] whereas modern scholars such as SIRCAR and MAJUMDAR consider Rāmapāla's reign to have lasted for fifty-three years.[128] The latest records known so far from Rāmapāla's time of rule are the Chandimau image inscription dated in his forty-second regnal year[129] and a *Pañcarakṣā* manuscript written in

---

[125] As BHIKKHU PĀSĀDIKA kindly pointed out to me in a private communication, "in Indien – insbesondere in Nālandā, wo der bekannte Buddha-Jünger Sāriputta geboren wurde – war es vermutlich nicht Sitte wie in Sri Lanka heute noch, daß die Mönche sehr oft Namen der bekanntesten Schüler des Buddha als Ordinationsnamen erhielten bzw. noch erhalten (am häufigsten „Ānanda")"; cf. RHYS DAVIDS 1897, pp. 39–40.

[126] This reference is found on the last line of fol. 3Ib which is damaged at the end, whereas the next folio is not preserved (cf. the transcript in ch. 2.1.1 above). The beginning of the sentence (*śrīmanNālandīyāryamahāsaṃgha°*) reminds of the inscriptions on the official seals discovered at Nālandā (*Nālandā-mahāvihārīya-ārya-bhikṣu-saṅghasya*) and Somapura (*śrīSomapure mahavihārīya-ārya-bhikṣusaṁghasya*) [cited in DUTT 1962, pp. 330 and 374, respectively].

[127] See CHIMPA/CHATTOPADHYAYA 1970, p. 314.

[128] See SIRCAR 1976, p. 209; MAJUMDAR 1971, pp. 161–162.

[129] See BANERJI 1933, p. 39 and plate V (b); cf. HUNTINGTON 1984, pp. 68–69 and fig. 75 (see also *ibid.*, p. xvii).

the fifty-third year of his reign.[130] The last stanza in the *Candrālaṃkāra* manuscript confirms now that Rāmapāla's rule lasted at least forty-four years. According to SIRCAR's chronology of the Pāla dynasty, Rāmapāla commenced his reign in the year AD 1072. Thus, the year indicated in the stanza would correspond to AD 1116.[131] This date most likely relates in some specific way to the time of completion of the *Candrālaṃkāra*.[132] Therefore, if Sāriputta is indeed the author of this treatise, it will have to be assumed that the *Candrālaṃkāra* was written rather in his youth, for at the time of king Parakkamabāhu I (1153–1186) he must have already been an elderly much respected religious leader and scholar.[133]

It cannot be decided unequivocally whether the Bhaikṣukī manuscript itself was also written in AD 1116 and, if not, how much later it was finished. The answer to this question depends to a great extent on the supposed relationship between Sāriputta and the author of the last stanza in the manuscript. It will perhaps be not too far-fetched to assume that this *codex unicus* is the first clean copy of Sāriputta's treatise prepared by a professional scribe and proofread by the author himself. After the final stanza of the treatise the scribe probably felt it necessary

---

[130] See BANERJEE 1969, pp. 61–63, and BANERJEE 1975, p. 110, note 35. Lately HIDAS offered a brief description of this manuscript with further references (see HIDAS 2008, pp. 73–74). For an outline of Rāmapāla's reign see MAJUMDAR 1943, pp. 155–156, and MAJUMDAR 1971, pp. 146–155. For a convenient overview of the differing chronological systems for the Pāla dynasty see HUNTINGTON 1984, pp. 29–37; see also *ibid.*, pp. 67–69 and 231–234.

[131] The date as given in the stanza is difficult to interpret, since it is apparently both incomplete and corrupt. Skt. *māghāṃśake daśasu* may have been thought to mean "on the tenth day in the [month of] Māgha".

[132] According to BECHERT, the *Candrālaṃkāra* was composed in the second half of the twelfth century (see BECHERT 1987, p. 9). This dating seems, however, to be just a rough guess probably based on the fact that Sāriputta is best known for his activities during the reign of king Parakkamabāhu I (1153–1186).

[133] That Sāriputta was held in high regard in the second half of the twelfth century is indicated in the *Cūlavaṃsa* where it is mentioned that "[f]or the thera named Sāriputta who persevered firmly in discipline, he [i.e. king Parakkamabāhu I] erected a vast (and) glorious pāsāda with rooms, terraces and chambers" at the Jetavana Vihāra (*Cūlavaṃsa* 78.34, tr. GEIGER/RICKMERS 1930, p. 105; cf. CROSBY 2006, pp. 52–54).

to name the author explicitly and record the date in which the treatise and, respectively, its authorized master copy were completed. The word *abhilikhyamāne* in particular seems to indicate that this final stanza was most likely penned by a scribe and not by the author himself.[134]

The date indicated in the last stanza serves in any case as a *terminus post quem* for the preparation of this manuscript. It follows that this codex cannot have been written earlier than the second decade of the twelfth century. On palaeographic and historical grounds, it seems likely that the Bhaikṣukī manuscript of the *Candrālaṃkāra* was indeed prepared still within the twelfth century.

### 2.1.6 The fate of the *Candrālaṃkāra* manuscript

The fact that the inscriptions in the Bhaikṣukī script were unearthed mainly in Eastern Bihar suggests that this script had apparently a rather limited geographical distribution. The language used in the inscriptions and in the *Maṇicūḍajātaka* manuscript indicates furthermore that the script was in use particularly by a group of Hīnayāna Buddhists of the Sāṃmitīya school,[135] or, as SIRCAR has put it, it was "prevalent among the Buddhist monks of the eastern regions of North India during the early

---

[134] In this context it is worth comparing the colophon of a manuscript of the *Aṣṭasāhasrikāprajñāpāramitā* written at Nālandā in the fifteenth year of Rāmapāla's reign: *mahārājādhirājaparameśvarapavamabhaṭṭārakaparamasaugata(?)-śrīmadrāmapāladevapravarddhamānavijayarājye pañcādaśame samvatsare vyabhilikhyamānapatrāṅkenāpi samvat 15 | vaiśākhe dine kṛṣṇasaptamyāṃ | asti Magadhaviṣaye śrīnālandavasin (?) lekhaka Ahanakuṇḍena bhaṭṭārakaiḥ Prajñāpāramitā likhitā* | (see WINTERNITZ/KEITH 1905, p. 250, no. 1428–MS. Sansk. a. 7 (R); the manuscript certainly reads °*parama*° i.o °*pavama*° and possibly °*mane yatrāṅkenāpi* i.o. °*manapatrāṅkenāpi*); cf. also *Proceedings* 1900, pp. 39–40 and 69–70 for ŚĀSTRĪ's and BLOCH's comments on the colophon of another manuscript of the *Aṣṭasāhasrikāprajñāpāramitā* written at Nālandā in the sixth year of Mahīpāla's reign. In the colophon of the latter codex the phrase *abhilikhyamāne* occurs.

[135] Cf. SKILLING 1997, pp. 108–113, esp. p. 112: "We may therefore conclude that the Sāmmatīyas were responsible for the inscriptions, and that the language is that of their canon: that is, that Monghyr District was indeed the major Sāmmatīya centre [...]"; see also NAMIKAWA 1993, pp. 151–166, OKANO 1998, pp. 13–18, and HANISCH 2006, p. 135.

medieval period, especially at Uddaṇḍapura (modern Biharsharif in the Patna District of Bihar)".[136] Bihar Sharif is just a stone's throw from the main cites where inscriptions in the Bhaikṣukī script have been discovered.

Although only one dated inscription has been found so far, the general belief that these inscriptions belong to a period between the eleventh and twelfth centuries seems to be justified. This assumption is moreover supported by the Bhaikṣukī manuscripts that turned up in Nepal and Tibet, since they contain texts which were composed not earlier than the twelfth century. The *Maṇicūḍajātaka* was written by the Buddhist grammarian and poet Sarvarakṣita who also authored the *Mahāsaṃvartanīkathā*.[137] He lived in the twelfth century[138] and was a contemporary of Sāriputta, the proposed author of the *Candrālaṃkāra*. For palaeographic and historical reasons it is unlikely that the Bhaikṣukī manuscripts of the *Maṇicūḍajātaka* and the *Candrālaṃkāra* were written later than the twelfth century or the beginning of the thirteenth century.[139]

It is well known that during the twelfth century the Buddhist universities in India suffered a pitiful fate. As STEINKELLNER has summarized in his *Tale of Leaves*, "Muslim raids swept through Northern India with steadily increasing pressure during this period. The great centres of Buddhist learning as for example in the Pāla realm, were destroyed near the turn to the thirteenth century, and with them their libraries: Odantapura, Vikramaśīla, Somapura, and Jagaddala."[140] At the threat of

---

[136] SIRCAR 1966, p. 79; SIRCAR's localization is most probably based on al-Bīrūnī's information that the Bhaikṣukī script was "used in Uduṇpûr in Pûrvadeśa" (SACHAU 1887–88, vol. I, p. 173; see ch. 1.1 above).

[137] See ed. OKANO 1998.

[138] See OKANO 1998, pp. 10–18.

[139] For the same reasons OKANO's assumption that the manuscript of the *Abhidharmasamuccayakārikā* found by TUCCI in Gongkar was written after 1435 in the Nalendra monastery in Tibet appears to me highly unlikely.

[140] STEINKELLNER 2004, p. 9; cf. also WADDELL 1892, pp. 19–22, DUTT 1962, pp. 354–380, and WARDER 1980, pp. 506–516.

the Muslim newcomers, many Indian scholars and monks were forced to run for their lives bringing with them their most valuable books. Some went to Eastern Bengal, Nepal and further to Tibet, others found shelter in the valleys of Burma and beyond.[141]

It could well be that during this troublesome time the *Candrālaṃkāra* manuscript was rescued by fleeing Buddhists and brought to the safety of Kathmandu, where one portion of it has survived till modern times. The history of the manuscript until the day BENDALL purchased 34 leaves of it in 1884 is, however, shrouded in darkness. There is no information about the circumstances under which the manuscript fragment was purchased, nor are we told anything about its original owner. Whereas BENDALL's portion ended its long and precipitous journey in the Cambridge University Library where it is presently kept, we know that at least 23 more folios remained in Kathmandu. In 1971 these folios were still available in the private collection of Dr Mānavajra Vajrācārya who allowed the IASWR to photograph the whole portion. Since then, all trace of 21 of these folios has unfortunately been lost. As mentioned above, recently Dr Madhuvajra Vajrācārya confirmed that only two folios have remained in his father's library, and these are probably the same two leaves photographed by the NGMPP in 1983.

FIGURE 7: Terracotta panel from the Somapura Mahāvihāra

[141] See LUCE/TIN HTWAY 1976, p. 206, and BHIKKHU PĀSĀDIKA 2006, p. 472; cf. RAY 1936.

## 2.2 Further Traces of the Bhaikṣukī Script

In the course of my study of the *Candrālaṃkāra* manuscript I quite unexpectedly discovered further traces of the Bhaikṣukī script in an old palm-leaf manuscript written in Proto-Bengali script[142] of the eleventh century. This is the afore-mentioned codex of Ratnamati's *Cāndravyākaraṇapañjikā* photographed by Sāṅkṛtyāyana in Tibet in the summer of 1937, which is said to be kept nowadays in the Nor bu liṅ ka monastery in Lhasa.[143] I had the opportunity to see a reproduction of Sāṅkṛtyāyana's photographs, many of them of quite poor quality and some completely illegible. Though 36 folios are missing, this is the most complete manuscript of Ratnamati's voluminous work known to exist.[144] When I checked this valuable codex, I was surprised to discover below the original letter-numerals at the left-hand margin on the verso side of each leaf a secondary pagination written in the Bhaikṣukī script.[145]

It can hardly be a mere coincidence that in a rare manuscript of Ratnamati's *Cāndravyākaraṇapañjikā* written in Proto-Bengali script of the eleventh century, Bhaikṣukī letter-numerals of the same type have been added like those in the Bhaikṣukī manuscript containing a commentary on this very same work by Ratnamati. Although the similarity

---

142 For the term "Proto-Bengali" see Dimitrov 2002, pp. 29–33.

143 See Hu-von Hinüber 2006, pp. 286 and 320 (MS no. 149); cf. Bandurski 1994, p. 106.

144 Originally the manuscript consisted of 266 folios, of which 36 folios (fols. 26, 53–60, 81–89 and 91–108) seem to have already been missing at the time of filming. Thus, 230 folios have been preserved (fols. 1–25, 27–52, 61–80, 90 and 109–266). However, due to some unlucky misplacement of leaves the recto sides of fols. 194–203 and the verso sides of fols. 124–133 have not been photographed. Instead, the recto sides of fols. 124–133 and the verso sides of fols. 194–203 have been retaken. Fols. 61–67 and 204–212 have also been photographed twice. Similarly, the recto side of fol. 12 appears twice on the photographs, whereas the verso side is missing.

145 This second pagination has already been noticed by Bandurski who was, however, not able to identify the script (see Bandurski 1994, p. 105).

of the fairly uniform Bhaikṣukī characters cannot be a conclusive argument, the fact of their extremely rare occurrence in written documents and the established connection between the texts transmitted in the two codices leave hardly any doubt that the Proto-Bengali manuscript of the *Cāndravyākaraṇapañjikā* and the Bhaikṣukī manuscript of the *Candrālaṃkāra* are related. However, we can only hypothesize about the exact nature of this relationship.

The most sensational theory is in any case that the scholar who composed the *Candrālaṃkāra* had studied Ratnamati's work from this very same Proto-Bengali manuscript and possibly he or someone working together with him wrote in the margin the Bhaikṣukī letter-numerals. The Bhaikṣukī pagination may have appeared at the start of the work on the *Cāndravyākaraṇapañjikā*, when this scholar added letter-numerals in his own script in order to avoid bringing the leaves of the Proto-Bengali manuscript into disorder. Thus, it is possible that by some incredible twists and turns of fate the working materials of the author of the *Candrālaṃkāra* have been preserved in Tibet. In this case it would indeed be tempting to consider the Bhaikṣukī manuscript of the *Candrālaṃkāra* an autograph or an authorized clean copy written in the first quarter of the twelfth century. If internal evidence confirms this hypothesis, this codex will prove to be of exceptional importance in the fields of Indian grammar, palaeography, and manuscriptology alike. The analysis of the internal evidence so far neither clearly supports nor denies the possibility of this manuscript being a master copy from an original draft.[146]

Another possible explanation is that while studying the *Candrālaṃkāra* a few years after the commentary itself was written, some unknown scholar who must have used the Bhaikṣukī script as his native script consulted the Proto-Bengali manuscript of the *Cāndravyākaraṇa-*

---

[146] It is noteworthy that the Bhaikṣukī manuscript of the *Candrālaṃkāra* contains many corrections which seem to have been made by the scribe himself. The copyist who prepared this manuscript was either admirably self-critical and conscientious, or there was someone else sitting next to him who was helping to correct the "slips of the pen".

*pañjikā* and added the secondary pagination to avoid confusion of the leaves during his work with this codex.

A third theory is that the Bhaikṣukī letter-numerals were added in the Proto-Bengali manuscript independent of the *Candrālaṃkāra* and possibly even before the latter commentary was written. This scenario does not exclude the possibility that the same Proto-Bengali manuscript was later used by the author of the *Candrālaṃkāra*.

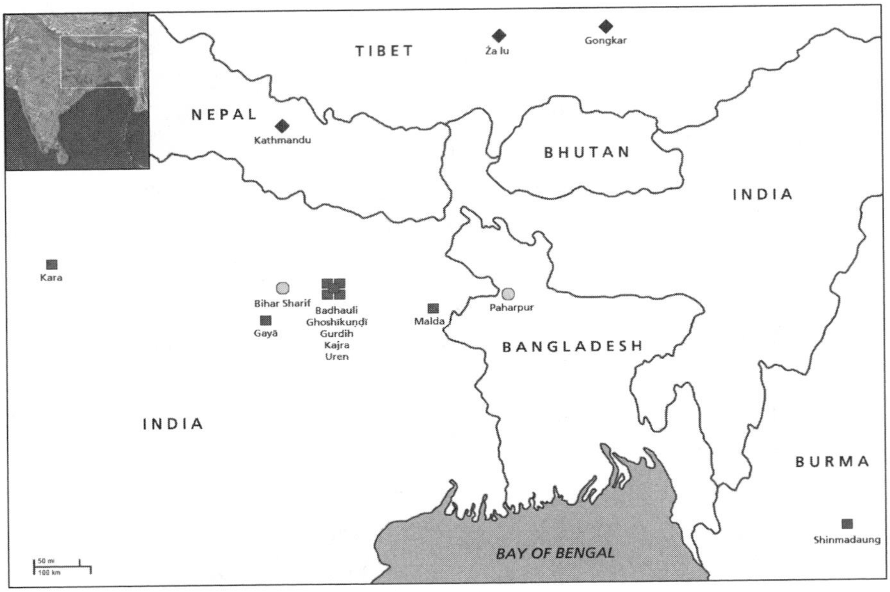


MAP 1: Sites of inscriptions (■) and manuscripts (◆) in the Bhaikṣukī script, and other places (○) where this script has reportedly been used.

## 2.3 Letter-Numerals in the Bhaikṣukī Script

Thanks to the manuscript of the *Cāndravyākaraṇapañjikā*, we have now a large set of more than 200 letter-numerals in the Bhaikṣukī script. The availability of such a large number of letter-numerals is almost a miracle, if one considers that until now we have at our disposal a total of only 69 folios written in this script.

In the following table all letter-numerals from Sāṅkṛtyāyana's photographs are reproduced. Since the quality of these photographs is in many cases quite poor and some of the letter-numerals are hardly legible or damaged, touching up the images and retouching the characters was inevitable. The letter-numerals for the following numbers can be seen more or less clearly: 2–11, 13–25, 27–51, 62–80, 109–123, 134–220, 222–230, 232–244, 246–247, 249–262, and 264. In a few cases significant parts of these characters are missing due to a physical damage (e.g. fols. 61, 221, 231, 265–266). On fols. 245, 248, and 263 the letter-numerals for 145, 148 and 163, respectively, have been written by mistake. On fols. 1, 52, and 90 no letter-numerals in the Bhaikṣukī script have been added. It is believed that despite these shortcomings, the table drawn up below offers a fairly precise and thorough impression of the system of the letter-numerals in the Bhaikṣukī script. Even though some characters are missing, with the help of the preserved letter-numerals now the whole system can be reconstructed easily.

**Table of the letter-numerals in the Bhaikṣukī script**

| 1 | 2 | 3 | 4 | 5 | 6 | 7 | 8 | 9 | 10 |
|---|---|---|---|---|---|---|---|---|---|

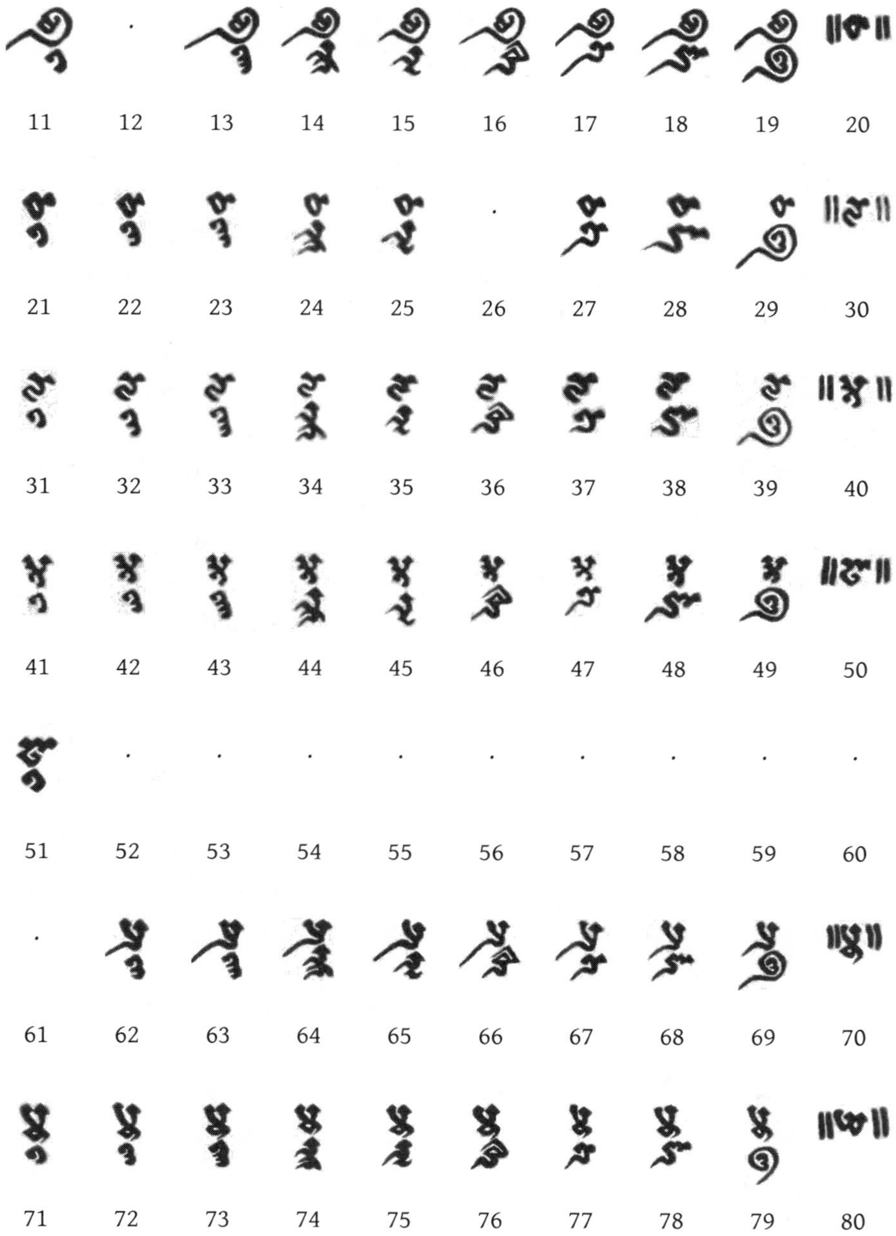
11 12 13 14 15 16 17 18 19 20
21 22 23 24 25 26 27 28 29 30
31 32 33 34 35 36 37 38 39 40
41 42 43 44 45 46 47 48 49 50
51 52 53 54 55 56 57 58 59 60
61 62 63 64 65 66 67 68 69 70
71 72 73 74 75 76 77 78 79 80

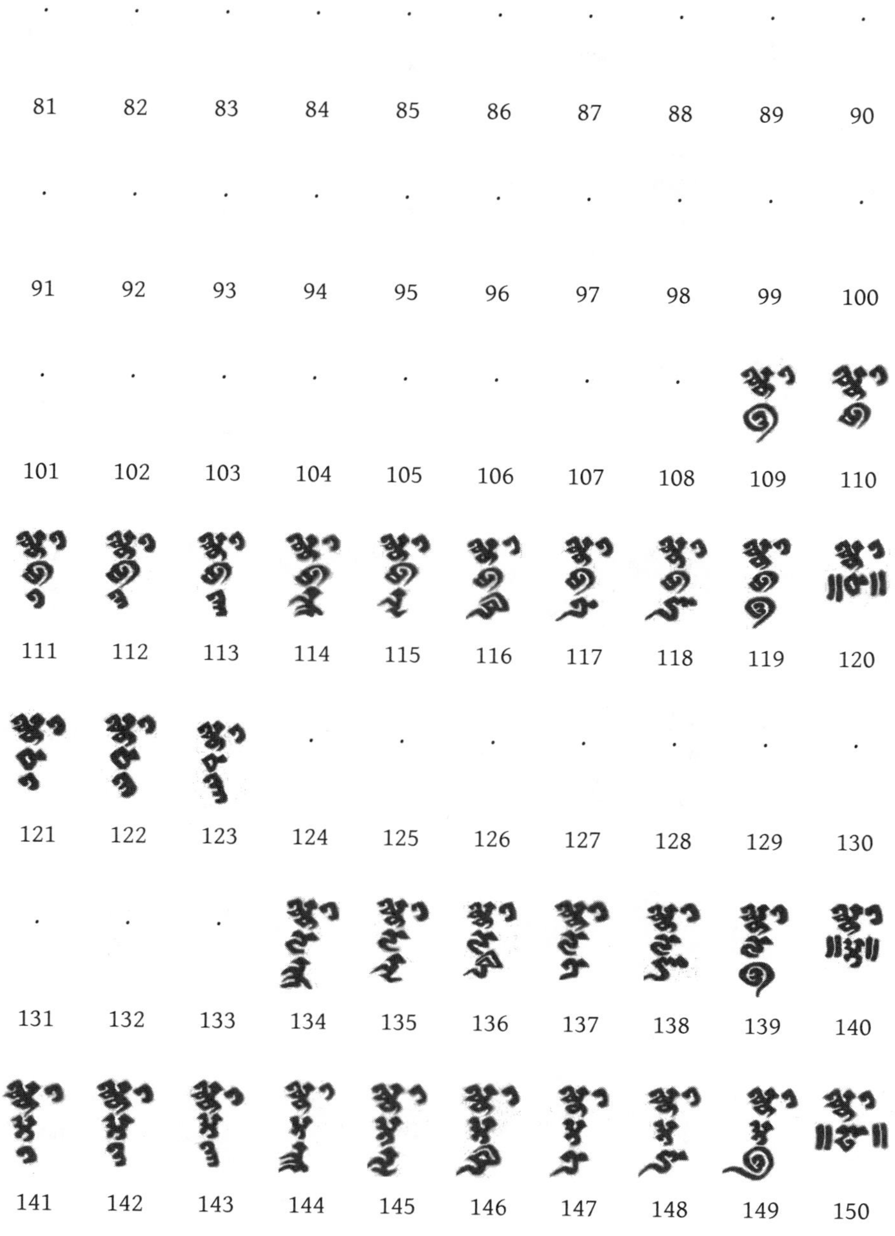
81 82 83 84 85 86 87 88 89 90
91 92 93 94 95 96 97 98 99 100
101 102 103 104 105 106 107 108 109 110
111 112 113 114 115 116 117 118 119 120
121 122 123 124 125 126 127 128 129 130
131 132 133 134 135 136 137 138 139 140
141 142 143 144 145 146 147 148 149 150

151 152 153 154 155 156 157 158 159 160

161 162 163 164 165 166 167 168 169 170

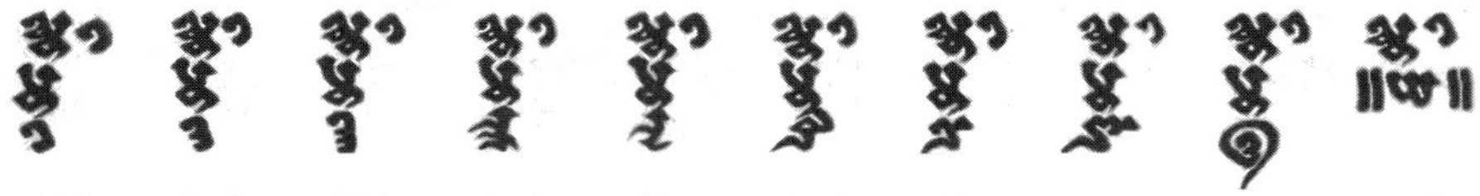

171 172 173 174 175 176 177 178 179 180

181 182 183 184 185 186 187 188 189 190

191 192 193 194 195 196 197 198 199 200

201 202 203 204 205 206 207 208 209 210

211 212 213 214 215 216 217 218 219 220

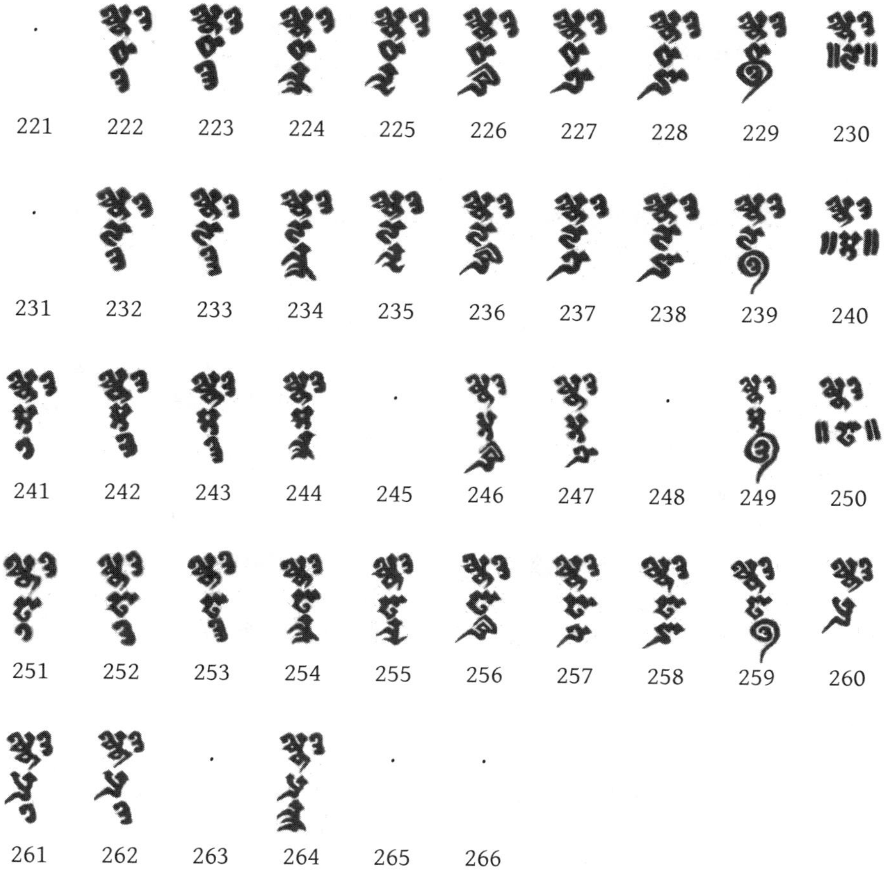


Due to the paucity of the available material, until very recently it has not been possible to describe adequately the system of the letter-numerals used in the Bhaikṣukī manuscripts.[147] The new discovery allows us now to see that this system closely follows the principles known from other manuscripts from Bengal and Nepal written in the same period.[148] A general feature of this system is that each digit is written on a separate line, so that when a number consists of more than one digit, the characters

[147] Cf. Hanisch 2006, p. 113.

[148] Cf. Bühler 1896, pp. 74–79.

signifying the smallest digit, the ten, the hundred, etc. are written vertically one under the other with the smallest digit at the bottom.

The numbers from 1 to 3 are represented by characters which appear as cursive forms of one, two, and three lines, respectively, written in the same style as the proper Bhaikṣukī letters. The letter-numeral for 1 (cf. 21) looks very similar to the syllable *ga* without the characteristic arrow-head. The letter-numerals (2) and (3) resemble the syllable *na* and the geminate *nna*, respectively. It is important to stress, however, that no complete identity between the letter-numerals and the regular letters has been aimed at, for this would have been against the general principle of the system. Although the resemblance to actual letters is obviously not coincidental, the identity with them is carefully avoided.

The simple numbers from 4 to 9 and the whole numbers 10, 20, 30, etc. are also represented by characters which bear some similarity to particular basic and conjunct letters in the Bhaikṣukī script. For example, (4) recalls the form of *lka* (cf. *lkā*), (5) resembles *tu*, (6) looks similar to *rī*, (7) is a stylized *ga*, (8) is similarly a stylized *ṭa*, and in (9) the characteristic element of an initial *u* can be seen. The similarity to individual characters is also evident when one compares (10) with *m* at the end of a word, (20) with *dha*, (30) with *la*, (40) with the ligature *pta*, (50) with *ḍha*, (60) with an initial *ṛ*, (70) with both *ṛ* and a subscribed *(m)bha*, as well as both (80) and (90) with *ya*.

Some of these characters or elements thereof are similar to the letter-numerals written in the Proto-Bengali script in the same manuscript. This is obviously the case with the letter-numerals for 4, 5, 7, 9, 20, 30, 40, 60, 70, 80, 90, and their combinations. As for the Proto-Bengali letter-numerals, they significantly resemble those found by Bendall in four manuscripts written in the first half of the eleventh century (kept now in Cambridge, Or. 1464, 1643, 1683, and 1688).[149] This substantiates

[149] Cf. the table of letter-numerals in Bendall 1883; see also *idid.*, pp. xxv, 101–102, 151–152 and 172.

the assumption that the *Cāndravyākaraṇapañjikā* manuscript discovered in Tibet was written in the eleventh century, probably in its first half.

Since in the eleventh and twelfth centuries the Bhaikṣukī script was used in a locality adjacent to or even overlapping with the geographical area where the distinct forms of the Bengali script were developing, the resemblance between the Proto-Bengali and the Bhaikṣukī letter-numerals might be due to the direct contact between the two scripts. Particularly noteworthy is the similarity between the Bhaikṣukī letter-numerals for 1 to 3 and the corresponding characters used in a manuscript from Bengal written in circa AD 1054 (Or. 1688).[150] It is nonetheless quite possible that the Bhaikṣukī letter-numerals have developed initially independent of the Proto-Bengali script. This may explain certain archaic features which connect the Bhaikṣukī letter-numerals with the characters used in the ancient Brāhmī script.

Besides the obvious similarities between the Bhaikṣukī and the Proto-Bengali letter-numerals used in the *Cāndravyākaraṇapañjikā* manuscript, there are also conspicuous differences concerning some general features of the two sets. Thus, whereas in the Proto-Bengali script a circle for zero is used for the whole tens (10, 20, 30, etc.), in the Bhaikṣukī letter-numerals there is no symbol for the zero. Instead double *daṇḍas* are written on both sides of the character for the ten.[151] Another interesting difference is the way the hundreds are written in both scripts. In the Proto-Bengali script two characters very much resembling the syllables *lu* and *lū* are used for 100 and 200, respectively, as is the common practice in other manuscripts from Bengal and Nepal written in the same period.[152] The Bhaikṣukī letter-numerals  (100) and  (200)[153] consist, on the other hand, of two elements written one

[150] Cf. BENDALL 1883, p. 175, and the table of letter-numerals therein.

[151] In the case of the letter-numerals for 110, 210, and 260 these *daṇḍas* are missing.

[152] Cf. BÜHLER 1896, p. 76.

[153] Since fol. 100 of the *Cāndravyākaraṇapañjikā* manuscript is missing, the Bhaikṣukī letter-numeral for the whole number 100 and its Proto-Bengali equivalent cannot be seen. On fols. 198–210 no letter-numerals in the Proto-Bengali script are written.

next to the other. The element on the left side resembles the conjunct letter *sbhe*, to the right of which the characters for 1 and 2, respectively, are added. The unattested letter-numeral for 300 most probably was written in a similar multiplicative way with the character for 3 on the right side, and 400 had on its right side the letter-numeral for 4. Similarly, the letter-numerals for 500, 600, 700, 800, and 900 can be reconstructed. This manner of writing the hundreds recalls the corresponding forms of the letter-numerals used in inscriptions.[154] It may be considered a conservative, if not archaic feature of the Bhaikṣukī letter-numerals.

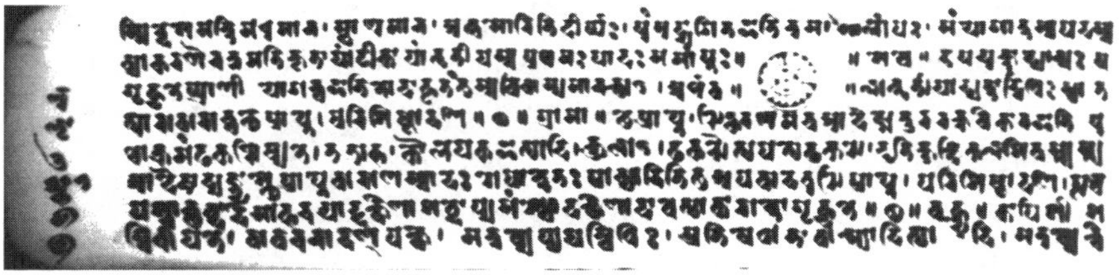

FIGURE 8: Fol. 119b (left part) of a manuscript of the *Cāndravyākaraṇapañjikā*

[154] Cf. BÜHLER 1896, p. 77.

## 2.4 The Order of the Folios of the Candrālaṃkāra Manuscript

The unexpected discovery of the Bhaikṣukī letter-numerals in the Proto-Bengali manuscript of the *Cāndravyākaraṇapañjikā* helps us to put in order the preserved folios of the *Candrālaṃkāra* manuscript which in the course of time have been thrown in disarray. Not only did the rare Bhaikṣukī script pose an obstacle to those who were willing to read this manuscript, but its poor state of preservation also made it a formidable task to properly order the leaves. Most of the leaves from the Cambridge portion are broken at the left-hand margin, so that the pagination on the reverse side of each leaf is either completely missing or only some hardly legible traces of it can be recognized. However, even the few preserved folio numbers posed problems because until recently the system of the Bhaikṣukī letter-numerals was by and large unclear. To add to the confusion, in the Kathmandu portion two different folios bearing one and the same letter-numeral were observed.

The quickest way to find the right place for every piece of the jigsaw puzzle is to identify all quotations from the *sūtra* text of the *Cāndravyākaraṇa*. These quotations, namely the *pratīka*s, are given in an abbreviated form and are easily identifiable, since they are always well set off between double *daṇḍa*s. Thus, even when the folio numbers are missing, from the sequence of the *pratīka*s a reliable conclusion regarding the order in which the leaves containing these quotations were originally put can be drawn. It is necessary to rely on the broader context only when there are no *pratīka*s on the leaf, as is the case with three leaves of the Cambridge portion and another four leaves from the Kathmandu portion of the manuscript.

It was Liebich who more than a century ago first suggested to rearrange the leaves of the Cambridge portion of the manuscript. He observed that the Arabic numbers added by a modern hand[155] in the upper

[155] These numbers were actually added by Bendall himself and reflect the (dis)-order in which the leaves were at the time he purchased the manuscript in Kathmandu

middle part on the verso side of each leaf do not indicate the proper order. With the exception of the three leaves from this portion on which no *pratīkas* are available and two more leaves with *pratīkas* which have either been unnoticed or not properly identified, LIEBICH indicated the correct sequence of the leaves.[156] However, since the arrangement of the leaves was discussed only in a brief footnote, it remained for a long time unnoticed, and even in recent publications LIEBICH was not credited adequately with his successful efforts.

While studying the Bhaikṣukī manuscript of the *Maṇicūḍajātaka*, HANISCH carefully re-examined the *Candrālaṃkāra* manuscript and compiled a list of the *sūtras* from the *Cāndravyākaraṇa* cited there.[157] On the basis of his preliminary analysis, HANISCH was able to determine the proper sequence of all leaves containing *pratīkas*, with the exception of one folio on which the single available *pratīka* was already wrongly identified by LIEBICH.[158]

---

(see BENDALL 1886, p. 123, note 2). The numbers 13 and 14 are written on one and the same folio (on its recto and verso side, respectively), and by mistake the number 22 was given twice on two different folios.

[156] LIEBICH 1895, p. 40, note 1: "Die richtige Reihenfolge ist diese (die Gedankenstriche zeigen die Lücken an): 1, 4, 29, 30, 31, 5, 12 – 14 – 21, 18, 20, 25 – 8 – 24, 23, 11, 28, 27, 26 – 34, 33, 32, 22, 15 – 10, 16, 17, 9, 22, 19 –. [...] Es fehlen, 2, 3, 6, 7 und 13." From the leaves which LIEBICH could not put in order, nos. 3 and 7 come before no. 1, no. 2 fills the gap (not noticed by LIEBICH) between nos. 1 and 4, no. 6 fills another gap (also unnoticed by LIEBICH) between nos. 31 and 5, and no. 13 is actually the recto side of no. 14. Besides this, one leaf is missing between nos. 9 and 22*, and no. 21 was not ordered correctly.

[157] See HANISCH 2007, pp. 150–155. In this "Alphabetical list of sūtras of the *Cāndravyākaraṇa* explained in the *Candrālaṃkāra*" the *sūtras* which are commented upon, but of which no *pratīkas* are available due to missing folios, are not indicated. Only after a thorough examination of the material it may become possible to identify all the *sūtras* which have been dealt with on the available folios. Besides this, it should be mentioned that although missing in HANISCH's list, the *pratīkas* of the following *sūtras* are in fact available in the preserved part of the *Candrālaṃkāra* manuscript: Cān. 1.1.151, 5.4.76, 6.1.62–66, 6.1.68, 6.2.10, 6.2.36, 6.4.6, and possibly also 6.4.35.

[158] LIEBICH did not order BENDALL's leaf no. 21 (fol. 23$^{I}$) properly, most probably because he had assumed that *ekāca* on this leaf is the abbreviation of Cān. 5.4.130 (*ekāco*

Neither LIEBICH nor HANISCH, however, were able to entirely reconstruct the actual folio numbers. Moreover, six leaves without *pratīkas* remained "unidentified".[159] Soon after I started working on the *Candrālaṃkāra* manuscript, the study of the context allowed me to order these folios. Besides this, it became clear that for some unknown reason the folios of this manuscript were arranged in two distinct units. These two units are marked graphically as separate manuscripts and each bears its own pagination.

The first folio of the first part is missing. On both the left-hand and the right-hand margins of the recto side as well as around the binding hole of the second folio vertical ruling lines are drawn. The last preserved folio of this part, probably fol. 31ᴵ, ends with the beginning of the commentary on the second section of the first chapter. We can only speculate whether this part of the manuscript contained the commentary up to the end of the fourth chapter and how many folios it comprised altogether.

What is certain is that the commentary on the fifth and sixth chapters was copied as if it had been another manuscript. This part of the text begins on the verso side of a leaf the recto side of which was initially blank.[160] On the verso side of this folio and on the recto side of the next one vertical ruling lines are drawn in the same way as on fol. 2ᴵ of the first part. The commentary on the fifth chapter is preceded by an invocation (*namo Mañjunāthāya*) and the pagination starts anew. The folio numbers on the first two leaves of this part are brocken off. There

*'śviśriḍīśīñūyvādiṣaṭkāt)*. Actually, the *sūtra* abbreviated here is Cān. 1.1.40 (*ekāco halādeḥ kriyārthād bhṛśābhīkṣṇye yaṅ*).

[159] Since the seventh folio without *pratīkas* contains the colophon of the work, it was immediately clear that this is the last leaf of the whole manuscript. Recently HANISCH rightly suggested the correct position and folio number of fol. 8ᴵ (see HANISCH 2007, p. 148, note 53).

[160] Later it was filled up by a second hand in Newari script. The text, namely ten stanzas in the Anuṣṭubh metre written in more or less corrupt Sanskrit, appears to have been copied from some astrological treatise from a section in which constellations are dealt with.

are, however, traces of the letter-numerals on fol. $3^{II}$ and on some of the subsequent folios. Interestingly, the commmentary on the sixth chapter is headed by another invocation (*namo Buddhāya*),[161] although the text does not begin on a new folio and the pagination is continued until the end of the manuscript. On the verso side of fol. $73^{II}$ (probably the ante-penultimate leaf of the manuscript with the commentary on the last *sūtra* of the *Cāndravyākaraṇa* commencing on it) vertical lines can also be observed. It appears that such lines were drawn only on the initial and final leaves of each manuscript unity.

As a result of this curious distribution of the *Candrālaṃkāra* in (at least) two "manuscripts" written most probably by one and the same hand, on the preserved folios we have two incomplete sets of letter-numerals, one set from 1 to 31, and another set from 1 to 75. With the help of the newly discovered set of the Bhaikṣukī letter-numerals in the *Cāndravyākaraṇapañjikā* manuscript we can verify the pagination of the *Candrālaṃkāra* manuscript and reconstruct the missing letter-numerals on each folio, with only few doubtful cases remaining. Thus, we are now ultimately in a position to put all the leaves in their original order.

### 2.4.1 Concordance to the Cambridge microfilm copy

The microfilm master copy of the *Candrālaṃkāra* manuscript in the Cambridge University Library (Or. 1278) bears the number 14101. The microfilm copy used for the purposes of this study was prepared in May 2006. This microfilm comprises of 37 exposures, the first two of which contain a copyright notice and a library card with the classmark of the manuscript. In the first column of the following concordance the number of the exposure and the position of the side of the leaf to be seen on it (either top [t] or bottom [b]) are indicated. In the second column the corresponding Arabic numbers written on the verso (v) side of the leaf are given. Only in one case a number has also been added on the recto (r)

[161] Perhaps a different invocation was placed at the beginning of the commentary on each chapter.

side. The third column contains the actual folio number with an indication of its recto (a) or verso (b) side. It is important to note that fol. 41$^{II}$a has been omitted by mistake; instead, fol. 41$^{II}$b has been photographed twice on exps. 8b and 9t.

| Exp. | No. | Fol. | Exp. | No. | Fol. | Exp. | No. | Fol. |
|---|---|---|---|---|---|---|---|---|
| 1 | 1r | 1$^{II}$a | 13t | 12r | 11$^{II}$a | 24b | 24v | 44$^{II}$b |
| 2t | 1v | 1$^{II}$b | 13b | 13 | 17$^{II}$a | 25t | 24r | 44$^{II}$a |
| 2b | 2v | 2$^{II}$b | 14t | 14 | 17$^{II}$b | 25b | 25v | 37$^{II}$b |
| 3t | 2r | 2$^{II}$a | 14b | 15v | 57$^{II}$b | 26t | 25r | 37$^{II}$a |
| 3b | 3v | 2$^{I}$b | 15t | 15r | 57$^{II}$a | 26b | 26v | 49$^{II}$b |
| 4t | 3r | 2$^{I}$a | 15b | 16v | 60$^{II}$b | 27t | 26r | 49$^{II}$a |
| 4b | 4r | 3$^{II}$a | 16t | 16r | 60$^{II}$a | 27b | 27v | 48$^{II}$b |
| 5t | 4v | 3$^{II}$b | 16b | 17v | 61$^{II}$b | 28t | 27r | 48$^{II}$a |
| 5b | 5v | 9$^{II}$b | 17t | 17r | 61$^{II}$a | 28b | 28v | 47$^{II}$b |
| 6t | 5r | 9$^{II}$a | 17b | 18v | 35$^{II}$b | 29t | 28r | 47$^{II}$a |
| 6b | 6v | 8$^{II}$b | 18t | 18r | 35$^{II}$a | 29b | 29v | 4$^{II}$b |
| 7t | 6r | 8$^{II}$a | 18b | 19v | 65$^{II}$b ? | 30t | 29r | 4$^{II}$a |
| 7b | 7v | 19$^{I}$b | 19t | 19r | 65$^{II}$a ? | 30b | 30v | 6$^{II}$b |
| 8t | 7r | 19$^{I}$a | 19b | 20v | 36$^{II}$b | 31t | 30r | 6$^{II}$a |
| 8b | 8v | 41$^{II}$b | 20t | 20r | 36$^{II}$a | 31b | 31v | 7$^{II}$b |
| 9t | 8v | 41$^{II}$b | 20b | 21v | 23$^{I}$b | 32t | 31r | 7$^{II}$a |
| 9b | 9v | 62$^{II}$b | 21t | 21r | 23$^{I}$a | 32b | 32v | 55$^{II}$b |
| 10t | 9r | 62$^{II}$a | 21b | 22v | 56$^{II}$b | 33t | 32r | 55$^{II}$a |
| 10b | 10v | 59$^{II}$b ? | 22t | 22r | 56$^{II}$a | 33b | 33v | 54$^{II}$b |
| 11t | 10r | 59$^{II}$a ? | 22b | 22*v | 64$^{II}$b ? | 34t | 33r | 54$^{II}$a |
| 11b | 11v | 46$^{II}$b | 23t | 22*r | 64$^{II}$a ? | 34b | 34v | 53$^{II}$b |
| 12t | 11r | 46$^{II}$a | 23b | 23v | 45$^{II}$b | 35 | 34r | 53$^{II}$a |
| 12b | 12v | 11$^{II}$b | 24t | 23r | 45$^{II}$a | | | |

### 2.4.2 Concordance to the Stony Brook microfiche copy

On the IASWR microfiche of the Kathmandu portion of the *Candrālaṃkāra* manuscript (LMhj-000, 035-1/1; MBB-1971-35) there are altogether 25 exposures. If the microfiche is placed in a landscape orientation with the first exposure in the upper left corner, these 25 exposures will be positioned on 4 rows and 7 columns. On row 1, column 1 the IASWR card is reproduced. On row 1, column 2 the catalogue card with the descriptive information about the manuscript can be seen. Thereafter follow the 23 exposures of the filmed manuscript with its leaves positioned vertically, each leaf side being either to the left (l) or to the right (r) on the exposure. The verso side of fol. 75$^{II}$ has not been filmed.[162] In the following concordance the number of each exposure, the row, the column, and the actual folio number are given.

| Exp. | Row | Col. | Fol. | Exp. | Row | Col. | Fol. | Exp. | Row | Col. | Fol. |
|---|---|---|---|---|---|---|---|---|---|---|---|
| 1 | 1 | 3 | 5$^{II}$b | 9l | 2 | 4 | 25$^{II}$a | 16r | 3 | 4 | 16$^{I}$b |
| 2l | 1 | 4 | 40$^{II}$a | 9r | 2 | 4 | 19$^{II}$b | 17l | 3 | 5 | 71$^{II}$a |
| 2r | 1 | 4 | 5$^{II}$a | 10l | 2 | 5 | 27$^{II}$a | 17r | 3 | 5 | 13$^{I}$b |
| 3l | 1 | 5 | 22$^{I}$a | 10r | 2 | 5 | 25$^{II}$b | 18l | 3 | 6 | 3$^{I}$b |
| 3r | 1 | 5 | 40$^{II}$b | 11l | 2 | 6 | 28$^{I}$a | 18r | 3 | 6 | 71$^{II}$b |
| 4l | 1 | 6 | 21$^{II}$a | 11r | 2 | 6 | 27$^{II}$b | 19l | 3 | 7 | 31$^{II}$a |
| 4r | 1 | 6 | 22$^{I}$b | 12l | 2 | 7 | 73$^{II}$a ? | 19r | 3 | 7 | 3$^{I}$a |
| 5l | 1 | 7 | 26$^{II}$a | 12r | 2 | 7 | 28$^{I}$b | 20l | 4 | 1 | 70$^{II}$b |
| 5r | 1 | 7 | 21$^{II}$b | 13l | 3 | 1 | 18$^{II}$b | 20r | 4 | 1 | 31$^{II}$b |
| 6l | 2 | 1 | 8$^{I}$a | 13r | 3 | 1 | 73$^{II}$b ? | 21l | 4 | 2 | 23$^{II}$a |
| 6r | 2 | 1 | 26$^{II}$b | 14l | 3 | 2 | 31$^{I}$b ? | 21r | 4 | 2 | 70$^{II}$a |
| 7l | 2 | 2 | 16$^{II}$a | 14r | 3 | 2 | 18$^{II}$a | 22l | 4 | 3 | 13$^{II}$a |
| 7r | 2 | 2 | 8$^{I}$b | 15l | 3 | 3 | 16$^{I}$a | 22r | 4 | 3 | 23$^{II}$b |
| 8l | 2 | 3 | 19$^{II}$a | 15r | 3 | 3 | 31$^{I}$a ? | 23l | 4 | 4 | 75$^{II}$a ? |
| 8r | 2 | 3 | 16$^{II}$b | 16l | 3 | 4 | 13$^{I}$a | 23r | 4 | 4 | 13$^{II}$b |

### 2.4.3 The original order of the folios

In the following list all folios from both parts of the *Candrālaṃkāra* manuscript preserved in Cambridge and Kathmandu are given in their original consecutive order. A dotted line indicates that one or more folios are missing. Most of the folio numbers given here have been reconstructed with a fair degree of certainty. Only in a few doubtful cases a question mark was deemed necessary to be added. Besides the infor-

[162] This side of the folio, which was initially blank, can be seen on the microfilm prepared by the NGMPP (Reel no.: E 1518/4). It was filled up by a later hand with three lines containing an invocation and the complete alphabet followed by some more scribbles ending with the word *kamalapatrākṣa*, all this written in a kind of script which bears some distant similarity with the Gujarati script. A third hand has added one more line written in late Newari script (Pracalitākṣara).

mation concerning the copies of the two parts of the manuscript, all *pratīkas* identified in the manuscript by HANISCH and a few more located by me afterwards have been indicated. It can now easily be seen that only one third (10 folios) of the sub-sub-commentary on the first section of the first chapter and about two thirds (47 folios) of the sub-sub-commentary on the last two chapters of the *Cāndravyākaraṇa* have been preserved.

| Fol. | Exp. | No. | Row | Col. | *Candrālaṃkāra* ad Cān. |
|---|---|---|---|---|---|
| $2^{I}$a | 4t | 3r | | | no *pratīkas* |
| $2^{I}$b | 3b | 3v | | | no *pratīkas* |
| $3^{I}$a | 19r | | 3 | 7 | no *pratīkas* |
| $3^{I}$b | 18l | | 3 | 6 | no *pratīkas* |
| $8^{I}$a | 6l | | 2 | 1 | no *pratīkas* |
| $8^{I}$b | 7r | | 2 | 2 | no *pratīkas* |
| $13^{I}$a | 16l | | 3 | 4 | no *pratīkas* |
| $13^{I}$b | 17r | | 3 | 5 | no *pratīkas* |
| $16^{I}$a | 15l | | 3 | 3 | *1.1.7–8, 11* |
| $16^{I}$b | 16r | | 3 | 4 | *1.1.13–15* |
| $19^{I}$a | 8t | 7r | | | *1.1.22* |
| $19^{I}$b | 7b | 7v | | | no *pratīkas* |
| $22^{I}$a | 3l | | 1 | 5 | *1.1.34–36* |
| $22^{I}$b | 4r | | 1 | 6 | *1.1.37, 39* |
| $23^{I}$a | 21t | 21r | | | *1.1.40* |
| $23^{I}$b | 20b | 21v | | | no *pratīkas* |
| $28^{I}$a | 11l | | 2 | 6 | *1.1.70, 72, 76–77* |
| $28^{I}$b | 12r | | 2 | 7 | *1.1.78, 80* |
| $31^{I}$a ? | 15r | | 3 | 3 | *1.1.104, 106, 108–110, 118, 120, 123* |
| $31^{I}$b ? | 14l | | 3 | 2 | *1.1.126, 132, 136, 143, 1.1* |
| $1^{II}$a | 1 | 1r | | | initially blank |
| $1^{II}$b | 2t | 1v | | | *5.1.1* |
| $2^{II}$a | 3t | 2r | | | no *pratīkas* |
| $2^{II}$b | 2b | 2v | | | no *pratīkas* |
| $3^{II}$a | 4b | 4r | | | no *pratīkas* |
| $3^{II}$b | 5t | 4v | | | *5.1.3–4, 6* |
| $4^{II}$a | 30t | 29r | | | *5.1.7, 10, 12, 14–15* |
| $4^{II}$b | 29b | 29v | | | *5.1.19–20, 28, 34–35, 37, 41* |

| Fol. | Exp. | No. | Row | Col. | *Candrālaṃkāra* ad Cān. |
|---|---|---|---|---|---|
| 5$^{II}$a | 2r | | 1 | 4 | *5.1.44, 48–49, 52* |
| 5$^{II}$b | 1 | | 1 | 3 | *5.1.53–59* |
| 6$^{II}$a | 31t | 30r | | | *5.1.60–61* |
| 6$^{II}$b | 30b | 30v | | | *5.1.62–63, 65–68* |
| 7$^{II}$a | 32t | 31r | | | *5.1.69–70, 73, 77* |
| 7$^{II}$b | 31b | 31v | | | *5.1.78–81* |
| 8$^{II}$a | 7t | 6r | | | no *pratīkas* |
| 8$^{II}$b | 6b | 6v | | | no *pratīkas* |
| 9$^{II}$a | 6t | 5r | | | *5.1.85–86, 88–89, 91–92* |
| 9$^{II}$b | 5b | 5v | | | *5.1.93–95, 98, 100* |
| 11$^{II}$a | 13t | 12r | | | *5.1.119, 124–125, 127, 131* |
| 11$^{II}$b | 12b | 12v | | | *5.1.132–135, 137* |
| 13$^{II}$a | 22l | | 4 | 3 | *5.2.2, 4* |
| 13$^{II}$b | 23r | | 4 | 4 | *5.2.5–6, 11, 14, 16, 20–21* |
| 16$^{II}$a | 7l | | 2 | 2 | *5.2.76, 78, 81, 85, 88, 90* |
| 16$^{II}$b | 8r | | 2 | 3 | *5.2.91–93, 95, 100–103, 105* |
| 17$^{II}$a | 13b | 13 | | | *5.2.108–109, 111, 115, 119, 126–128* |
| 17$^{II}$b | 14t | 14 | | | *5.2.129, 132, 137–138, 140–141, 143, 145* |
| 18$^{II}$a | 14r | | 3 | 2 | *5.2.146–147, 5.2, *5.3.1* |
| 18$^{II}$b | 13l | | 3 | 1 | *5.3.2–4, 7–8, 10* |
| 19$^{II}$a | 8l | | 2 | 3 | *5.3.11–13* |
| 19$^{II}$b | 9r | | 2 | 4 | *5.3.14, 18–19* |
| 21$^{II}$a | 4l | | 1 | 6 | *5.3.28, 30, 34–35, 37–38* |
| 21$^{II}$b | 5r | | 1 | 7 | *5.3.39–41, 48, 53, 55–57, 61* |
| 23$^{II}$a | 21l | | 4 | 2 | *5.3.80, 82, 84, 87–89* |
| 23$^{II}$b | 22r | | 4 | 3 | *5.3.90–93, 95–96, 98–99* |
| 25$^{II}$a | 9l | | 2 | 4 | *5.3.124–126, 130–134* |
| 25$^{II}$b | 10r | | 2 | 5 | *5.3.135–140* |
| 26$^{II}$a | 5l | | 1 | 7 | *5.3.141–142, 147–149, 151, 153* |
| 26$^{II}$b | 6r | | 2 | 1 | *5.3.155, 157–158, 160 -161, 164, 166–167* |
| 27$^{II}$a | 10l | | 2 | 5 | *5.3.169, 171–174* |
| 27$^{II}$b | 11r | | 2 | 6 | *5.3, 5.4.1* |
| 31$^{II}$a | 19l | | 3 | 7 | *5.4.58, 66–68, 70, 76* |
| 31$^{II}$b | 20r | | 4 | 1 | *5.4.77–81* |
| 35$^{II}$a | 18t | 18r | | | *5.4.139–140, 154, 156–157* |
| 35$^{II}$b | 17b | 18v | | | *5.4.158, 160–161, 163–165* |
| 36$^{II}$a | 20t | 20r | | | *5.4.167, 170–172, 175, 5.4, 6.1.1* |
| 36$^{II}$b | 19b | 20v | | | *6.1.2–4* |

| Fol. | Exp. | No. | Row | Col. | *Candrālaṃkāra* ad Cān. |
|---|---|---|---|---|---|
| $37^{II}$a | 26t | 25r | | | *6.1.5, 7* |
| $37^{II}$b | 25b | 25v | | | *6.1.10–14* |
| $40^{II}$a | 2l | | 1 | 4 | *6.1.54–57* |
| $40^{II}$b | 3r | | 1 | 5 | *6.1.59, 61* |
| $41^{II}$a | – | – | | | *6.1.62–65* |
| $41^{II}$b | 9t | 8v | | | *6.1.66, 68* |
| $44^{II}$a | 25t | 24r | | | *6.2.4, 6, 8* |
| $44^{II}$b | 24b | 24v | | | *6.2.10, 12–14, 16–17, 19, 21* |
| $45^{II}$a | 24t | 23r | | | *6.2.23* |
| $45^{II}$b | 23b | 23v | | | *6.2.25–28* |
| $46^{II}$a | 12t | 11r | | | *6.2.29–30, 32–33, 36–37, 39* |
| $46^{II}$b | 11b | 11v | | | *6.2.41, 43, 45–46, 48* |
| $47^{II}$a | 29t | 28r | | | *6.2.51–52, 58–59, 74–75* |
| $47^{II}$b | 28b | 28v | | | *6.2.76–79* |
| $48^{II}$a | 28t | 27r | | | *6.2.80–81, 84–85, 91–94, 96* |
| $48^{II}$b | 27b | 27v | | | *6.2.97, 99, 102, 104–106, 109* |
| $49^{II}$a | 27t | 26r | | | *6.2.110–111* |
| $49^{II}$b | 26b | 26v | | | *6.2.113, 117* |
| $53^{II}$a | 35 | 34r | | | *6.3.2, 4, 6* |
| $53^{II}$b | 34b | 34v | | | *6.3.7–8, 10* |
| $54^{II}$a | 34t | 33r | | | *6.3.11–14* |
| $54^{II}$b | 33b | 33v | | | *6.3.15–17* |
| $55^{II}$a | 33t | 32r | | | *6.3.19–24* |
| $55^{II}$b | 32b | 32v | | | *6.3.25–27* |
| $56^{II}$a | 22t | 22r | | | no *pratīkas* |
| $56^{II}$b | 21b | 22v | | | *6.3.28* |
| $57^{II}$a | 15t | 15r | | | *6.3.29–30* |
| $57^{II}$b | 14b | 15v | | | *6.3.31–34* |
| $59^{II}$a ? | 11t | 10r | | | *6.3.64–69* |
| $59^{II}$b ? | 10b | 10v | | | *6.3.70–75* |
| $60^{II}$a | 16t | 16r | | | *6.3.76–78, 80–81, 83, 87, 91–92* |
| $60^{II}$b | 15b | 16v | | | *6.3.94–96, 100* |
| $61^{II}$a | 17t | 17r | | | *6.3.102, 106, 108, 111, 114–115, 118* |
| $61^{II}$b | 16b | 17v | | | *6.3.122, 128, 131, 133, 6.3, 6.4.1* |
| $62^{II}$a | 10t | 9r | | | no *pratīkas* |
| $62^{II}$b | 9b | 9v | | | *6.4.2–6, 9* |
| $64^{II}$a ? | 23t | 22*r | | | *6.4.19, 21–23* |
| $64^{II}$b ? | 22b | 22*v | | | *6.4.24–25, 27–28, 31, 33* |

| Fol. | Exp. | No. | Row | Col. | *Candrālaṃkāra* ad Cān. |
|---|---|---|---|---|---|
| 65$^{II}$a ? | 19t | 19r | | | *6.4.35 ?, 38* |
| 65$^{II}$b ? | 18b | 19v | | | *6.4.39, 41, 44, 46–47* |
| 70$^{II}$a | 21r | | 4 | 2 | *6.4.114–115* |
| 70$^{II}$b | 20l | | 4 | 1 | *6.4.116–118, 121–123* |
| 71$^{II}$a | 17l | | 3 | 5 | *6.4.125, 127, 129–130* |
| 71$^{II}$b | 18r | | 3 | 6 | *6.4.132–133, 135–136* |
| 73$^{II}$a ? | 12l | | 2 | 7 | *6.4.154–156* |
| 73$^{II}$b ? | 13r | | 3 | 1 | *6.4.157–158* |
| 75$^{II}$a ? | 23l | | 4 | 4 | colophon |
| 75$^{II}$b ? | - | | | | initially blank |

FIGURE 9: A brass image of Buddha from Gayā

# CHAPTER THREE

## Script Tables

## 3.1 Tables of the Bhaikṣukī Script

Until recently scholars willing to read the scant material written in the Bhaikṣukī script were compelled to content themselves with the rather basic script table prepared by Bendall and the selected characters reproduced from there a few years later by Bühler. The insufficient documentation of this script, due both to the relatively limited number of characters, namely 112, and the poor quality of the reproductions, combined with the paucity of handwritten material, did not facilitate in-depth studies of the Bhaikṣukī script. Not only the manuscripts, but also the epigraphical material in this script has received hardly any attention and remained largely unnoticed and unmentioned even in the most comprehensive works on Indian palaeography and epigraphy written in the twentieth century. Consequently, in the course of time the Bhaikṣukī script was nearly forgotten. So much so that more than a century after Bendall deciphered the script, the necessity of "deciphering" the script anew was felt in the West. The study of the Bhaikṣukī manuscript of the *Maṇicūḍajātaka* undertaken by Hahn and Hanisch in 2004 soon resulted, among other things, in two script tables, a preliminary one of 109 characters and another revised and slightly enlarged table containing 115 characters extracted from the *Maṇicūḍajātaka* manuscript, and ten more characters from the Kathmandu portion of the *Candrālaṃkāra* manuscript.[163]

Here a further step towards a more detailed documentation of the Bhaikṣkukī script is being made. In the script tables drawn up below more than 750 characters and symbols from the *Candrālaṃkāra* manuscript have been put together. Besides the basic letters, the tables include a large number of conjuncts, some of which occur only in grammatical texts. Various examples of diacritic vowels have also been included. The great majority of the characters have been extracted from

---

[163] See Hahn 2005, pp. 702–701, and Hanisch 2006, pp. 119–120.

the Cambridge portion of the *Candrālaṃkāra* manuscript, the copy of which is of much better quality than the Kathmandu portion and thus proves more suitable and useful for the purposes of palaeographic analysis. The material presented here should ultimately facilitate the study of the history of the Bhaikṣukī script with respect to its origin, development, and relation to other Indian scripts.

The letters are arranged according to a system which I originally developed for the presentation of the Old Bengali letters.[164] This arrangement has the advantage of allowing the script tables to be used not only as a rich database for palaeographic study, but also as a practical tool for quick reference when reading materials written in the same or similar form of the script. The characters are systematically arranged in the following groups:

1. Basic letters, i.e. the vowels in initial position and the consonants with an inherent *-a*.
2. Conjunct consonants arranged according to the last consonant disregarding a semi-vowel which may follow. The arrangement is made according to the phonetic nature of the last consonant, starting with the velars, palatals, etc. Subgroups of the conjuncts with a following nasal, a following semi-vowel, a following sibilant, a following fricative *-h-*, and the conjuncts with geminates are also included here.
3. Diacritic vowels in open syllables with the structure CV.
4. *Anusvāra*, *visarga*, *avagraha*, *virāma*, and other symbols, including the figure-numerals.[165]
5. Characters which look similar and may be confused.
6. All the characters of the previous groups arranged in strict alphabetical order with additional information about the word from which each character has been extracted and its position on the folio.[166]

---

[164] See DIMITROV 2002, pp. 56–71.

[165] Most of the figure-numerals can only be observed in a few marginal notes where the line for an insertion is indicated. The few letter-numerals preserved in this manuscript have not been extracted here, since they are identical with the Bhaikṣukī characters found in the Proto-Bengali manuscript discussed above (see ch. 2.3 above).

[166] In addition, the folio numbers of the characters from the Kathmandu portion are underlined.

## 3.1.1 Basic letters

### 3.1.1.1 Initial vowels

| 𑰀 | 𑰁 | 𑰂 | 𑰃 | 𑰄 | 𑰅 | 𑰆 | 𑰇 | 𑰈 | 𑰊 | 𑰋 | 𑰌 | 𑰍 |
|---|---|---|---|---|---|---|---|---|---|---|---|---|
| *a* | *ā* | *i* | *ī* | *u* | *ū* | *ṛ* | *ṝ* | *ḷ* | *e* | *ai* | *o* | *au* |

### 3.1.1.2 Consonants

| | | | | |
|---|---|---|---|---|
| 𑰎 | 𑰏 | 𑰐 | 𑰑 | 𑰒 |
| *ka* | *kha* | *ga* | *gha* | *ṅa* |
| 𑰓 | 𑰔 | 𑰕 | 𑰖 | 𑰗 |
| *ca* | *cha* | *ja* | *jha* | *ña* |
| 𑰘 | 𑰙 | 𑰚 | 𑰛 | 𑰜 |
| *ṭa* | *ṭha* | *ḍa* | *ḍha* | *ṇa* |
| 𑰝 | 𑰞 | 𑰟 | 𑰠 | 𑰡 |
| *ta* | *tha* | *da* | *dha* | *na* |
| 𑰢 | 𑰣 | 𑰤 | 𑰥 | 𑰦 |
| *pa* | *pha* | *ba* | *bha* | *ma* |

| | | | |
|---|---|---|---|
| 𑰧 | 𑰨 | 𑰩 | 𑰪 |
| *ya* | *ra* | *la* | *va* |
| 𑰫 | 𑰬 | 𑰭 | 𑰮 |
| *śa* | *ṣa* | *sa* | *ha* |

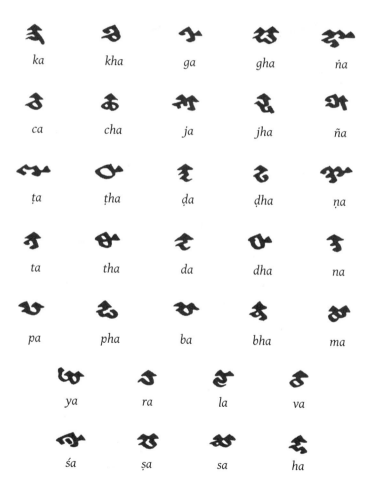

## 3.1.2 Conjunct consonants

### 3.1.2.1 Conjuncts with a following velar stop

#### 3.1.2.1.1 -*k*-

*ṅka* *ṅkā* *ṅki* *tka* *pkri* *rkā* *lkā* *ṣka* *skā* *skṛ*

#### 3.1.2.1.2 -*g*-

*ṅga* *ṅgī* *ṅge* *ṅgo* *dgu* *dgo* *dgau*

#### 3.1.2.1.3 -*gh*-

*dgha* *dgho* *rgha* *rghā*

### 3.1.2.2 Conjuncts with a following palatal stop

#### 3.1.2.2.1 -*c*-

*ñca* *ñcā* *rccha* *ścā* *ścu* *śce* *ścai* *ścau*

#### 3.1.2.2.2 -*ch*-

*ccha* *cchāṃ* *cche* *cchvo* *rccha*

3.1.2.2.3 *-j-*

*gja* *ṅjī* *ñja* *rjñā*

3.1.2.2.4 *-jh-*

*jjha*

## 3.1.2.3 Conjuncts with a following retroflex stop

3.1.2.3.1 *-ṭ-*

*ṣṭa* *ṣṭā* *ṣṭi* *ṣṭī* *ṣṭu* *ṣṭe* *ṣṭya* *ṣṭyā*

3.1.2.3.2 *-ṭh-*

*ṣṭha* *ṣṭhi* *ṣṭhī* *ṣṭhe*

3.1.2.3.3 *-ḍ-*

*ṇḍa* *ṇḍū* *ṇḍvā*

3.1.2.3.4 *-ḍh-*

*ḍḍhau*

## 3.1.2.4 Conjuncts with a following dental stop

3.1.2.4.1 *-t-*

*ktaṃ* *ktā* *kti* *ktu* *ktau* *ktyā* *ctvaṃ* *ṭtvaṃ* *ṭtvā* *nta*

*ntā nti ntu ntya ntyā ntyo ntyau ntrye pta pti*

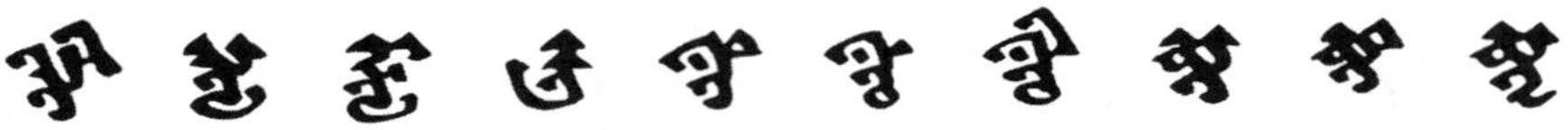

*ptau ptya ptyā rtṛ śti śtva śtve sta sti stu*

*stū stṛ stṝ ste stau stye stra strī stvi*

3.1.2.4.2 ***-th-***

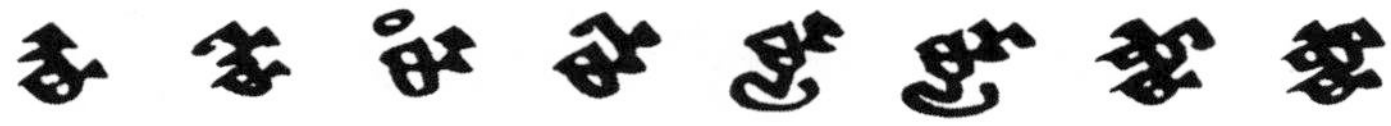

*ntha nthe rthaṃ rthe rthya rthyā sthā sthi*

3.1.2.4.3 ***-d-***

*nda ndyo ndra ndri ndre bda bdā bde bdo rda*

*rdṛ rde rdo rddha rdvi*

3.1.2.4.4 ***-dh-***

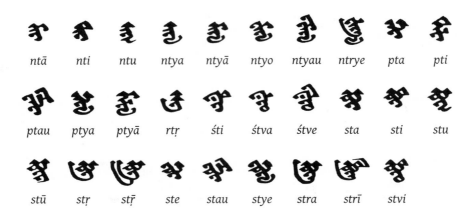

*gdha ddha ddhā ddhi ddhuṃ ddhe ddhya ddhyā ndhā ndhi*

*ndhu* *ndhe* *bdha* *bdhā* *bdhe* *rddha*

#### 3.1.2.5 Conjuncts with a following labial stop

##### 3.1.2.5.1 -*p*-

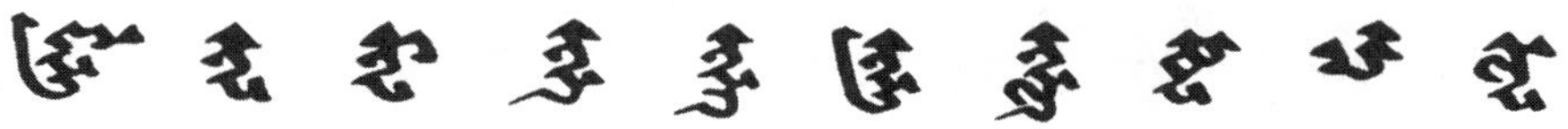

*ṭpra* *tpa* *tpā* *tpu* *tpū* *tpra* *tplu* *mpa* *rpa* *lpa*

*lpā* *lpi* *lpo* *ṣpa* *ṣpu* *ṣpo* *spa* *spṛ*

##### 3.1.2.5.2 -*ph*-

*tsphu* *sphā* *sphu* *spho*

##### 3.1.2.5.3 -*b*-

*mba* *mbā* *rbbha*

##### 3.1.2.5.4 -*bh*-

*jbha* *jbhā* *jbhyāṃ* *dbhā* *dbhya* *mbha* *mbhe* *rbbha* *rbhū*

### 3.1.2.6 Conjuncts with a following nasal

#### 3.1.2.6.1 -ṅ-    3.1.2.6.2 -ñ-

*kṅi*    *jña*  *jñā*  *jñe*  *rjñā*

#### 3.1.2.6.3 -ṇ-

*kṇa*  *kṣṇa*  *kṣṇyaṃ*  *bṇi*  *vṇi*

#### 3.1.2.6.4 -n-

*gna*  *gnā*  *gni*  *gno*  *ṅni*  *tna*  *pno*  *bhnā*  *mnā*  *mni*

*rna*  *śne*  *śnu*  *sni*  *hna*

#### 3.1.2.6.5 -m-

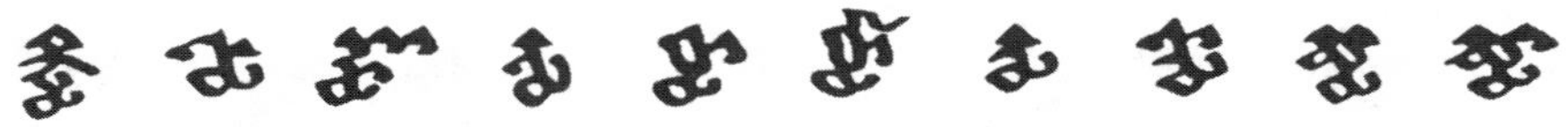

*kṣmi*  *gma*  *ṅmā*  *tma*  *dhmā*  *dhmo*  *nma*  *nmo*  *sma*  *smā*

*smi*  *sme*  *hma*  *hmā*  *hmo*

### 3.1.2.7 Conjuncts with a following semi-vowel

#### 3.1.2.7.1 -*y*-

ktyā kya kye kyo kṣṇyaṃ kṣya kṣyā kṣye khya khyā
khye khyai ṅyā ṅyu ṅyū ṅye ṅsyā cya jbhyāṃ jya
ṭyi ḍyi ṇṇya ṇya ttyā tya tyā tyu tye tsya
ddhya ddhyā dbhya dya dye dyo dvyā dhya dhyā dhyu
dhye dhyai ntya ntyā ntyo ntyau ntrye ndyo nya nyu
nyo ptya ptyā pya pyā pyu bhya bhyu mya myāṃ
rthya rthyā rya ryā ryi ryu rye rvyu rṣyā rhya
lya lye vya vyā vyu vye vyo śya ṣṭya ṣṭyā
ṣya ṣyā stye sya syā sye syai syo hya hyā

3.1.2.7.2 *-r-*

*kra* *kri* *krī* *kre* *ggra* *ggrā* *ghrā* *ṅggra* *jggra* *jri*

*ṭpra* *ḍhra* *tpra* *tra* *trā* *tri* *tre* *trai* *dra* *dru*

*dvru* *ntrye* *ndra* *ndri* *ndre* *pkri* *pra* *prā* *pri* *pre*

*pro* *bru* *bhra* *bhrū* *vra* *śra* *śri* *śrī* *śru* *śrū*

*śre* *śro* *śrau* *śryu* *stra* *strī* *sra* *hra* *hrī*

3.1.2.7.3 *-l-*

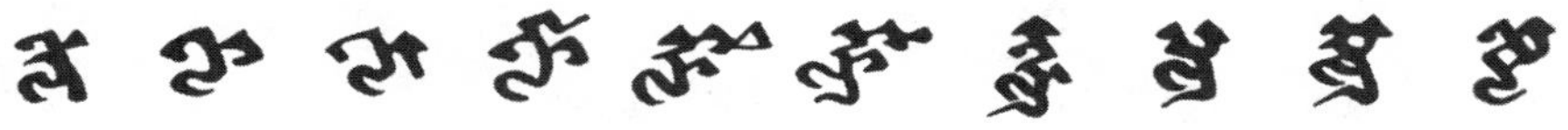

*kle* *glā* *glā* *glo* *ṅli* *ṅlu* *tplu* *plu* *blu* *mle*

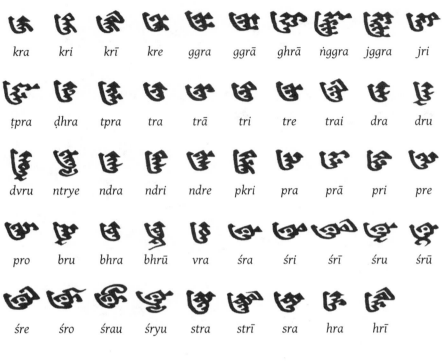

*rli* *vlu* *śle* *ślo* *hlā*

### 3.1.2.7.4 *-v-*

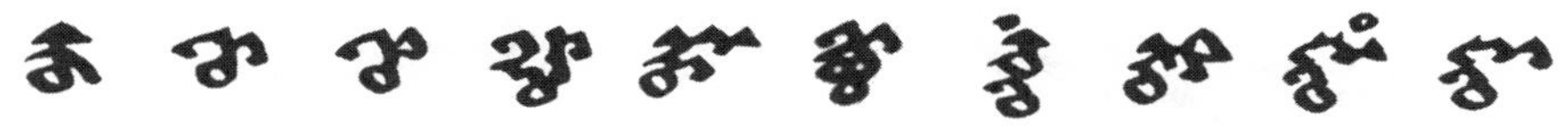

*kva* *gvā* *gvi* *ghvo* *ṅva* *cchvo* *ctvaṃ* *jvi* *ṭtvaṃ* *ṭtvā*

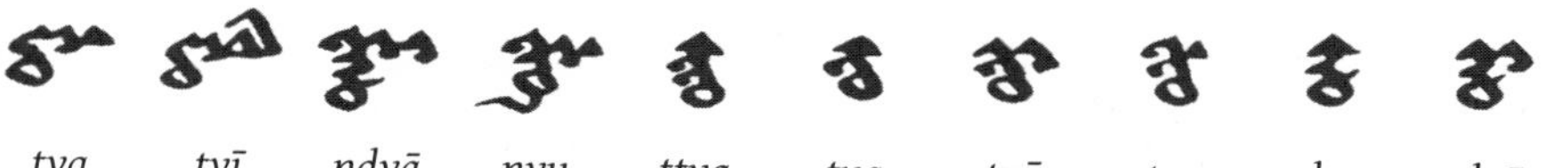

*ṭva* *ṭvī* *ṇḍvā* *ṇvu* *ttva* *tva* *tvā* *tve* *dva* *dvā*

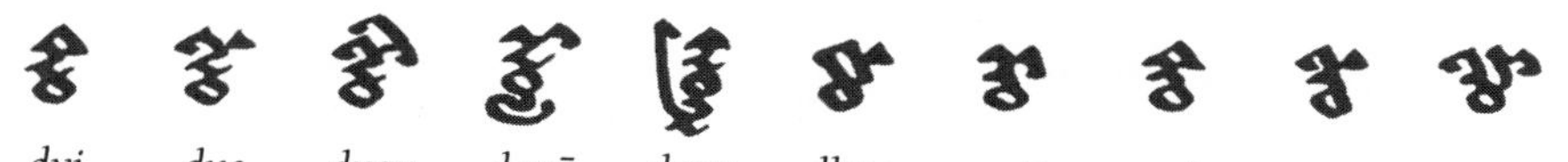

*dvi* *dve* *dvau* *dvyā* *dvru* *dhva* *nvā* *nvi* *nve* *pvo*

*mva* *mvā* *mvi* *mvṛ* *yvā* *yve* *rdvi* *rvyu* *lvā* *lvi*

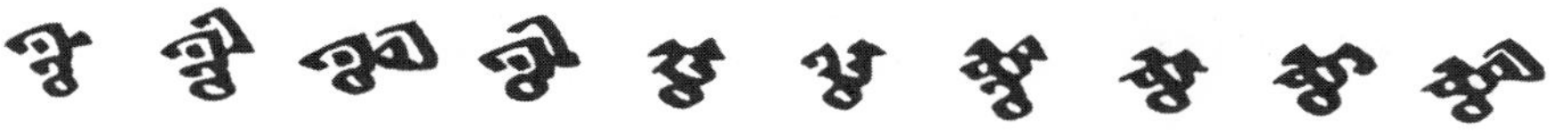

*śtva* *śtve* *śvī* *śve* *ṣva* *ṣve* *stvi* *sva* *svā* *svī*

*sve* *svo* *svau* *hva* *hvā*

## 3.1.2.8 Conjuncts with a following sibilant

### 3.1.2.8.1 *-ś-*

*ṅśa* *ṅśā* *ṅśi* *rśa*

3.1.2.8.2 -ṣ-

*kṣa kṣā kṣi kṣī kṣu kṣe kṣo kṣṇa kṣṇyaṃ kṣmi*

*kṣya kṣyā kṣye rṣā rṣi rṣe rṣyā*

3.1.2.8.3 -s-

*ksa ṅsi ṅsyā ṇsaṃ tsa tsu tsau tsya nsa nsī*

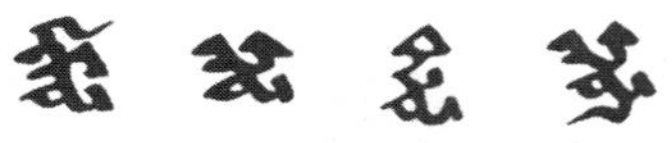

*nso psa psi psu*

### 3.1.2.9 Conjuncts with a fricative *-h-*

*nha rha rhya*

### 3.1.2.10 Conjuncts with a geminate

*ṅggra cca ccā cco jggra jji ṇṇa ṇṇya tta ttā*

*tti ttu ttū tte ttau ttyā ttva ddi ddṛ ddo*

*ddyu ddve nna nni nno ppi mma yya yyo rgga*

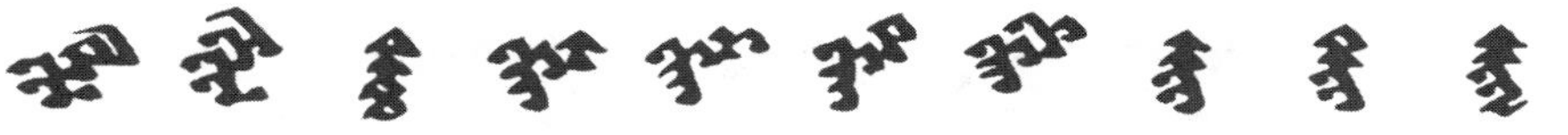

*rggī rggau rcci rṇṇa rṇṇā rṇṇi rṇṇo rtta rtti rttu*

*rddi rdde rnna rnni rmma rlli rllo rvva rvvā rvvi*

*rvve llo vvi*

### 3.1.3 Diacritic vowels

3.1.3.1 -*ā*

*kā khā ghā ṅā cā jā ṭā ṭhā ḍā ṇā*

*tā thā dā dhā nā pā bā bhā mā yā*

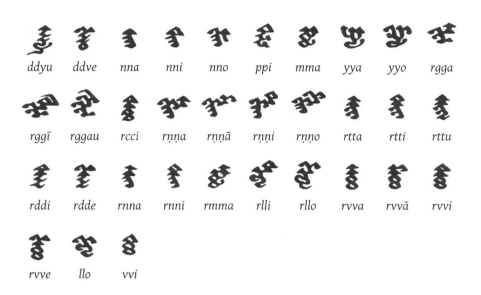

*rā lā vā śā ṣā sā hā*

### 3.1.3.2 -*i*

*ki khi gi ṅi ci ji jhi ñi ṭi ṭhi*

*ḍi ḍhi ṇi ti di dhi ni pi bhi mi*

*yi ri li vi śi ṣi si hi*

### 3.1.3.3 -*ī*

*kī khī cī jī ñī ṭī ṇī tī dī dhī*

*nī pī bhī mī rī lī vī śī sī hī*

### 3.1.3.4 -*u*

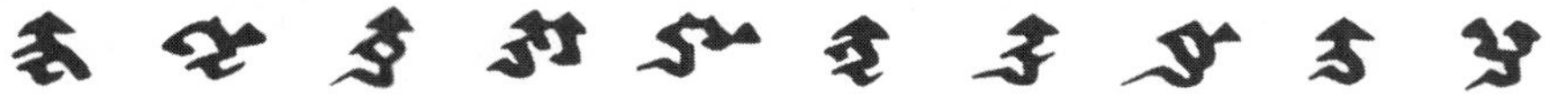

*ku gu cu ju ṭu tu du dhu nu pu*

*phu bu bhu mu yu ru lu vu śu ṣu*

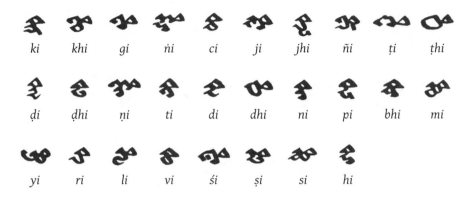

*su hu*

### 3.1.3.5 -ū

*gū cū jū tū dū dhū nū pū bhū mū*

*yū rū lū śū sū hū*

### 3.1.3.6 -ṛ

*kṛ gṛ jṛ tṛ dṛ nṛ pṛ bhṛ mṛ rṛ*

*vṛ sṛ śṛ hṛ*

### 3.1.3.7 -ṝ

*kṝ gṝ nṝ*

### 3.1.3.8 -ḷ

*dḷ*

### 3.1.3.9 -e

*ke ge ce che je ṭe ṭhe ḍhe ṇe te*

*the de dhe ne pe bhe me ye re le*

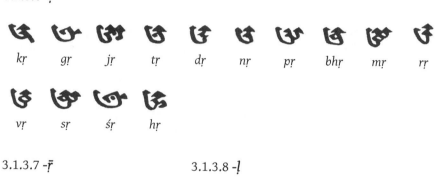

*ve śe ṣe se he*

3.1.3.10 -*ai*

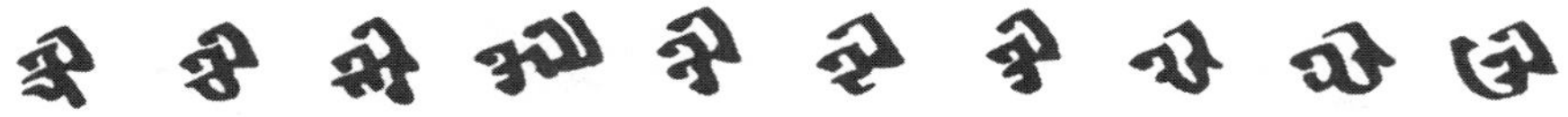

*kai cai jai ṇai tai dai nai pai yai rai*

*vai śai sai hai*

3.1.3.11 -*o*

*ko go ṅo co jo ño ṭo ṭho ṇo to*

*tho do dho no po bo bho mo yo ro*

*lo vo śo ṣo so*

3.1.3.12 -*au*

*gau cau ḍhau ṇau dau dhau nau pau bhau yau*

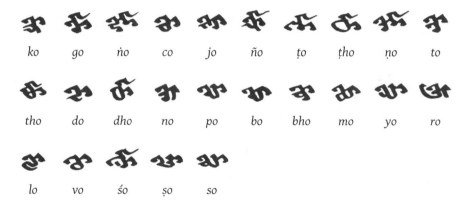

*lau vau śau sau*

### 3.1.4 Anusvāra, visarga, avagraha, virāma, and other symbols

*kaṃ ṇaṃ taṃ daṃ naṃ paṃ yaṃ raṃ laṃ vaṃ*

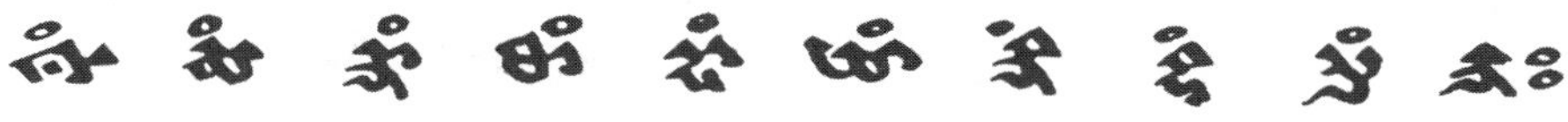

*śaṃ saṃ kāṃ thāṃ pāṃ yāṃ kiṃ hiṃ puṃ kaḥ*

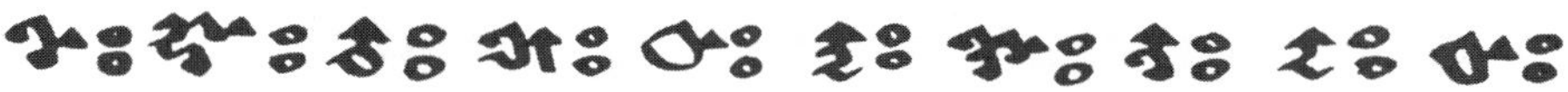

*gaḥ ṅaḥ caḥ ñaḥ ṭhaḥ ḍaḥ ṇaḥ taḥ daḥ dhaḥ*

*naḥ paḥ maḥ yaḥ raḥ vaḥ śaḥ ṣaḥ saḥ k*

*j t t n n p m m ṃ ṃ*

*m̐ ḥ ’ ṭ* ⁝ ⁞⁞ | || | ×^

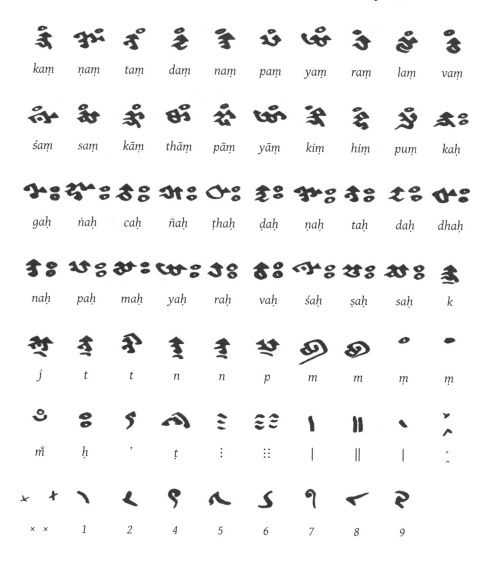

× × 1 2 4 5 6 7 8 9

### 3.1.5 Similar characters

a pu u o ū au
ḷ le kṛ kra kha ce
khyā vyo ga śa ggra trai
gna ne ṅa hā ca va
ṭha dha ḍa nda ḍha da
ḍhi pi ṇa nā tu tpa
dṛ dra pū plu pṛ pra
pe ye bha ru bhṛ bhra
ma sa lpo llo vṛ vra
śṛ śra hū hna hṛ hra

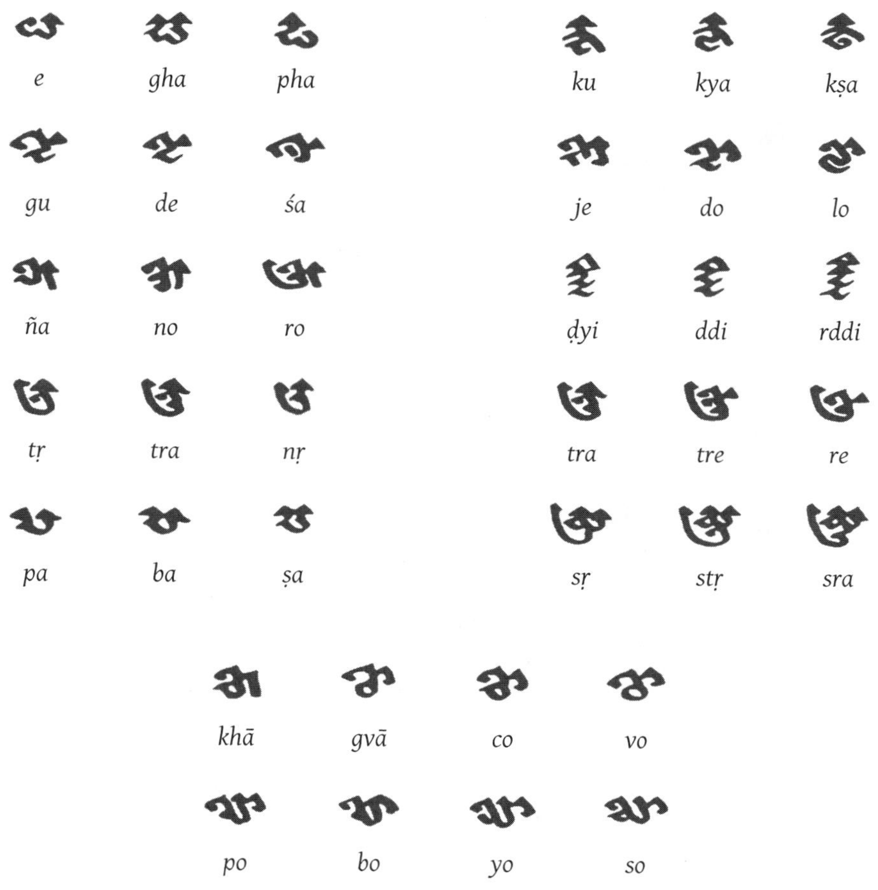
e
gha
pha
ku
kya
kṣa
gu
de
śa
je
do
lo
ña
no
ro
ḍyi
ddi
rddi
tṛ
tra
nṛ
tra
tre
re
pa
ba
ṣa
sṛ
stṛ
sra
khā
gvā
co
vo
po
bo
yo
so

### 3.1.6 Characters in alphabetical order

A

1.  a (*asati*, 6$^{\text{II}}$b$^{9}$)

Ā

2.  ā (*āvṛtti°*, 2$^{\text{II}}$a$^{10}$)

I

3.  i (*iti*, 2$^{\text{II}}$b$^{3}$)

Ī

4.  ī (*īṣad°*, 4$^{\text{II}}$b$^{1}$)

U

5.  u (*uttaratrā°*, 4$^{\text{II}}$a$^{2}$)

Ū

6.  ū (*ūpa*, 11$^{\text{II}}$a$^{10}$)

Ṛ

7.  ṛ (*ṛṇam*, 9$^{\text{II}}$a$^{10}$)

Ṝ

8.  ṝ (*ṝlvādi°*, 4$^{\text{II}}$a$^{10}$)

Ḷ

9.  ḷ (*ṛ ḷ ity*, 11$^{\text{II}}$b$^{2}$)

E

10.  e (*ata eva*, 1$^{\text{II}}$b$^{2}$)

AI

11.  ai (*aikārthya°*, 4$^{\text{II}}$a$^{4}$)

O

12.  o (*omāṅor*, 9$^{\text{II}}$a$^{8}$)

AU

13.  au (*au*[*kā*]*re*, 11$^{\text{II}}$a$^{7}$)

K

14.  ka (*vācakatvan*, 19$^{\text{I}}$b$^{2}$)

15.  k (*kñitīty*, 6$^{\text{II}}$b$^{9}$)

16.  kaṃ (*jñāpakaṃ*, 4$^{\text{II}}$a$^{5}$)

17.  kaḥ (*ṛkaḥ*, 8$^{\text{II}}$a$^{1}$)

18.  kā (*adhikārād*, 1$^{\text{II}}$b$^{2}$)

| | | |
|---|---|---|
| 19. |  | kāṃ (*ākāṃkṣā*, $1^{II}b^{10}$) |
| 20. |  | ki (*kim*, $1^{II}b^{5}$) |
| 21. |  | kiṃ (*kiṃ*, $4^{II}b^{10}$) |
| 22. |  | kī (*yakīti*, $23^{I}a^{1}$) |
| 23. |  | ku (*akurvvatā*, $6^{II}b^{1}$) |
| 24. |  | kṛ (*kṛtvāpi*, $19^{I}b^{5}$) |
| 25. |  | kṝ (*kṝbhyaḥ*, $36^{II}a^{4}$) |
| 26. |  | ke (*ke*, $9^{II}a^{1}$) |
| 27. |  | kai (°*ṇaikaikasya*, $8^{II}a^{7}$) |
| 28. |  | ko (*iko*, $4^{II}b^{8}$) |
| 29. |  | kṅi (*kṅitīty*, $7^{II}b^{4}$) |
| 30. |  | kṇa (*vṛkṇa*, $4^{II}b^{9}$) |
| 31. |  | ktaṃ (*yuktaṃ*, $19^{I}a^{1}$) |
| 32. |  | ktā (*yuktāḥ*, $23^{I}a^{8}$) |
| 33. |  | kti (°*uktidoṣaḥ*, $23^{I}b^{9}$) |
| 34. |  | ktu (*vaktum*, $19^{I}a^{7}$) |
| 35. |  | ktau (*dviruktau*, $49^{II}b^{8}$) |
| 36. |  | ktyā (°*yuktyā*, $3^{II}b^{9}$) |
| 37. |  | kya (*kyajādi*°, $4^{II}a^{4}$) |
| 38. |  | kye (*śakye*, $7^{II}b^{4}$) |
| 39. |  | kyo (*śakyo*, $7^{II}b^{6}$) |
| 40. |  | kra (*vikraya*, $7^{II}b^{7}$) |
| 41. |  | kri (*kriyata*, $2^{I}b^{7}$) |
| 42. |  | krī (*krīṅjī*, $6^{II}a^{1}$) |
| 43. |  | kre (*vikretavya*, $7^{II}b^{8}$) |
| 44. |  | kle (°*kleśatvena*, $2^{I}b^{2}$) |
| 45. |  | kva (*kva cid*, $23^{I}b^{4}$) |
| 46. |  | kṣa (°*lakṣaṇam*, $1^{II}b^{2}$) |
| 47. |  | kṣā (*kṣāyituṃ*, $7^{II}b^{6}$) |
| 48. |  | kṣi (*rakṣitena*, $8^{II}a^{8}$) |
| 49. |  | kṣī (*upakṣīṇe*, $8^{II}a^{7}$) |
| 50. |  | kṣu (*bhikṣutvena*, $2^{I}b^{4}$) |
| 51. |  | kṣe (*kṣeptuṃ*, $2^{I}a^{2}$) |
| 52. |  | kṣo (*dakṣo*, $2^{I}a^{7}$) |

53.  kṣṇa (*ukṣṇaḥ*, $27^{II}a^{9}$)

54.  kṣṇyaṃ (*ābhikṣṇyaṃ*, $53^{II}a^{4}$)

55.  kṣmi (*lakṣmi*, $46^{II}b^{8}$)

56.  kṣya (*vakṣyamāṇa°*, $23^{I}a^{7}$)

57.  kṣyā (*vakṣyāmi*, $4^{II}a^{5}$)

58.  kṣye (*avakṣyepa*, $11^{II}a^{5}$)

59.  ksa (*luk san°*, $2^{II}b^{10}$)

## KH

60.  kha (*likhana°*, $6^{II}a^{9}$)

61.  khā (*duḥkhāt*, $65^{II}a^{1}$)

62.  khi (*khitī*, $13^{II}a^{8}$)

63.  khī (*nakhīnām*, $18^{II}b^{8}$)

64.  khya (*°vyākhyayā*, $7^{II}a^{5}$)

65.  khyā (*°saṃkhyāyāḥ*, $1^{II}b^{1}$)

66.  khye (*°mukhyeneti*, $4^{II}b^{7}$)

67.  khyai (*saṃkhyaikā°*, $9^{II}b^{1}$)

## G

68.  ga (*bhagavatas*, $2^{I}b^{3}$)

69.  gaḥ (*prayogaḥ*, $23^{I}b^{9}$)

70.  gi (*°yogino*, $41^{II}b^{2}$)

71.  gu (*°guṇaś*, $19^{I}a^{9}$)

72.  gū (*śryugūrṇṇoḥ*, $35^{II}a^{4}$)

73.  gṛ (*gṛhī*, $2^{I}b^{2}$)

74.  gṝ (*gṝ śabde*, $36^{II}a^{4}$)

75.  ge (*°bhāge*, $2^{II}b^{2}$)

76.  go (*°candragomī*, $2^{II}a^{7}$)

77.  gau (*gauṇatvān*, $2^{II}a^{8}$)

78.  ggra (*ggrahaṇaṃ*, $23^{I}a^{1}$)

79.  ggrā (*saṃggrāmaya°*, $19^{I}a^{7}$)

80.  gja (*pṛthagja[no]*, $2^{I}a^{3}$)

81.  gdha (*snigdhatarā*, $8^{II}b^{8}$)

82.  gna (*nagna*, $60^{II}a^{5}$)

83.  gnā (*nagnāndheti*, $60^{II}a^{5}$)

84.  gni (*tenāgnicin*, $7^{II}a^{2}$)

85.  gno (*lagno*, $60^{II}a^{6}$)

86.  gma (*tigma°*, $17^{II}b^{7}$)

87.  glā (*glānir*, $60^{II}a^{1}$)

88.  glā (*glānāv*, $60^{II}a^{1}$)

89.  glo (*pṛthaglopasyā°*, $25^{II}a^{8}$)

90.  gvā (*lug vā*, $6^{II}a^{5}$)

91.  gvi (*°lugvidhau*, $4^{II}b^{6}$)

## GH

92.  gha (*ghañ{a}*, $2^{I}a^{5}$)

93.  ghā (*vyāghāto*, $7^{II}a^{8}$)

94.  ghrā (*ghrādhmor*, $41^{II}b^{5}$)

95.  ghvo (*laghvor*, $13^{I}a^{3}$)

## Ṅ

96.  ṅa (*ṅamo*, $3^{II}a^{1}$)

97.  ṅaḥ (*laṅaḥ*, $19^{I}a^{6}$)

98.  ṅā (*taṅānā*, $19^{I}a^{3}$)

99.  ṅi (*luṅi*, $9^{II}a^{6}$)

100.  ṅo (*omāṅor*, $9^{II}a^{8}$)

101.  ṅka (*nāśaṅkanīyaḥ*, $6^{II}a^{1}$)

102.  ṅkā (*śaṅkā*, $9^{II}b^{1}$)

103.  ṅki (*āśaṅkitaṃ*, $2^{II}b^{9}$)

104.  ṅga (*prasaṅga*, $3^{II}b^{3}$)

105.  ṅgī (*ṅgīkarttavyaḥ*, $19^{I}b^{5}$)

106.  ṅge (*ntaraṅge*, $7^{II}a^{3}$)

107.  ṅgo (*°prasaṅgo*, $23^{I}a^{9}$)

108.  ṅggra (*atiṅggrahaṇe*, $6^{II}b^{8}$)

109.  ṅjī (*krīṅjī*, $6^{II}a^{1}$)

110.  ṅni (*adeṅniṣedhā°*, $23^{II}b^{10}$)

111.  ṅmā (*āṅmāṅaś*, $7^{II}a^{6}$)

112.  ṅyā (*ṅyā*, $6^{II}b^{6}$)

113.  ṅyu (*caṅyu*, $40^{II}b^{4}$)

114.  ṅyū (*ṅyūṇaḥ*, $46^{II}b^{8}$)

115.  ṅye (*liṅy ed*, $6^{II}b^{9}$)

116. ṅli (*caṅliṭor*, $2^{II}b^{9}$)

117. ṅlu (*yaṅluky*, $41^{II}b^{5}$)

118. ṅva (*māṅvat*, $7^{II}a^{6}$)

119. ṅśa (°*viṅśati*°, $75^{II}a^{5}$)

120. ṅśā (*aṅśād*, $4^{II}a^{7}$)

121. ṅśi (*tiṅśiti*, $44^{II}a^{8}$)

122. ṅsi (*liṅsi*, $45^{II}b^{2}$)

123. ṅsyā (*adeṅ syāt{a}*, $45^{II}a^{10}$)

## C

124. ca (*upacaritaḥ*, $1^{II}b^{2}$)

125. caḥ (*acaḥ*, $3^{II}b^{3}$)

126. cā (*vicārā*°, $6^{II}a^{9}$)

127. ci (*ucitam*, $4^{II}b^{2}$)

128. cī (°*[v]ācī*, $23^{I}a^{6}$)

129. cu (*cu[ṭu]tu*, $71^{II}b^{1}$)

130. cū (*cūrṇṇi*°, $11I^{I}a^{1}$)

131. ce (°*cetasāṃ*, $2^{II}b^{6}$)

132. cai (*caivaṃ*, $23^{I}b^{5}$)

133. co (°*vaikāco*, $4^{II}a^{2}$)

134. cau (*cau*, $18^{II}a^{3}$)

135. cca (*niyamāc ca*, $23^{I}a^{9}$)

136. ccā (*dviruccāraṇe*, $3^{II}a^{5}$)

137. cco (*yac coktam*, $8^{II}b^{2}$)

138. ccha (°*pṛcchaka*, $4^{II}b^{2}$)

139. cchāṃ (*icchāṃ*, $19^{I}b^{9}$)

140. cche (*vyavacchedāt*, $1^{II}b^{6}$)

141. cchvo (*cchvor*, $19^{II}b^{7}$)

142. ctvaṃ (*ectvaṃ*, $9^{II}a^{6}$)

143. cya (°*vācyatayā*, $2^{II}b^{5}$)

## CH

144. cha (*chavi*, $64^{II}b^{8}$)

145. che (*che*, $7^{II}a^{5}$)

## J

146. ja (*prayojanā*°, $4^{II}a^{4}$)

147.  j (*ajdantya°*, $6^{II}a^{7}$)

148.  jā (*jāti°*, $1^{II}b^{10}$)

149.  ji (*uttejitum*, $19^{I}a^{5}$)

150.  jī (*°jītyāder*, $6^{II}a^{9}$)

151.  ju (*saṃjugopiṣate*, $19^{I}a^{6}$)

152.  jū (*mṛjū*, $36^{II}b^{2}$)

153.  jṛ (*jṛbhrama*, $25^{II}a^{6}$)

154.  je (*ādaij evā°*, $4^{II}a^{6}$)

155.  jai (*jaitvana*, $25^{II}a^{10}$)

156.  jo (*cajoḥ*, $6^{II}b^{1}$)

157.  jggra (*aijggrahaṇam*, $37^{II}b^{10}$)

158.  jji (*aujjijhad*, $3^{II}b^{6}$)

159.  jjha (*ajjhanoḥ*, $4^{II}a^{5}$)

160.  jña (*yajña°*, $7^{II}b^{6}$)

161.  jñā (*jñānaṃ*, $2^{I}a^{5}$)

162.  jñe (*jñeyaṃ*, $11^{II}a^{6}$)

163.  jbha (*aijbhavituṃ*, $37^{II}b^{9}$)

164.  jbhā (*aijbhā*, $37^{II}b^{9}$)

165.  jbhyāṃ (*°majbhyāṃ*, $8^{II}b^{6}$)

166.  jya (*prayujyante*, $2^{II}b^{3}$)

167.  jri (*jri*, $6^{II}a^{2}$)

168.  jvi (*sujvidhir*, $2^{II}a^{10}$)

## JH

169.  jha (*jhalo*, $2^{I}a^{9}$)

170.  jhi (*ujjijhiṣaty*, $3^{II}b^{5}$)

## Ñ

171.  ña (*nañas*, $11^{II}a^{5}$)

172.  ñaḥ (*vyeñaḥ*, $4^{II}a^{8}$)

173.  ñi (*ñitvan*, $23^{I}a^{2}$)

174.  ñī (*ghañīti*, $17^{II}b^{9}$)

175.  ño (*dhāño*, $48^{II}a^{8}$)

176.  ñca (*pañcamy°*, $3^{II}b^{2}$)

177.  ñcā (*°vañ cācā°*, $4^{II}a^{2}$)

178.  ñja (*°vyañjanā°*, $1^{II}b^{6}$)

## Ṭ

179.  ṭa (*āṭiṭad*, $4^{II}a^{6}$)

180.  ṭā (*iṭā*, $6^{II}b^{7}$)

181.  ṭi (*aṭiṭyiṣaty*, $3^{II}b^{5}$)

182.  ṭī (*ṭīkā*°, $2^{II}b^{1}$)

183.  ṭu (*vaṭur*, $4^{II}b^{5}$)

184.  ṭe (*ṭeṣṭhīvyata*, $6^{II}a^{8}$)

185.  ṭo (*liṭor*, $3^{II}b^{7}$)

186.  ṭtvaṃ (*aniṭtvaṃ*, $45^{II}b^{2}$)

187.  ṭtvā (*seṭtvāt*, $36^{II}a^{5}$)

188.  ṭpra (*dhuṭprasa*°, $6^{II}a^{7}$)

189.  ṭyi (*aṭiṭyiṣaty*, $3^{II}b^{5}$)

190.  ṭva (*khaṭvarṣir*, $8^{II}a^{1}$)

191.  ṭvī ([*kha*]*ṭvīyā*, $6^{II}b^{7}$)

## ṬH

192.  ṭha (*pāṭhas*, $8^{II}b^{5}$)

193.  ṭhaḥ (*pāṭhaḥ*, $8^{II}b^{6}$)

194.  ṭhā (°*pāṭhān*, $3^{II}b^{8}$)

195.  ṭhi (*paṭhitaṃ*, $23^{I}a^{2}$)

196.  ṭhe (*pāṭhe*, $19^{I}a^{3}$)

197.  ṭho (*pāṭho*, $3^{II}b^{9}$)

## Ḍ

198.  ḍa (°*ḍatamajbhyāṃ*, $8^{II}b^{6}$)

199.  ḍaḥ (*ḍaḥ*, $6^{II}a^{7}$)

200.  ḍā (*laḍādayaḥ*, $23^{I}a^{3}$)

201.  ḍi (*lloḍ ity a*°, $2^{I}b^{6}$)

202.  ḍḍhau (°*liḍ ḍhaukata*, $64^{II}a^{1}$)

203.  ḍyi (*aḍiḍyiṣatīti*, $3^{II}b^{5}$)

## ḌH

204.  ḍha (*rūḍhatvāt{a}*, $23^{I}b^{2}$)

205.  ḍhi (*rūḍhitvād*, $4^{II}b^{3}$)

206.  ḍhe (*ḍhenādau*, $17^{II}b^{3}$)

207.  ḍhau (*ḍaḍhau*, $64^{II}a^{1}$)

208.  ḍhra (*ḍhranimitto*, $17^{II}b^{5}$)

## Ṇ

209.  ṇa (*ggrahaṇam*, $7^{II}a^{2}$)

210.  ṇaṃ (°*ggrahaṇaṃ*, $6^{II}a^{6}$)

211.  ṇaḥ (*gauṇaḥ*, $2^{II}b^{10}$)

212.  ṇā (°*antareṇāva*°, $1^{II}b^{8}$)

213.  ṇi (*yaṇika*, $7^{II}b^{3}$)

214.  ṇī (*praṇītaś*, $2^{I}b^{7}$)

215.  ṇe (°*uccāraṇe*, $3^{II}a^{6}$)

216.  ṇai (*pūrvveṇaikam*, $6^{II}b^{1}$)

217.  ṇo (*ke* 〈'〉*ṇo*, $9^{II}a^{1}$)

218.  ṇau (*ṇau*, $21^{II}a^{1}$)

219.  ṇḍa (*muṇḍasya*, $5^{II}b^{10}$)

220.  ṇḍū (*kaṇḍūr*, $6^{II}b^{2}$)

221.  ṇḍvā (*kaṇḍvādi*, $6^{II}b^{2}$)

222.  ṇṇa (°*tvāṇ ṇatvaṃ*, $3^{II}a^{1}$)

223.  ṇṇya (*ghuṇṇyator*, $6^{II}b^{1}$)

224.  ṇya (*prāṇyaṅga*°, $4^{II}b^{6}$)

225.  ṇvu (*ṇvul*, $4^{II}b^{2}$)

226.  ṇsaṃ (*yaṇsaṃyogā*°, $60^{II}a^{1}$)

## T

227.  ta (*dyotakā*, $23^{I}a^{6}$)

228.  taṃ (°*sahitaṃ*, $1^{II}b^{6}$)

229.  taḥ (*tataḥ*, $19^{I}a^{4}$)

230.  t (*vyavadhānāt*, $4^{II}a^{4}$)

231.  t (*paratvāt*, $45^{II}a^{3}$)

232.  tā (*caritārthayor*, $8^{II}a^{3}$)

233.  ti (*jahātīti*, $2^{I}a^{9}$)

234.  tī (*dvitīye*, $2^{II}b^{3}$)

235.  tu (*vodhayitum*, $4^{II}a^{5}$)

236.  tū (*tūbhayathāpy*, $3^{II}a^{1}$)

237.  tṛ (*tṛtīyasya*, $8^{II}b^{7}$)

238.  te (*teṣāṃ*, $2^{I}a^{5}$)

239.  tai (°*kṛtaivā*°, $7^{II}a^{6}$)

240.  to (*nighāto*, $7^{II}a^{9}$)

241.  tka (*tat katham*, $2^{II}a^{2}$)

242.  tta (*anudāttatvaṃ*, $3^{II}a^{3}$)

243.  ttā (*anutpattāv*, $4^{II}a^{3}$)

244.  tti (°*vṛttiḥ*, $4^{II}b^{3}$)

245.  ttu (*paścāt tuk{a}*, $7^{II}a^{8}$)

246.  ttū (*yat tūktaṃ*, $8^{II}a^{8}$)

247.  tte (*abhidhatteḥ*, $2^{II}a^{8}$)

248.  ttau (*vṛttau*, $7^{II}b^{8}$)

249.  ttyā (*anuvṛttyā*, $4^{II}a^{8}$)

250.  ttva (*asattva*°, $2^{II}b^{1}$)

251.  tna (*prayatna*°, $1^{II}b^{9}$)

252.  tpa (*utpatyabhāvād*, $19^{I}a^{6}$)

253.  tpā (*etenotpādita*, $2^{I}a^{3}$)

254.  tpu (°*vāt puki*, $41^{II}b^{5}$)

255.  tpū (°*śāt pūrvvasmin*, $7^{II}a^{3}$)

256.  tpra (°*vat prakāśata*, $19^{I}b^{2}$)

257.  tplu (*paścāt pluta*°, $65^{II}b^{4}$)

258.  tma (°*ātmakam*, $3^{II}a^{6}$)

259.  tya (°*pratyaya*°, $23^{I}a^{9}$)

260.  tyā (*pravṛtyā*, $1^{II}b^{9}$)

261.  tyu (*pīty uktaṃ*, $3^{II}a^{9}$)

262.  tye (*pratyekam*, $8^{II}a^{8}$)

263.  tra (°*sūtram*, $8^{II}b^{10}$)

264.  trā (*tatrāpi*, $23^{I}a^{5}$)

265.  tri (*dvitri*°, $2^{II}b^{3}$)

266.  tre (*mātre*, $23^{I}a^{9}$)

267.  trai (*trailokya*°, $2^{I}b^{3}$)

268.  tva (*dvitvam*, $19^{I}a^{7}$)

269.  tvā (°*viṣayatvāc*, $2^{I}b^{3}$)

270.  tve (°*kleśatvena*, $2^{I}b^{2}$)

271.  tsa (°*antāt sana*, $19^{I}a^{5}$)

272.  tsu (°*antāt suv*°, $19^{I}b^{4}$)

273.  tsau (*ot sau*, $11^{II}a^{8}$)

274.  tsphu (°*āt sphurer*, $5^{II}b^{5}$)

275.  tsya (*matsyasya*, $26^{\mathrm{II}}a^{8}$)

## TH

276.  tha (*prathama°*, $3^{\mathrm{II}}b^{5}$)

277.  thā (*anyathā*, $19^{\mathrm{I}}a^{7}$)

278.  thāṃ (*kathāṃ*, $9^{\mathrm{II}}a^{3}$)

279.  the (*yatheṣṭam*, $3^{\mathrm{II}}b^{7}$)

280.  tho (*tathobhayaṃ*, $4^{\mathrm{II}}a^{6}$)

## D

281.  da (*kṛdantā*, $23^{\mathrm{I}}a^{3}$)

282.  daṃ (*idaṃ*, $19^{\mathrm{I}}b^{8}$)

283.  daḥ (*bhedaḥ*, $3^{\mathrm{II}}a^{4}$)

284.  dā (*ityādāv*, $23^{\mathrm{I}}b^{8}$)

285.  di (*duhadihetyādi*, $6^{\mathrm{II}}a^{5}$)

286.  dī (*dīrghasyeti*, $7^{\mathrm{II}}a^{9}$)

287.  du (*duhadihetyādi*, $6^{\mathrm{II}}a^{5}$)

288.  dū (*īdū*, $11^{\mathrm{II}}a^{5}$)

289.  dṛ (*dṛśyate*, $19^{\mathrm{I}}a^{1}$)

290.  dḷ (*ṛdḷty*, $9^{\mathrm{II}}b^{3}$)

291.  de (*°ādeśasya*, $2^{\mathrm{II}}b^{8}$)

292.  dai (*ādaij*, $4^{\mathrm{II}}a^{6}$)

293.  do (*°doṣaś*, $2^{\mathrm{I}}a^{1}$)

294.  dau (*°etyādau*, $3^{\mathrm{II}}a^{3}$)

295.  dgu (*tadguṇa°*, $1^{\mathrm{II}}b^{6}$)

296.  dgo (*udgo*, $23^{\mathrm{II}}b^{6}$)

297.  dgau (*°nād gauṇa°*, $3^{\mathrm{II}}a^{4}$)

298.  dgha (*°ādghasa*, $3^{\mathrm{II}}a^{8}$)

299.  dgho (*°ānudghoṣaṇāc*, $4^{\mathrm{II}}a^{5}$)

300.  ddi (*°gād diṣṭa°*, $6^{\mathrm{II}}a^{1}$)

301.  ddṛ (*°dād dṛśyate*, $17^{\mathrm{II}}a^{5}$)

302.  ddo (*°vād doṣa*, $6^{\mathrm{II}}a^{9}$)

303.  ddyu (*duddyuṣatīti*, $4^{\mathrm{II}}a^{7}$)

304.  ddve (*hrasvād dve*, $3^{\mathrm{II}}a^{1}$)

305.  ddha (*°siddhatvād*, $3^{\mathrm{II}}a^{2}$)

306.  ddhā (*siddhā*, $6^{\mathrm{II}}a^{1}$)

307.  ddhi (*taddhita*, 9$^{II}$a$^{3}$)

308.  ddhuṃ (*boddhuṃ*, 2$^{I}$b$^{1}$)

309.  ddhe (*°rthyād dhetor*, 19$^{I}$a$^{4}$)

310.  ddhya (*°siddhya°*, 4$^{II}$b$^{4}$)

311.  ddhyā (*°prasiddhyā*, 23$^{I}$b$^{2}$)

312.  dbhā (*°vadbhāvād*, 2$^{II}$a$^{3}$)

313.  dbhya (*rudbhyas*, 46$^{II}$a$^{9}$)

314.  dya (*upapadyata*, 3$^{II}$a$^{5}$)

315.  dye (*yady evam*, 4$^{II}$a$^{9}$)

316.  dyo (*dyotata*, 19$^{I}$b$^{2}$)

317.  dra (*dravyam*, 19$^{I}$b$^{2}$)

318.  dru (*vā dru*, 59$^{II}$a$^{1}$)

319.  dva (*dvayor*, 8$^{II}$a$^{4}$)

320.  dvā (*yadvā*, 2$^{II}$b$^{2}$)

321.  dvi (*dvirvacane*, 2$^{II}$b$^{1}$)

322.  dve (*dve*, 2$^{II}$b$^{10}$)

323.  dvau (*dvau*, 2$^{II}$b$^{6}$)

324.  dvyā (*dvyādi°*, 2$^{II}$b$^{7}$)

325.  dvru (*°vād vruvo*, 46$^{II}$a$^{7}$)

## DH

326.  dha (*vipratiṣedha*, 9$^{II}$a$^{3}$)

327.  dhaḥ (*vidhaḥ*, 4$^{II}$b$^{9}$)

328.  dhā (*°vidhānaṃ*, 23$^{I}$a$^{7}$)

329.  dhi (*bodhi°*, 2$^{I}$a$^{7}$)

330.  dhī (*°ābhidhīyata*, 2$^{II}$b$^{7}$)

331.  dhu (*°mādhurya°*, 19$^{I}$b$^{3}$)

332.  dhū (*asādhūnāṃ*, 8$^{I}$a$^{8}$)

333.  dhe (*°ābhidheyatayā*, 2$^{II}$a$^{1}$)

334.  dho (*virodhopa°*, 4$^{II}$a$^{6}$)

335.  dhau (*vidhau*, 2$^{I}$b$^{5}$)

336.  dhmā (*°padhmānī°*, 36$^{II}$b$^{6}$)

337.  dhmo (*ghrādhmor*, 41$^{II}$b$^{5}$)

338.  dhya (*sambadhyate*, 6$^{II}$b$^{3}$)

339.  dhyā (*sādhyāva°*, 19$^{I}$b$^{1}$)

340.  dhyu (*°dadhyuḥ*, $23^{\text{I}}\text{b}^{3}$)

341.  dhye (*mmadhye*, $8^{\text{II}}\text{b}^{6}$)

342.  dhyai (*adhyaiyātāṃ*, $3^{\text{II}}\text{b}^{1}$)

343.  dhva (*dhvaneḥ*, $2^{\text{II}}\text{a}^{4}$)

## N

344.  na (*vyavadhāna°*, $6^{\text{II}}\text{b}^{7}$)

345.  n (*evān*, $9^{\text{II}}\text{a}^{6}$)

346.  n (*yasmin*, $11^{\text{II}}\text{b}^{2}$)

347.  naṃ (*vyavadhānaṃ*, $4^{\text{II}}\text{b}^{2}$)

348.  naḥ (*naḥ*, $6^{\text{II}}\text{b}^{1}$)

349.  nā (*°vacanāt{a}*, $23^{\text{I}}\text{a}^{1}$)

350.  ni (*nirddeśāt*, $19^{\text{I}}\text{b}^{3}$)

351.  nī (*nāśaṅkanīyaḥ*, $6^{\text{II}}\text{a}^{1}$)

352.  nu (*°parānugatam*, $2^{\text{II}}\text{b}^{5}$)

353.  nū (*anūpaḥ*, $11^{\text{II}}\text{a}^{10}$)

354.  nṛ (*°nṛpater*, $75^{\text{II}}\text{a}^{5}$)

355.  nṝ (*nṝ*, $62^{\text{II}}\text{b}^{4}$)

356.  ne (*°prayojane*, $1^{\text{II}}\text{b}^{3}$)

357.  no (*noktaṃ*, $1^{\text{II}}\text{b}^{1}$)

358.  nai (*°tvenaiṅo*, $11^{\text{II}}\text{a}^{3}$)

359.  nau (*pīnau*, $4^{\text{II}}\text{b}^{5}$)

360.  nta (*°gantavyaḥ*, $8^{\text{II}}\text{b}^{1}$)

361.  ntā (*°cintāyām*, $1^{\text{II}}\text{b}^{4}$)

362.  nti (*bhavanti*, $23^{\text{I}}\text{a}^{3}$)

363.  ntu (*kin tu*, $2^{\text{II}}\text{b}^{7}$)

364.  ntya (*dantya°*, $6^{\text{II}}\text{a}^{8}$)

365.  ntyā (*antyāpe°*, $1^{\text{II}}\text{b}^{4}$)

366.  ntyo (*dantyoṣṭhayoḥ*, $8^{\text{II}}\text{b}^{8}$)

367.  ntyau (*dantyauṣṭha°*, $2^{\text{I}}\text{a}^{8}$)

368.  ntrye (*svātantryeṇa*, $62^{\text{II}}\text{a}^{9}$)

369.  ntha (*ggranthasyā°*, $2^{\text{I}}\text{b}^{5}$)

370.  nthe (*°ggranthena*, $7^{\text{II}}\text{a}^{5}$)

371.  nda (*°sundaraṃ*, $36^{\text{II}}\text{a}^{1}$)

372.  ndyo (*vandyo*, $2^{\text{I}}\text{b}^{2}$)

373.  ndra (°*candra*°, $2^{II}a^{7}$)

374.  ndri (°*endriya*°, $2^{II}a^{3}$)

375.  ndre (*cāndre*, $61^{II}b^{5}$)

376.  ndhā (*vandhā*, $4^{II}a^{7}$)

377.  ndhi (°*sambandhi*°, $8^{II}b^{8}$)

378.  ndhu (*vandhuṣv*, $4^{II}a^{7}$)

379.  ndhe (°*sambandhe*, $22^{I}b^{4}$)

380.  nna (*sannanta*°, $1^{II}b^{4}$)

381.  nni (*sann iti*, $4^{II}a^{1}$)

382.  nno (°*kṛṣṭan notta*°, $4^{II}a^{10}$)

383.  nma (*tanmate*, $6^{II}a^{10}$)

384.  nmo (°*n mokṣata*, $49^{II}a^{6}$)

385.  nya (*anyathā*, $23^{I}b^{6}$)

386.  nyu (*lūnyuḥ*, $11^{II}a^{1}$)

387.  nyo (*anyonya*°, $9^{II}b^{1}$)

388.  nvā (°*ānvākhyāne*, $2^{II}a^{4}$)

389.  nvi (*sanvidhānāt{a}*, $4^{II}a^{3}$)

390.  nve (*nanv evaṃ*°, $2^{I}a^{3}$)

391.  nsa (*napunsakatā*, $54^{II}a^{1}$)

392.  nsī (*apunsīty*, $54^{II}a^{2}$)

393.  nso (*punso*, $53^{II}a^{10}$)

394.  nha (*inhan*°, $19^{II}a^{7}$)

## P

395.  pa (°*lopa*°, $6^{II}b^{3}$)

396.  p (*matup*, $35^{II}a^{7}$)

397.  paṃ (*svarūpaṃ*, $41^{II}b^{8}$)

398.  paḥ (*nalopaḥ*, $7^{II}a^{4}$)

399.  pā (*pāribhāṣitaṃ*, $4^{II}b^{5}$)

400.  pāṃ (*vidhirūpāṃ*, $23^{I}b^{4}$)

401.  pi (*kvipi*, $6^{II}b^{2}$)

402.  pī (*apīti*, $19^{I}a^{3}$)

403.  pu (*pustake*, $19^{I}a^{2}$)

404.  puṃ (*puṃliṅgaḥ*, $2^{I}b^{8}$)

405.  pū (*pūrvvā*°, $23^{I}b^{2}$)

406.  pṛ (*pṛthag°*, $4^{II}a^{1}$)

407.  pe (*°pradīpe*, $6^{II}a^{2}$)

408.  pai (*°supaikā°*, $7^{II}b^{9}$)

409.  po (*kvipo*, $6^{II}b^{2}$)

410.  pau (*°lopau*, $2^{II}a^{2}$)

411.  pkri (*supkriyā°*, $9^{II}b^{3}$)

412.  pta (*saptamyāṃ*, $4^{II}b^{8}$)

413.  pti (*prāptir*, $41^{II}b^{4}$)

414.  ptau (*dīptau*, $2^{I}b^{9}$)

415.  ptya (*prāptyabhāvād*, $7^{II}b^{1}$)

416.  ptyā (*tṛptyā*, $54^{II}a^{9}$)

417.  pno (*prāpnoti*, $9^{II}b^{6}$)

418.  ppi (*ṭippitake*, $61^{II}b^{5}$)

419.  pya (*tathāpy atra*, $4^{II}a^{7}$)

420.  pyā (*lipyāḥ*, $2^{II}a^{5}$)

421.  pyu (*apy ubhayoḥ*, $8^{II}b^{3}$)

422.  pra (*prayoge*, $9^{II}b^{2}$)

423.  prā (*prārcchati*, $9^{II}b^{5}$)

424.  pri (*priyam*, $11^{II}a^{8}$)

425.  pre (*predidhad*, $9^{II}a^{5}$)

426.  pro (*prohyata*, $8^{II}b^{10}$)

427.  plu (*apluta*, $11^{II}a^{3}$)

428.  pvo (*kupvo*, $64^{II}b^{9}$)

429.  psa (*dhīpsatīti*, $49^{II}b^{8}$)

430.  psi (*hvālipsisicaḥ*, $28^{I}a^{2}$)

431.  psu (*supsupaikā°*, $7^{II}b^{9}$)

## PH

432.  pha (*viphalaṃ*, $2^{II}b^{1}$)

433.  phu (*phulla*, $60^{II}b^{1}$)

## B

434.  ba (*bahu°*, $6^{II}b^{9}$)

435.  bā (*°bāhulyāt*, $6^{II}a^{4}$)

436.  bu (*buddhiḥ*, $23^{I}b^{7}$)

437.  bo (*boddhuṃ*, $2^{I}b^{1}$)

438.  bṇi (*sub ṇici*, $9^{II}a^{7}$)

439.  bda (*śabda°*, $23^{I}a^{4}$)

440.  bdā (*°śabdā*, $2^{II}b^{3}$)

441.  bde (*°śabdena*, $2^{II}b^{7}$)

442.  bdo (*°śabdo*, $2^{II}b^{2}$)

443.  bdha (*°labdhasya*, $8^{II}a^{10}$)

444.  bdhā (*subdhātutve*, $4^{II}b^{3}$)

445.  bdhe (*labdhe*, $8^{II}a^{9}$)

446.  bru (*bruvaḥ*, $31^{II}b^{5}$)

447.  blu (*subluki*, $7^{II}a^{4}$)

## BH

448.  bha (*bhaviṣyati*, $7^{II}b^{5}$)

449.  bhā (*bhāva°*, $19^{I}b^{7}$)

450.  bhi (*vyabhicaraty*, $9^{II}a^{6}$)

451.  bhī (*bhīhrīhūnān*, $2^{II}b^{9}$)

452.  bhu (*bhuvo*, $31^{I}b^{8}$)

453.  bhū (*ābhūd*, $23^{I}a^{7}$)

454.  bhṛ (*bhṛśaṃ*, $23^{I}a^{4}$)

455.  bhe (*bhedāt{a}*, $2^{II}b^{1}$)

456.  bho (*bhojane*, $9^{II}b^{8}$)

457.  bhau (*bhauvādika°*, $6^{II}a^{4}$)

458.  bhnā (*kṣubhnādi°*, $3^{II}a^{2}$)

459.  bhya (*labhyata*, $7^{II}a^{10}$)

460.  bhyu (*°ābhyupagate*, $6^{II}a^{4}$)

461.  bhra (*bhraṃśu*, $4^{II}b^{3}$)

462.  bhrū (*bhrūśabdasya*, $46^{II}b^{9}$)

## M

463.  ma (*abhimataṃ*, $6^{II}b^{8}$)

464.  maḥ (*°ottamaḥ*, $11^{II}a^{1}$)

465.  m (*°artham*, $4^{II}a^{9}$)

466.  m (*uktam*, $3^{II}b^{7}$)

467.  mā (*ānumānikaṃ*, $8^{II}b^{9}$)

468.  mi (*°nimittam*, $3^{II}b^{10}$)

469.  mī (*kariṣyāmīti*, $23^{I}a^{8}$)

470.  mu (*°samudāye*, $1^{II}b^{4}$)

471.  mū (*°mūliyābhyāṃ*, $62^{II}b^{3}$)

472.  mṛ (*parāmṛṣan*, $3^{II}a^{1}$)

473.  me (*āgamenāpi*, $4^{II}b^{2}$)

474.  mo (*namo*, $2^{I}b^{5}$)

475.  mnā (*°nāmnā*, $2^{I}b^{7}$)

476.  mni (*°nāmni*, $4^{II}b^{7}$)

477.  mpa (*sampadādi*, $6^{II}b^{2}$)

478.  mba (*°sambandhāt{a}*, $23^{I}b^{8}$)

479.  mbā (*[vi]śiṣṭām bā*, $23^{I}b^{4}$)

480.  mbha (*sambhavati*, $9^{II}b^{2}$)

481.  mbhe (*cārambhe*, $2^{I}b^{1}$)

482.  mma (*°sammatam*, $4^{II}a^{2}$)

483.  mya (*pañcamya°*, $3^{II}b^{2}$)

484.  myāṃ (*saptamyāṃ*, $3^{II}b^{3}$)

485.  mle (*mlecchitavyam*, $8^{I}a^{9}$)

486.  mva (*pumvad°*, $7^{II}a^{8}$)

487.  mvā (*°mātram vā*, $23^{I}b^{4}$)

488.  mvi (*°samvijñānam*, $1^{II}b^{5}$)

489.  mvṛ (*samvṛtta*, $3^{II}a^{8}$)

Y

490.  ya (*yadi*, $6^{II}b^{7}$)

491.  yaṃ (*nāyaṃ*, $7^{II}a^{4}$)

492.  yaḥ (*viṣayaḥ*, $9^{II}a^{5}$)

493.  yā (*°dvayādeśe*, $2^{II}b^{4}$)

494.  yāṃ (*gaṇanāyāṃ*, $2^{II}b^{3}$)

495.  yi (*°darśayituṃ*, $9^{II}a^{1}$)

496.  yu (*ayuktaṃ*, $4^{II}b^{3}$)

497.  yū (*°vāyū*, $4^{II}b^{5}$)

498.  ye (*°dvayena*, $4^{II}b^{10}$)

499.  yai (*sam[u]dāyaikāca*, $1^{II}b^{9}$)

500.  yo (*°ābhidheyo*, $2^{II}b^{2}$)

501.  yau (*°yaugapadye*, $8^{II}a^{7}$)

502.  yya (*kṣayya*, $7^{II}b^{6}$)

503.  yyo (*krayyo*, $7^{II}b^{7}$)

504.  yvā (*yvāśabdasya*, $11^{II}a^{6}$)

505.  yve (*yved*, $11^{II}a^{6}$)

## R

506.  ra (°*āpara*°, $2^{II}a^{1}$)

507.  raṃ (*paraṃ*, $6^{II}a^{3}$)

508.  raḥ (*sāgaraḥ*, $23^{I}a^{4}$)

509.  rā (*upacārāt*, $4^{II}b^{5}$)

510.  ri (*pāribhāṣitaṃ*, $4^{II}b^{5}$)

511.  rī (*amarīmārjjata*, $41^{II}b^{1}$)

512.  ru (*dviruccāraṇe*, $3^{II}a^{4}$)

513.  rū (*niṣedharūpāṃ*, $23^{I}b^{4}$)

514.  rṛ (*ur ṛd*, $36^{II}a^{9}$)

515.  re (°*dvāreṇa*, $2^{II}a^{4}$)

516.  rai (°*dharair*, $2^{I}b^{2}$)

517.  ro (°*virodhinoś*, $23^{I}b^{8}$)

518.  rkā ([*upa*]*rkārīyati*, $11^{II}b^{5}$)

519.  rgga (°*yor ggamya*°, $11^{II}a^{9}$)

520.  rggī (*varggīyo*, $23^{I}a^{2}$)

521.  rggau (°*opamārggau*, $17^{II}b^{8}$)

522.  rgha (°*dīrghatve*, $6^{II}b^{4}$)

523.  rghā (*dīrghāntaḥ*, $9^{II}b^{2}$)

524.  rcci (’*rccite*, $7^{II}a^{1}$)

525.  rccha (*prarcchatīti*, $9^{II}b^{5}$)

526.  rjñā (°*siddher jñāpa*°, $6^{II}a^{1}$)

527.  rṇṇa (*varṇṇa*[*mā*]*tram*, $7^{II}a^{9}$)

528.  rṇṇā (°*varṇṇāśraye*, $8^{II}b^{10}$)

529.  rṇṇi (°*dhātor ṇṇico*, $7^{II}b^{5}$)

530.  rṇṇo (*śryugūrṇṇoḥ*, $35^{II}a^{4}$)

531.  rtṛ (°*kartṛtvāt*, $2^{I}b^{6}$)

532.  rtta (*anuvarttate*, $7^{II}a^{9}$)

533.  rtti (°*varttini*, $6^{II}b^{4}$)

534.  rttu (*karttum*, $8^{II}b^{1}$)

535.  rthaṃ (*evārthaṃ*, $4^{II}a^{5}$)

536.  rthe (*samānārthena*, $23^{I}b^{8}$)

537.  rthya (*vaiyarthya°*, $7^{II}b^{10}$)

538.  rthyā (*°sāmarthyād*, $19^{I}a^{2}$)

539.  rda (*°tor dantyau°*, $2^{I}a^{8}$)

540.  rdṛ (*dhetor dṛṣṭan*, $19^{I}a^{4}$)

541.  rde (*nirdeśād*, $9^{II}a^{6}$)

542.  rdo (*nirdoṣatvāc*, $2^{II}a^{6}$)

543.  rddi (*°nārddidhiṣaty*, $4^{II}a^{6}$)

544.  rdde (*nirddeśād*, $2^{II}b^{9}$)

545.  rddha (*ārddhadhā°*, $19^{I}a^{8}$)

546.  rdvi (*°der dvitīyasya*, $8^{II}a^{10}$)

547.  rna (*°ttir na*, $7^{II}b^{9}$)

548.  rnna (*°der nna*, $19^{I}a^{7}$)

549.  rnni ([*vi*]*dhir nnitya°*, $19^{I}a^{1}$)

550.  rpa (*śarpare*, $64^{II}a^{7}$)

551.  rbbha (*garbbhaḥ*, $\underline{27^{II}a}^{7}$)

552.  rbhū (*°rbhūta°*, $23^{I}a^{3}$)

553.  rmma (*°yor mmadhye*, $8^{II}b^{6}$)

554.  rya (*°kāryasyā°*, $7^{II}a^{8}$)

555.  ryā (*paryāye*, $7^{II}b^{9}$)

556.  ryi (*kāryitve*, $41^{II}b^{4}$)

557.  ryu (*°yor yuga°*, $8^{II}a^{3}$)

558.  rye (*nājānantarye*, $9^{II}a^{4}$)

559.  rli (*āśīrliṅ°*, $6^{II}b^{8}$)

560.  rlli (*°āśīrlliṅīti*, $7^{II}b^{5}$)

561.  rllo (*°por llopaḥ*, $6^{II}b^{7}$)

562.  rvyu (*°ter vyutpāda°*, $19^{I}b^{1}$)

563.  rvva (*°pūrvva°*, $2^{II}b^{2}$)

564.  rvvā (*pūrvvā°*, $23^{I}b^{2}$)

565.  rvvi (*nirvviṣayam*, $7^{II}b^{2}$)

566.  rvve (*pūrvveṇaikam*, $6^{II}b^{1}$)

567.  rśa (*°darśanād*, $3^{II}a^{4}$)

568.  rṣā (*prakarṣādy°*, $23^{I}b^{3}$)

569.  rṣi (*khaṭvarṣir*, $8^{II}a^{1}$)

570.  rṣe (°*prakarṣe*, 8$^{\rm II}$b$^{7}$)

571.  rṣyā (*cikīrṣyād*, 6$^{\rm II}$b$^{8}$)

572.  rha (°*ārhatvāt*, 4$^{\rm II}$a$^{3}$)

573.  rhya (*tarhy atiṅ*°, 6$^{\rm II}$b$^{8}$)

L

574.  la (°*lakṣaṇe*, 7$^{\rm II}$a$^{2}$)

575.  laṃ (*sakalaṃ*, 2$^{\rm II}$a$^{10}$)

576.  lā (*kālāpāḥ*, 9$^{\rm II}$b$^{9}$)

577.  li (*lipi*°, 2$^{\rm II}$a$^{8}$)

578.  lī (*valīti*, 3$^{\rm II}$b$^{6}$)

579.  lu (*lug*, 2$^{\rm II}$b$^{10}$)

580.  lū (*lūnyuḥ*, 11$^{\rm II}$a$^{1}$)

581.  le (*lekhaka*, 6$^{\rm II}$a$^{8}$)

582.  lo (*lokānandā*°, 2$^{\rm I}$b$^{6}$)

583.  lau (*laukika*°, 17$^{\rm II}$a$^{7}$)

584.  lkā (*upalkārīyatīti*, 11$^{\rm II}$b$^{5}$)

585.  lpa (*vikalpasya*, 4$^{\rm II}$b$^{8}$)

586.  lpā (°*alpārthasya*, 9$^{\rm II}$b$^{1}$)

587.  lpi (°*kalpitaṃ*, 3$^{\rm II}$a$^{7}$)

588.  lpo (*vi*《*ka*》*lpo*, 19$^{\rm I}$b$^{9}$)

589.  lya (*tulya*°, 9$^{\rm II}$b$^{9}$)

590.  lye (*śākalyena*, 23$^{\rm I}$a$^{4}$)

591.  llo (*llopo*, 23$^{\rm I}$a$^{1}$)

592.  lvā (*tālvādi*°, 2$^{\rm II}$a$^{3}$)

593.  lvi (*alvidhitvena*, 6$^{\rm II}$b$^{10}$)

V

594.  va (*vacanāt*, 9$^{\rm II}$b$^{7}$)

595.  vaṃ (°*gauravaṃ*, 1$^{\rm II}$b$^{9}$)

596.  vaḥ (°*dhātavaḥ*, 23$^{\rm I}$b$^{2}$)

597.  vā (°*kṛtavān*, 2$^{\rm II}$a$^{7}$)

598.  vi (*aviśeṣeṇa*, 23$^{\rm I}$a$^{8}$)

599.  vī (*vīpsā*°, 2$^{\rm II}$a$^{2}$)

600.  vu (*suvutpatteḥ*, 9$^{\rm II}$b$^{10}$)

601.  vṛ (°*vṛttiḥ*, 3$^{\rm II}$b$^{6}$)

602.  ve (*vety*, $4^{II}a^{8}$)

603.  vai (°*avayavaikāco*, $4^{II}a^{1}$)

604.  vo (*ivopa*°, $3^{II}a^{7}$)

605.  vau (*avayavau*, $2^{II}b^{4}$)

606.  vṇi (*suv ṇici*, $6^{II}a^{2}$)

607.  vya (*vikretavya*, $7^{II}b^{8}$)

608.  vyā (°*vyāpārā*°, $2^{II}a^{6}$)

609.  vyu (*vyutpattiḥ*, $2^{II}a^{5}$)

610.  vye (*karttavye*, $7^{II}a^{3}$)

611.  vyo (*vyoḥ*, $64^{II}b^{6}$)

612.  vra (*vrata*°, $2^{I}b^{2}$)

613.  vlu (*suvluka*, $4^{II}a^{3}$)

614.  vvi (*suvviṣaye*, $7^{II}a^{3}$)

## Ś

615.  śa (*dviśabdā*°, $2^{II}a^{1}$)

616.  śaṃ (*āśaṃsyate*, $2^{I}b^{4}$)

617.  śaḥ (°*nirddeśaḥ*, $4^{II}a^{1}$)

618.  śā (*nirddeśāt*, $9^{II}b^{7}$)

619.  śi (°*viśiṣṭa*°, $23^{I}b^{9}$)

620.  śī (*āśīrliṅ*, $6^{II}b^{8}$)

621.  śu (*bhraṃśu*, $4^{II}b^{3}$)

622.  śū (*śūṭhor*, $19^{II}b^{6}$)

623.  śṛ (*śṛṅgāṇi*, $3^{I}b^{1}$)

624.  śe (*viśeṣaṇatve*, $3^{II}b^{2}$)

625.  śai (*daśaitan*°, $62^{II}a^{7}$)

626.  śo (*śobhana*°, $7^{II}a^{7}$)

627.  śau (*ṣo[pa]deśau*, $6^{II}a^{10}$)

628.  ścā (*paścād*, $4^{II}a^{6}$)

629.  ścu (*dh[u]ṭi ścur*, $49^{II}a^{3}$)

630.  śce (°*guṇaś ceti*, $19^{I}a^{9}$)

631.  ścai (*itaś caikā*°, $9^{II}a^{3}$)

632.  ścau (*paraiś caurādi*°, $22^{I}a^{6}$)

633.  śti (*śtip*°, $41^{II}b^{3}$)

634.  śtva (*jaśtvanatve*, $7^{II}a^{3}$)

635.  śtve (*jaśtvena*, $64^{II}a^{1}$)

636.  śne (*praśne*, $60^{II}b^{7}$)

637.  śnu (*aśnuhīti*, $11^{II}a^{4}$)

638.  śya (*dṛśyate*, $19^{I}a^{1}$)

639.  śra (°*āśrayam*, $2^{II}a^{3}$)

640.  śri (*rājaśriyā*, $23^{I}a^{2}$)

641.  śrī (*rājaśrībhiḥ*, $53^{II}b^{10}$)

642.  śru (*śrutau*, $64^{II}a^{1}$)

643.  śrū (*śrūyata*, $8^{I}a^{9}$)

644.  śre (*śreyān{a}*, $2^{II}a^{6}$)

645.  śro (*śrotre*°, $2^{II}a^{3}$)

646.  śrau (°*śrautra*°, $2^{II}a^{9}$)

647.  śryu (*śryugūrṇṇoḥ*, $35^{II}a^{4}$)

648.  śle (*ślesma*°, $4^{II}b^{5}$)

649.  ślo (°*śloke*, $2^{I}b^{8}$)

650.  śvī (*śvī*, $35^{II}a^{3}$)

651.  śve (*śveḥ*, $4^{II}b^{7}$)

## Ṣ

652.  ṣa (°*viṣayā*°, $2^{II}b^{2}$)

653.  ṣaḥ (*doṣaḥ*, $3^{II}a^{6}$)

654.  ṣā (°*vibhāṣārthayā*, $4^{II}a^{8}$)

655.  ṣi (*pāribhāṣitaṃ*, $4^{II}b^{5}$)

656.  ṣu (*padeṣu*, $4^{II}b^{7}$)

657.  ṣe (*vipratiṣedhāt{a}*, $8^{II}a^{2}$)

658.  ṣo (*puruṣo*°, $11^{II}a^{1}$)

659.  ṣka (*naiṣkalyaṃ*, $65^{II}a^{1}$)

660.  ṣṭa (*bhṛṣṭa*, $4^{II}b^{4}$)

661.  ṣṭā (*viśiṣṭā*, $23^{I}b^{7}$)

662.  ṣṭi (*viśinaṣṭi*, $2^{I}a^{4}$)

663.  ṣṭī (*yaṣṭī*《*ḥ*》, $2^{I}b^{8}$)

664.  ṣṭu (°*ṣṭum*, $8^{II}b^{5}$)

665.  ṣṭe (*ācaṣṭe*, $23^{I}b^{2}$)

666.  ṣṭya (°*tuṣṭyartham*, $6^{II}a^{5}$)

667.  ṣṭyā (*tiṣṭyāsatīti*, $4^{II}b^{4}$)

668.  ṣṭha (*pratiṣṭhate*, $23^{I}b^{4}$)

669.  ṣṭhi (*niṣṭhitasyeti*, $4^{II}b^{9}$)

670.  ṣṭhī (*ṣṭhīvatīti*, $6^{II}a^{6}$)

671.  ṣṭhe (*iṣṭhe*, $26^{II}b^{6}$)

672.  ṣpa (*niṣpattaye*, $19^{I}a^{2}$)

673.  ṣpu (*dauṣpuruṣyam*, $65^{II}a^{1}$)

674.  ṣpo (*vāṣpo*, $22^{I}a^{4}$)

675.  ṣya (*bhaviṣyati*, $4^{II}b^{9}$)

676.  ṣyā (*kariṣyāmīti*, $23^{I}a^{8}$)

677.  ṣva (*triṣv api*, $4^{II}b^{7}$)

678.  ṣve (*°bahuṣv ekā°*, $8^{II}b^{7}$)

## S

679.  sa (*asammatam*, $11^{II}a^{1}$)

680.  saṃ (*saṃciketiṣati*, $19^{I}a^{6}$)

681.  saḥ (*pratibhāsaḥ*, $11^{II}b^{8}$)

682.  sā (*sāmānya°*, $4^{II}b^{6}$)

683.  si (*°siddhe*, $6^{II}b^{8}$)

684.  sī (*dāsīṣṭeti*, $6^{II}b^{9}$)

685.  su (*sucam*, $2^{II}b^{9}$)

686.  sū (*°sūtre*, $2^{II}a^{2}$)

687.  sṛ (*°sṛjītyāder*, $6^{II}a^{9}$)

688.  se (*samāse*, $11^{II}a^{9}$)

689.  sai (*saiva*, $2^{II}a^{10}$)

690.  so (*vasor*, $3^{II}a^{8}$)

691.  sau (*sautra°*, $23^{I}b^{1}$)

692.  skā (*°saṃskāra°*, $2^{II}a^{1}$)

693.  skṛ (*asaṃskṛtā°*, $8^{I}a^{5}$)

694.  sta (*pustake*, $19^{I}a^{2}$)

695.  sti (*°ñas tiṅy*, $11^{II}a^{5}$)

696.  stu (*vastuta*, $3^{II}a^{7}$)

697.  stū (*stūyamāna°*, $2^{I}b^{7}$)

698.  stṛ (*stṛstṝ*, $6^{II}a^{9}$)

699.  stṝ (*stṛstṝ*, $6^{II}a^{9}$)

700.  ste (*°cchedas tena*, $7^{II}b^{1}$)

701.  stau (*stauti*, 2$^{\mathrm{I}}$b$^{7}$)

702.  stye (*nāsty evety*, 2$^{\mathrm{II}}$b$^{5}$)

703.  stra (*sakṛcchāstra°*, 4$^{\mathrm{II}}$a$^{1}$)

704.  strī (*strītvād*, 19$^{\mathrm{I}}$b$^{7}$)

705.  stvi (*astv iti*, 2$^{\mathrm{I}}$b$^{5}$)

706.  sthā (*sthānivad°*, 2$^{\mathrm{II}}$a$^{3}$)

707.  sthi (*vyavasthitaṃ*, 23$^{\mathrm{I}}$a$^{7}$)

708.  sni (*snigdhatarā*, 8$^{\mathrm{II}}$b$^{8}$)

709.  spa (*paraspara°*, 23$^{\mathrm{I}}$b$^{8}$)

710.  spṛ (*spṛśa*, 44$^{\mathrm{II}}$a$^{7}$)

711.  sphā (*pusphārayiṣatīti*, 5$^{\mathrm{II}}$b$^{5}$)

712.  sphu (*cisphu*, 5$^{\mathrm{II}}$b$^{4}$)

713.  spho (*sphoṭo*, 8$^{\mathrm{I}}$a$^{2}$)

714.  sma (*vismaraṇa°*, 8$^{\mathrm{II}}$b$^{9}$)

715.  smā (*asmākaṃ*, 3$^{\mathrm{II}}$a$^{7}$)

716.  smi (*pūrvvasmin*, 7$^{\mathrm{II}}$a$^{3}$)

717.  sme (*smeḥ*, 5$^{\mathrm{II}}$b$^{10}$)

718.  sya (*antasya*, 4$^{\mathrm{II}}$b$^{3}$)

719.  syā (*dvitvasyāpy*, 2$^{\mathrm{II}}$b$^{2}$)

720.  sye (*tasyety*, 7$^{\mathrm{II}}$b$^{1}$)

721.  syai (*ekasyaivā°*, 1$^{\mathrm{II}}$b$^{4}$)

722.  syo (*°raktasyo°*, 23$^{\mathrm{I}}$b$^{6}$)

723.  sra (*sahasraṃ*, 17$^{\mathrm{II}}$a$^{10}$)

724.  sva (*svarūpa°*, 6$^{\mathrm{II}}$a$^{2}$)

725.  svā (*svārtha°*, 1$^{\mathrm{II}}$b$^{1}$)

726.  svī (*svīkṛtavān*, 2$^{\mathrm{II}}$a$^{7}$)

727.  sve (*hrasve*, 9$^{\mathrm{II}}$a$^{6}$)

728.  svo (*hrasvo*, 9$^{\mathrm{II}}$b$^{3}$)

729.  svau (*hrasvau*, 3$^{\mathrm{II}}$b$^{1}$)

## H

730.  ha (*āha*, 2$^{\mathrm{II}}$a$^{2}$)

731.  hā (*rahād*, 3$^{\mathrm{II}}$a$^{2}$)

732.  hi (*avihitasyaiva*, 23$^{\mathrm{I}}$a$^{1}$)

733.  hiṃ (*hiṃsyā*, 2$^{\mathrm{I}}$a$^{1}$)

734.  hī (*gṛhī*, $2^{I}b^{2}$)

735.  hu (*°bāhulyāt*, $6^{II}a^{4}$)

736.  hū (*hūnāṃ*, $2^{II}b^{10}$)

737.  hṛ (*°nodāhṛtāni*, $23^{I}a^{3}$)

738.  he (*hetunā*, $9^{II}a^{4}$)

739.  hai (*sahaika°*, $6^{II}b^{6}$)

740.  hna (*gṛhnaḥ*, $60^{II}a^{3}$)

741.  hma (*brāhmaṇya*, $7^{II}a^{4}$)

742.  hmā (*brahmā*, $37^{II}b^{5}$)

743.  hmo (*brāhmo*, $27^{II}a^{7}$)

744.  hya (*vāhya°*, $8^{II}a^{10}$)

745.  hyā (*°pragṛhyā*, $11^{II}a^{4}$)

746.  hra (*hrasvād*, $3^{II}a^{1}$)

747.  hrī (*bhīhrīhūnān*, $2^{II}b^{9}$)

748.  hlā (*āhlādane*, $2^{I}b^{9}$)

749.  hva (*vahvalpā°*, $9^{II}b^{1}$)

750.  hvā (*hvālipsisicaḥ*, $28^{I}a^{2}$)

## Symbols

751.  ’ *’bhinna*, $23^{I}a^{5}$ (*avagraha*)

752.  ṃ *saṃjñā°*, $23^{I}a^{9}$ (ring *anusvāra*)

753.  ṃ *evaṃ*, $9^{II}a^{4}$ (dot *anusvāra*)

754.  m̐ *°vām̐ś*, $2^{I}a^{1}$ (*candrabindu*)

755.  ḥ *°vihitāḥ*, $4^{II}b^{6}$ (*visarga*)

756.  ṭ *i ṭ ṭ ṭ ti*, $62^{II}a^{10}$ (deletion and filler character)

| | | | |
|---|---|---|---|
| 757. |  | ⁝ | *hrasva*:*ḥ*, 41$^{\mathrm{II}}$b$^{2}$ (deletion and filler symbol) |
| 758. |  | ⁝⁝ | °*ādaya*::*ḥ*, 2$^{\mathrm{I}}$a$^{5}$ (deletion and filler symbol) |
| 759. |  | \| | *syāt* \|, 7$^{\mathrm{II}}$b$^{8}$ (*daṇḍa*) |
| 760. |  | \|\| | *iti* \|\|, 7$^{\mathrm{II}}$b$^{8}$ (double *daṇḍa*) |
| 761. |  | ˈ | *ṭīkā* ˈ, 44$^{\mathrm{II}}$a$^{9}$ (“semi” *daṇḍa*) |
| 762. |  | $^{\times}_{\wedge}$ | *dhātu*$^{\times}_{\wedge}$*dīpaḥ*, 44$^{\mathrm{II}}$b$^{9}$ (*kākapada*) |
| 763. |  | × × | × *pra* ×, 44$^{\mathrm{II}}$b$^{\mathrm{margin}}$ (insertion) |
| 764. |  | 1 | number one, 54$^{\mathrm{II}}$a$^{\mathrm{margin}}$ |
| 765. |  | 2 | number two, 55$^{\mathrm{II}}$b$^{\mathrm{margin}}$ |
| 766. |  | 4 | number four, 62$^{\mathrm{II}}$a$^{\mathrm{margin}}$ |
| 767. |  | 5 | number five, 64$^{\mathrm{II}}$b$^{\mathrm{margin}}$ |
| 768. |  | 6 | number six, 46$^{\mathrm{II}}$a$^{\mathrm{margin}}$ |
| 769. |  | 7 | number seven, 45$^{\mathrm{II}}$b$^{\mathrm{margin}}$ |
| 770. |  | 8 | number eight, 73$^{\mathrm{II}}$a$^{\mathrm{margin}}$ |
| 771. |  | 9 | number nine, 9$^{\mathrm{II}}$b$^{\mathrm{margin}}$ |

## 3.2 Palaeographic peculiarities

In the end, a few observations about some palaeographic peculiarities of the *Candrālaṃkāra* manuscript should be made here. It is important to stress, though, that in this publication no attempt for a palaeographic study of the Bhaikṣukī script in the perspective of its historical evolution is being made. The aim is rather to fulfil one of the preconditions for such a study, and offer first a systematic documentation of the available palaeographic material.

### 3.2.1 Distinction between *ṛ* and *ra*

Contrary to Bendall who assumed that there is an "absence of distinction between *ṛi* medial and *ra* conjunct", which he moreover considered to be "archaic and noteworthy, especially in a treatise on grammar where it might be expected that the identity of words like *vṛita* and *vrata* would lead to serious confusions",[167] it should be noted that the scribe in fact subtly differentiates between these characters, as can now be easily seen at the hand of the script tables (cf. *kṛ* and *kra*, *dṛ* and *dra*, *pṛ* and *pra*, *bhṛ* and *bhra*, *vṛ* and *vra*, *śṛ* and *śra*, *sṛ* and *sra*, *hṛ* and *hra*).

### 3.2.2 The geminate *gg*

The scribe always writes the geminate *gg* instead of a single *g*, not only before *r* but also when it is followed by *ṛ*; e.g. *anuggrahas* (fol. $2^{\mathrm{I}}\mathrm{a}^{7}$), ***ggra**-haṇaṃ* (fol. $23^{\mathrm{I}}\mathrm{a}^{1}$). On one occasion *gṛ* has been written instead of *ggra*; cf. ***ggra**hagunaś* (fol. $19^{\mathrm{I}}\mathrm{a}^{9}$) and ***gṛ**haguhaś* (fol. $36^{\mathrm{II}}\mathrm{a}^{4}$).

---

[167] Bendall 1886, p. 113. The same assumption was made again lately (cf. Hanisch 2006, pp. 117–118). In the samples provided by Hanisch on p. 120, we read the characters *hṛ*, *kra*, *tra*, and *pra*, which are certainly different from *hra*, *kṛ*, *tṛ*, and *pṛ*, respectively. These characters are as a matter of fact clearly differentiated in both the *Candrālaṃkāra* and the *Maṇicūḍajātaka* manuscripts.

### 3.2.3 Gemination after *r*

In most cases, after *r* the following consonant is doubled; however, inconsistently single consonants also appear here and there, as can be seen in the script tables.

### 3.2.4 Confusion of *ṛ* and *ri*

The scribe infrequently confuses *ṛ* and *ri*, e.g. *anu**vṛ**ttini**vri**ttyartham* (fol. $4^{II}a^{9}$), *d**ri**ṣṭa*° i.o. *dṛṣṭa*° (fol. $7^{II}b^{4}$), ***tri**tīyaḥ* i.o. *tṛtīyaḥ* (fol. $61^{II}b^{6}$).

### 3.2.5 Initial *ī*

Initial *ī* is often not distinguished from its short counterpart, and hence *i* appears instead; e.g. ***i** ghrādhmoḥ* (fol. $41^{II}b^{5}$) i.o. ***ī** ghrādhmoḥ*.

### 3.2.6 Differentiation of *b* and *v*

The scribe is inconsistent with respect to differentiating between *b* and *v*. Sometimes he writes ***v**odhi*° (fol. $2^{I}a^{3}$) and a few lines below ***b**odhi*° (fol. $2^{I}a^{7}$); cf. also ***v**odhayitum* (fol. $4^{II}a^{5}$), ***v**odhayati* (fol. $5^{II}b^{8}$) and ***b**odhi*° (fol. $75^{II}a^{4}$). This inconsistency can also be observed within a single line, e.g. *[vi]śiṣṭām bā kriyāṃ kriyāmātram vā* (fol. $23^{I}b^{4}$).

### 3.2.7 Interchange of sibilants

An interchange of the sibilants can also be observed, though not particularly often; e.g. *°āpabhraṃsa°* (fol. $3^{I}a^{6}$) i.o. *°āpabhraṃśa°*, *V[ā]caṣpatiḥ* (fol. $3^{I}b^{4}$) i.o. *Vācaspatiḥ*, *paribhāsā°* (fol. $8^{II}a^{2}$) i.o. *paribhāṣā°*, *pratisedha°* (fol. $8^{II}b^{9}$) i.o. *pratiṣedha°*, *°niśedhārtham* (fol. $9^{II}b^{5-6}$) i.o. *°niṣedhārtham*.

### 3.2.8 Confusion of *kṣ* and *kh*

Very rarely *kṣ* and *kh* are confused; e.g. *saṃ**khy**[e]pa°* (fol. $3^{I}b^{6}$) i.o. *saṃ**kṣ**epa°*.

### 3.2.9 Final consonant

The scribe uses two alternative ways for indicating that a consonant should be read without an inherent vowel *-a*. Either a *virāma* symbol is used, such as is usually written in other Indian scripts; or a specially modified *akṣara* is written which comprises the proper character and a kind of diacritical mark which resembles the Bhaikṣukī *dīrghamātra* of *ī*. Quite often, though, neither of these two techniques is applied, so that only considerations of grammar and context may help us to decide whether the inherent vowel *-a* should be disregarded.

## 3.3 Conclusion

The few remarks about the Bhaikṣukī manuscript of the *Candrālaṃkāra*, and the extensive script tables provided in this publication will suffice to read with ease and confidence other manuscripts and epigraphic materials written in the Bhaikṣukī script. We can only hope that more such materials are still preserved and will surface out somewhere. Despite their precarious history, the Bhaikṣukī manuscripts and inscriptions discovered so far maintain this hope. It may well be that more spectacular discoveries lie just ahead of us …

**Postscript**

A new contribution to the study of the Bhaikṣukī script has been presented by Hanisch in the exquisite first volume of the *Manuscripta Buddhica* (*Sanskrit Texts from Giuseppe Tucci's Collection.* Part I. Edited by Francesco Sferra. Roma 2009, pp. 195–342) published in the beginning of January 2010. This book became available only a few days before the present study was submitted for printing, and it was thus impossible to utilize it here. However, since my work has been mentioned once there (p. 197, note 8), I take the opportunity to clarify one point which otherwise may have remained unclear. Major parts of the present book were completed by the end of February 2008, and a detailed report, including a preliminary version of this study, was submitted to the director of the Arrow-headed Script Project by the end of April 2008.

*This is the story of Taffimai Metallumai carved on an old tusk a very long time ago by the Ancient Peoples. [...] The tusk was part of an old tribal trumpet that belonged to the Tribe of Tegumai. The pictures were scratched on it with a nail or something, and then the scratches were filled up with black wax, but all the dividing lines and the five little rounds at the bottom were filled with red wax. When it was new there was a sort of network of beads and shells and precious stones at one end of it; but now that has been broken and lost—all except the little bit that you see. The letters round the tusk are magic—Runic magic,—and if you can read them you will find out something rather new ...*

Rudyard Kipling
*Just So Stories for Little Children*

# APPENDIX

## Facsimile Edition of the Candrālaṃkāra Manuscript

The Cambridge and the Kathmandu portions of the *Candrālaṃkāra* manuscript have been split up and kept at two different places for more than a century. Moreover, as mentioned above, the present location of 21 folios of the Kathmandu portion is not known. Thus, it has become even less likely that the material, which has survived since the twelfth century when the manuscript was most probably written, will ever be physically joined together again. Since even today the material is not easily available and the preserved leaves in Cambridge are still in disorder, it was thought worth offering here a facsimile edition of this valuable manuscript with the folios properly arranged.

The colour images of the Cambridge portion were prepared on February 28, 2008 at the Cambridge University Library. The original photographs are of superb quality and allow us to get an exact impression of the current state of preservation of the material. The extremely high expenses for these photographs were covered by the German Research Foundation and the Department of Indology and Tibetology at the University of Marburg.[168] The images of the Cambridge MS Or. 1278 are reproduced by kind permission of the Syndics of Cambridge University Library.

Of the Kathmandu portion we have at our disposal only black and white images prepared by way of digitization of the IASWR microfiche. The photographs were taken on August 17, 1971 in Kathmandu, and the the master copy of the IASWR is at present stored in the Alderman Library of the University of Virginia. For the purposes of this publication a copy of the microfiche kept at the University Library in Göttingen was

[168] It is frustrating to estimate that the total cost of the 34 colour images amounts to more than seven times Nepal's gross national income per capita for the year 2006.

used. The photographs of the Kathmandu portion are, alas, of quite poor quality. Fols. $23^{\text{II}}$ and $75^{\text{II}}$ from this portion of the manuscript are reproduced from the NGMPP's microfilm copy prepared on June 8, 1983.

Even though the images of the material presented here vary in quality, it is believed that the advantages of rejoining the manuscript and making it generally available to the interested public justify the decision to offer a facsimile of the largest portion of handwritten material in the Bhaikṣukī script known so far.

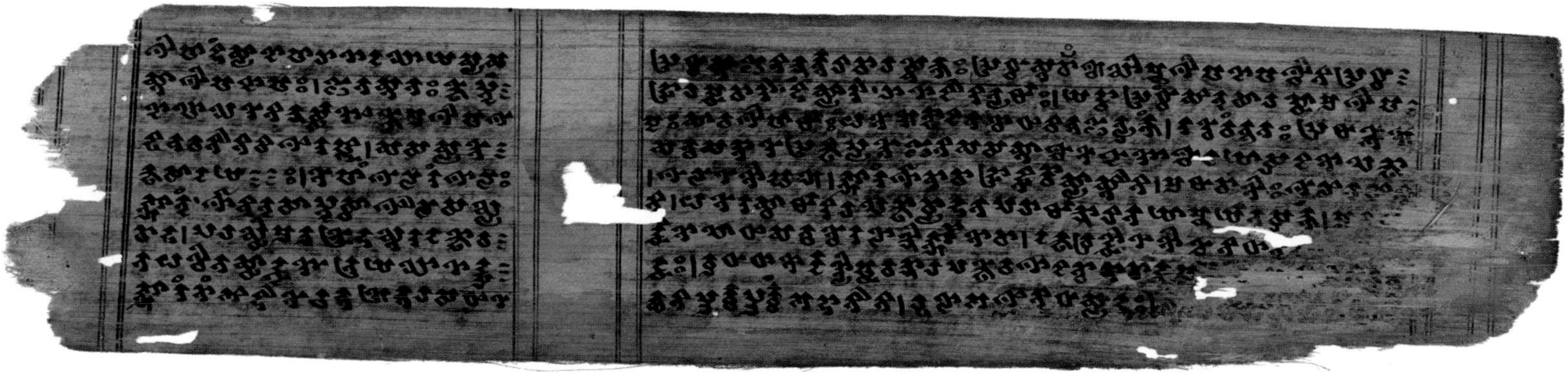

fol. 2Ia

fol. 2ʳb

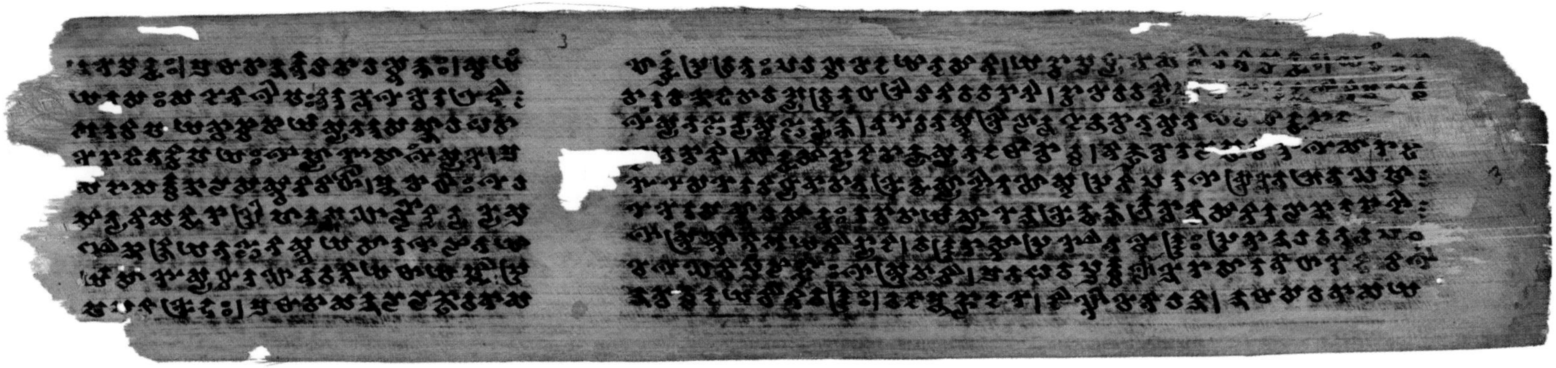

fol. 3ʳa

fol. 3Ib

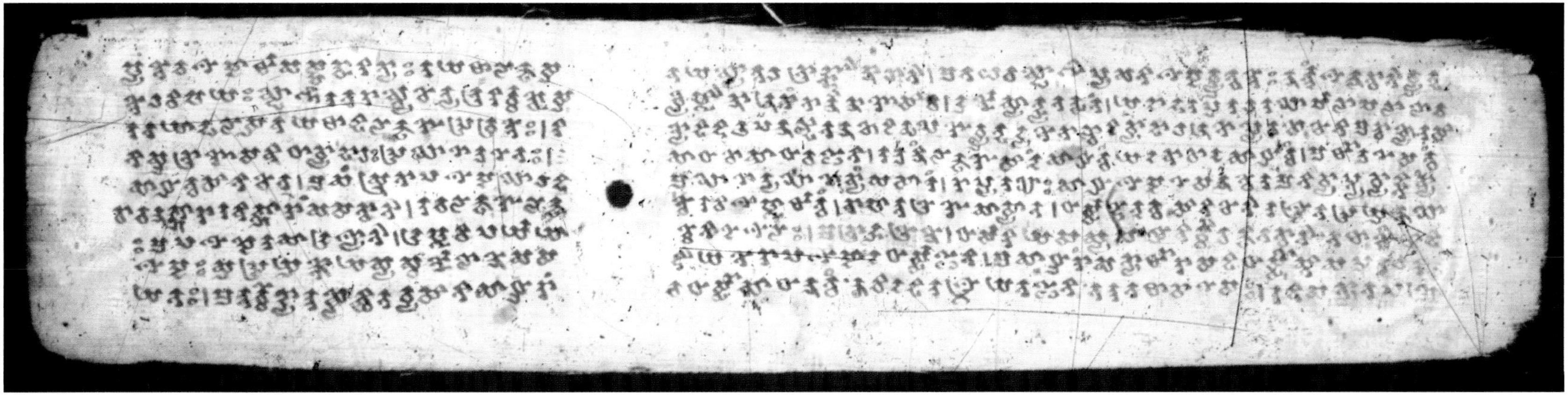

fol. 8Ia

fol. 8Ib

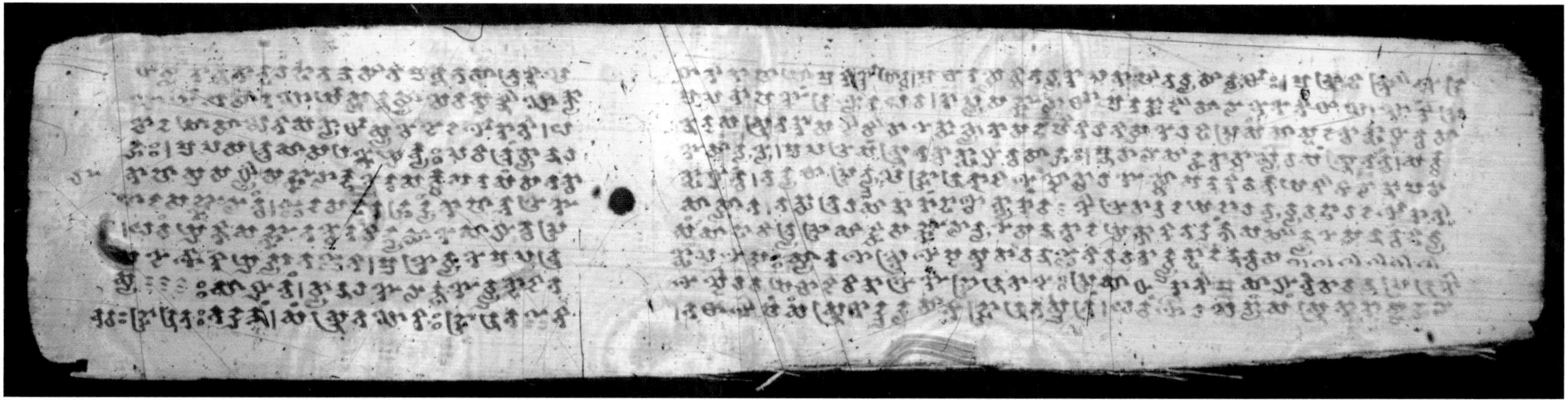

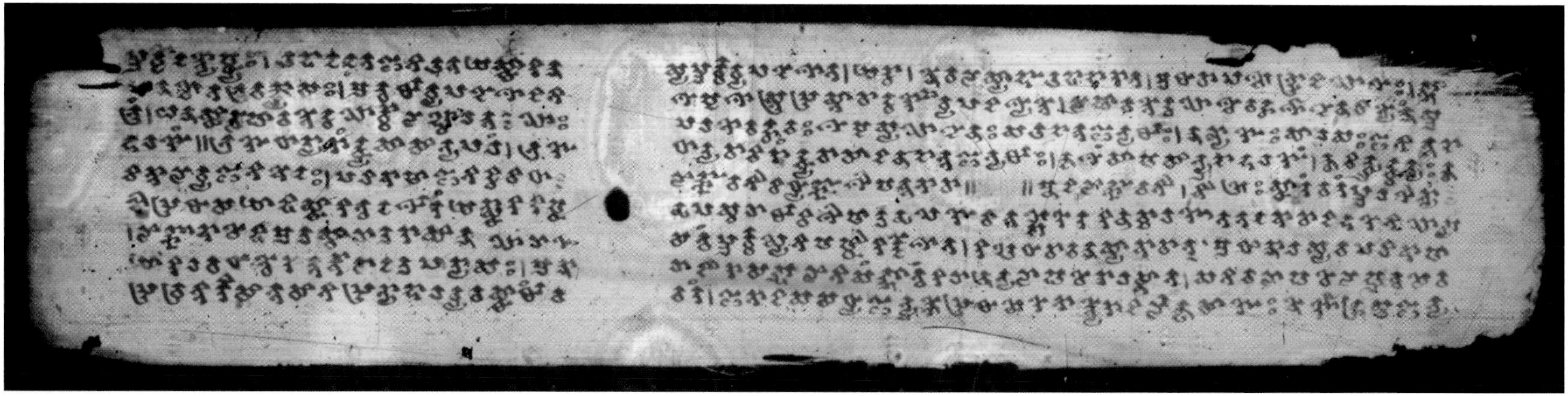

fol. 13Ia

fol. 13ˡb

fol. 16ˡa

fol. 16Ib

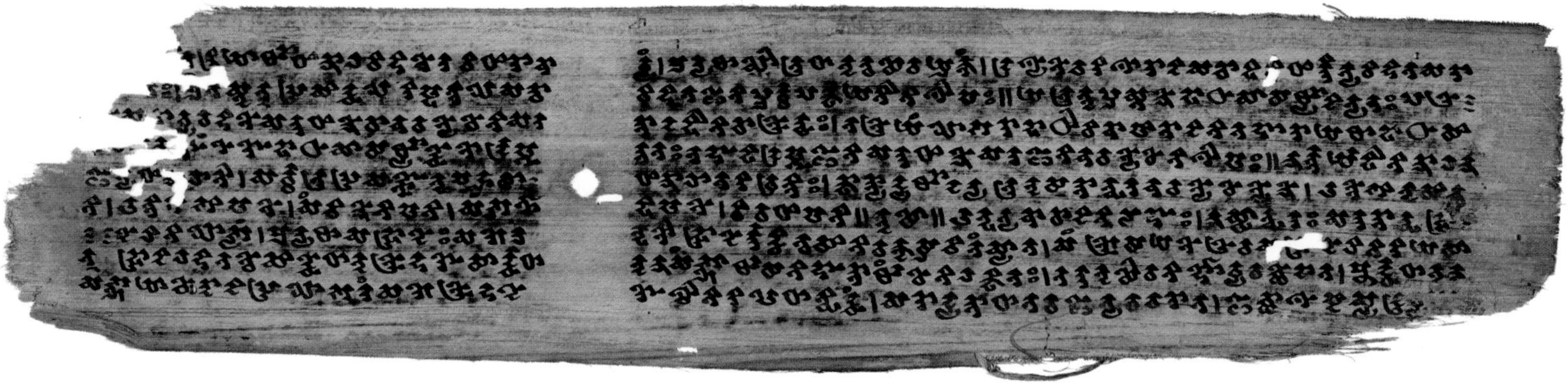

fol. 19Ia

fol. 19ᴵb

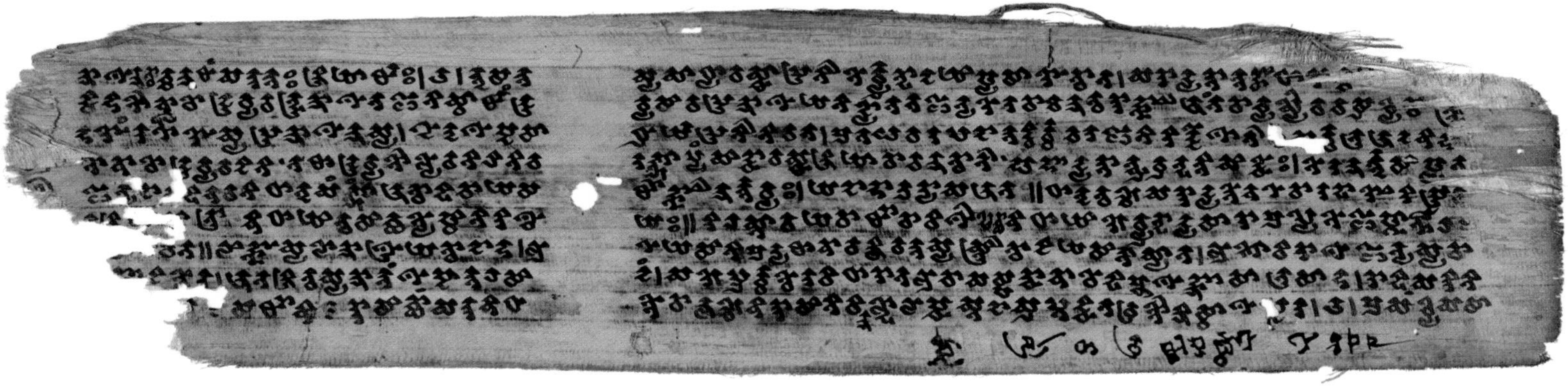

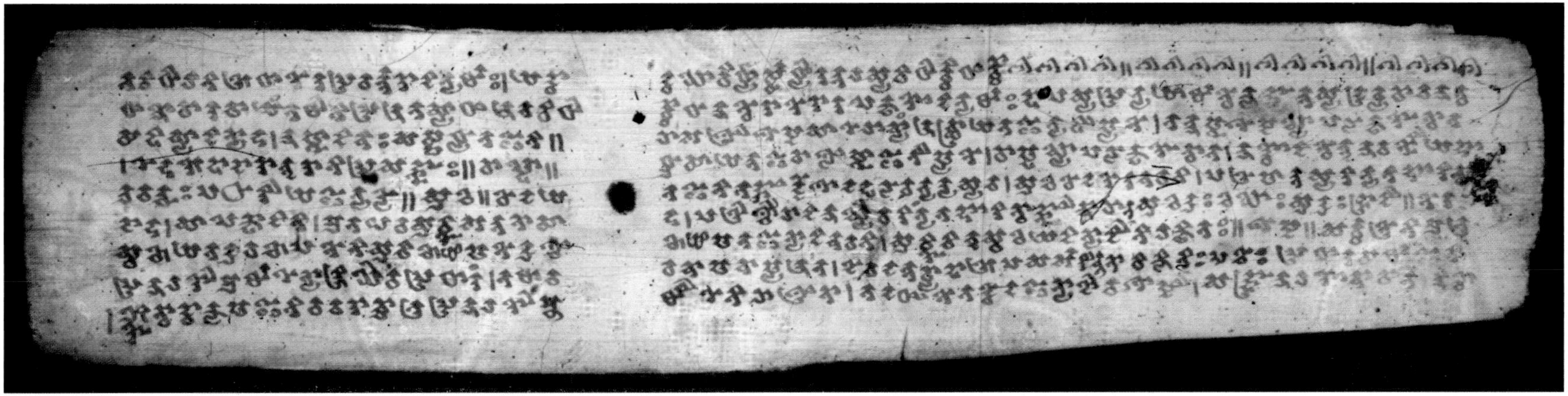

fol. 22ᴵa

fol. 22[I]b

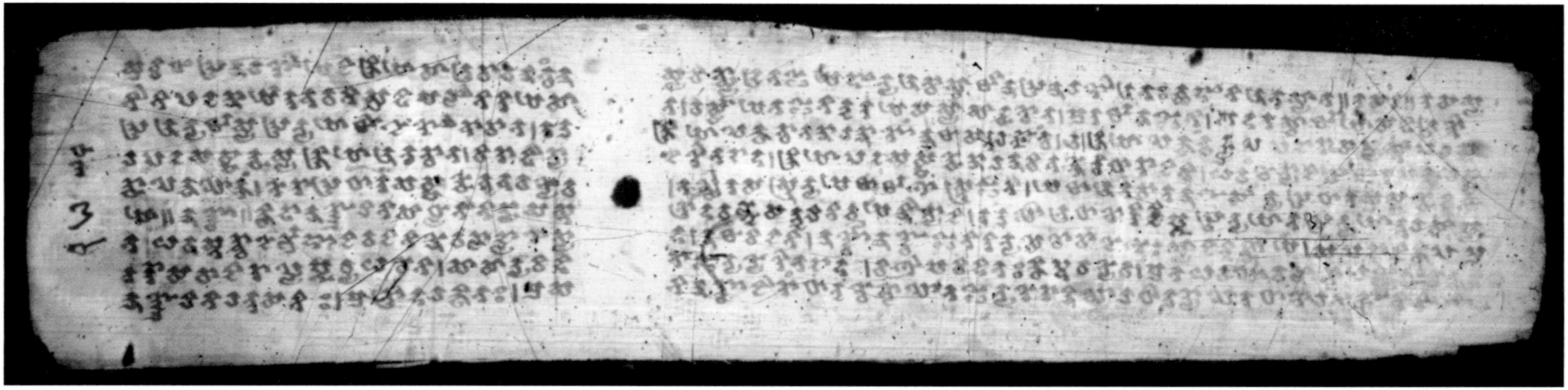

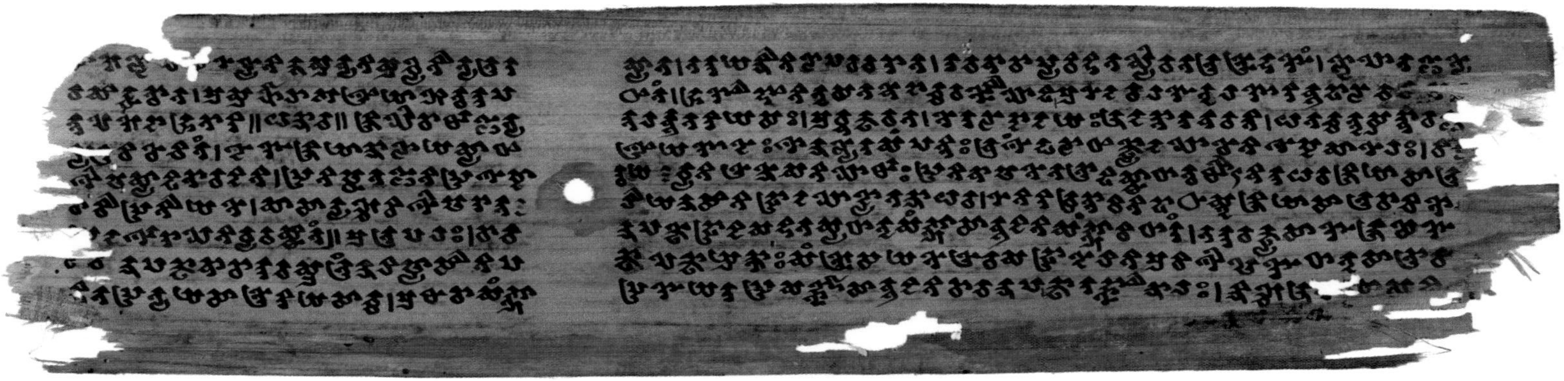

fol. 23[I]a

fol. 23ᴵb

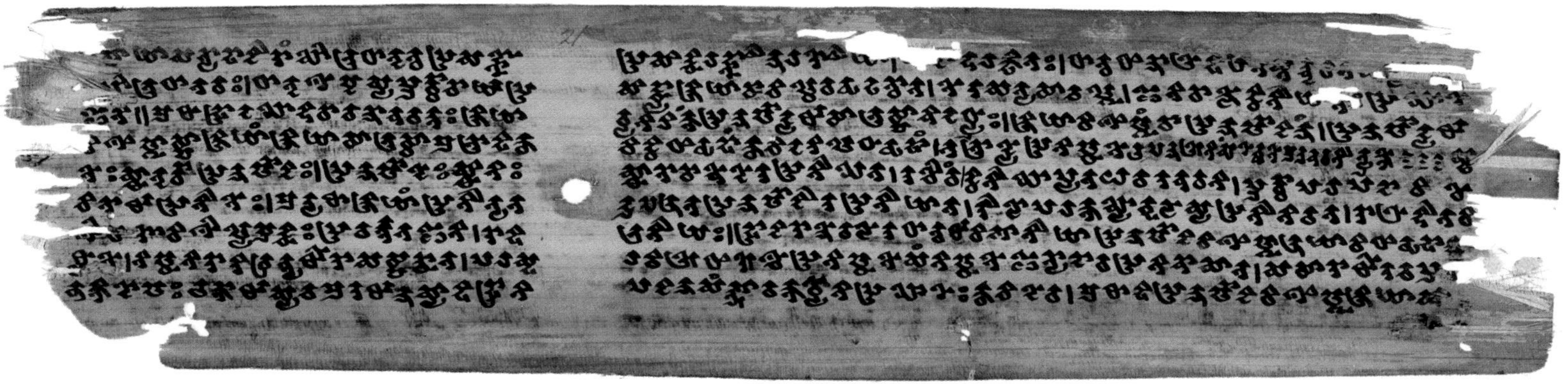

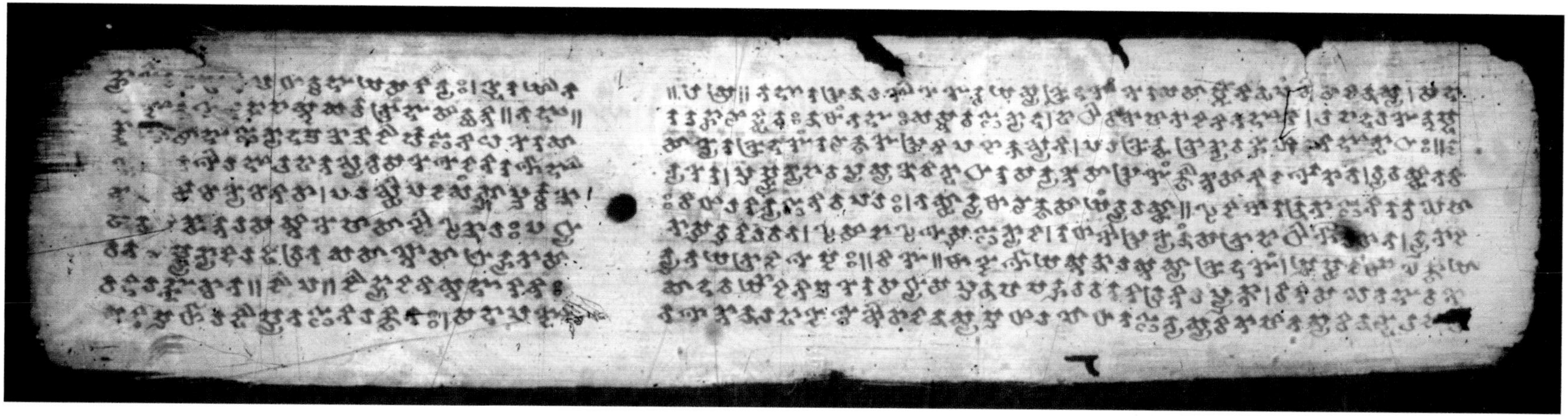

fol. 28ᴵa

fol. 28ᴵb

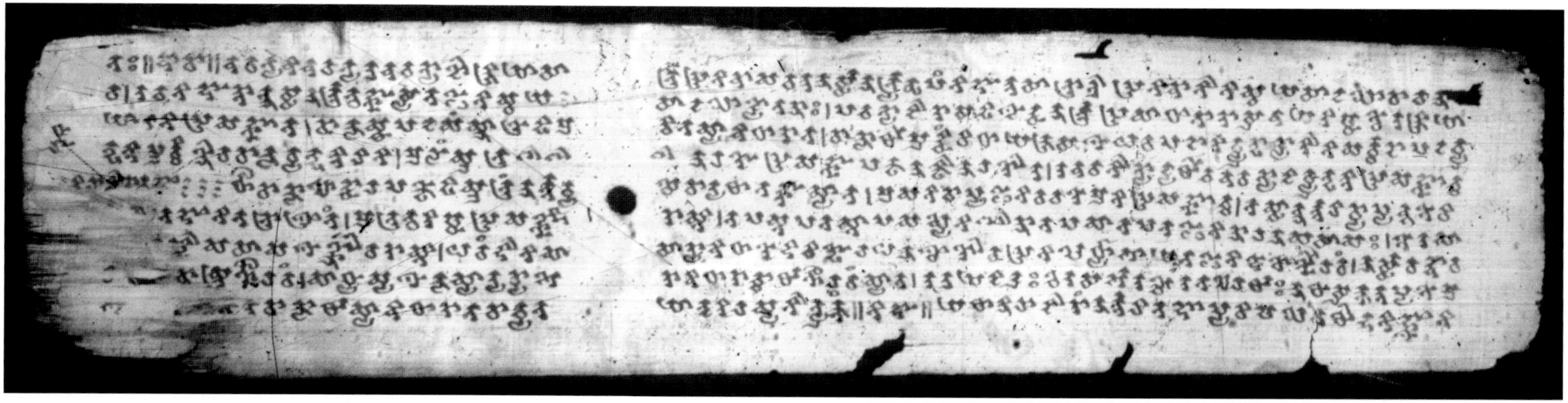

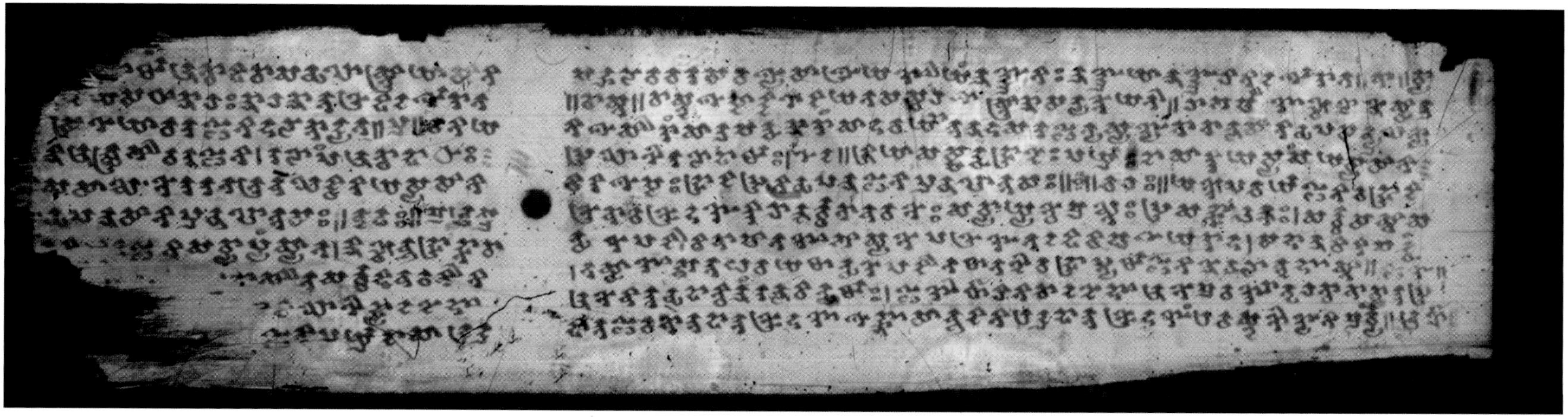

fol. 31ᴵa

fol. 31Ib

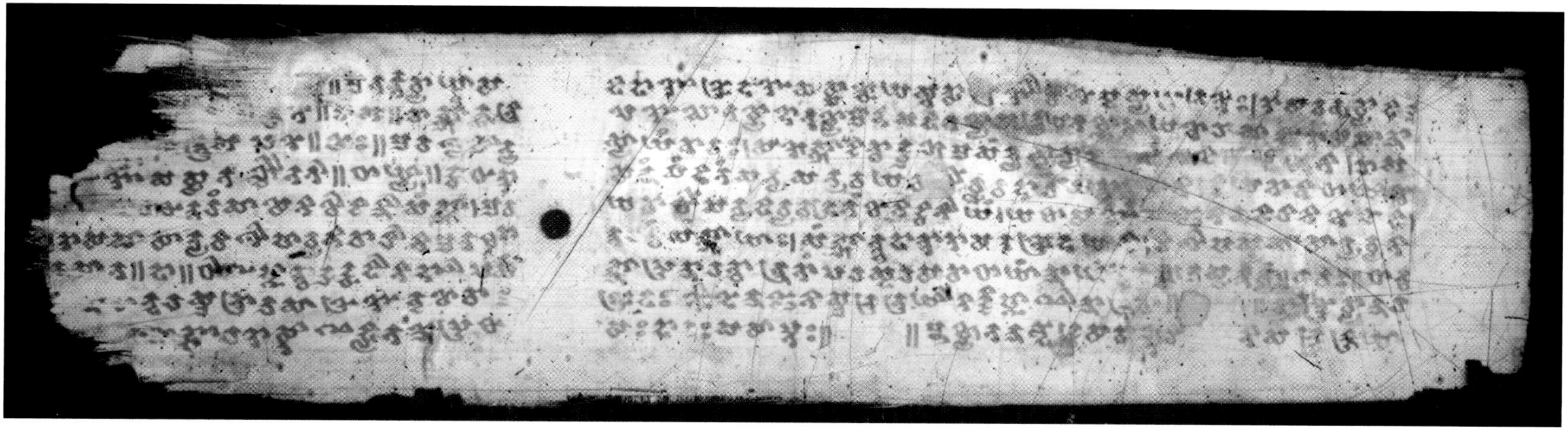

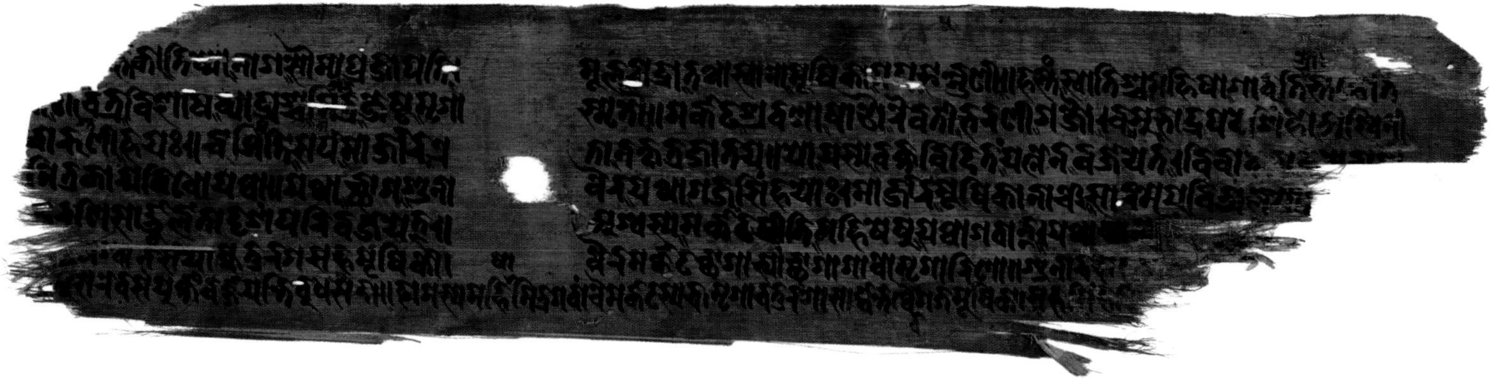

fol. 1IIa

fol. 1IIb

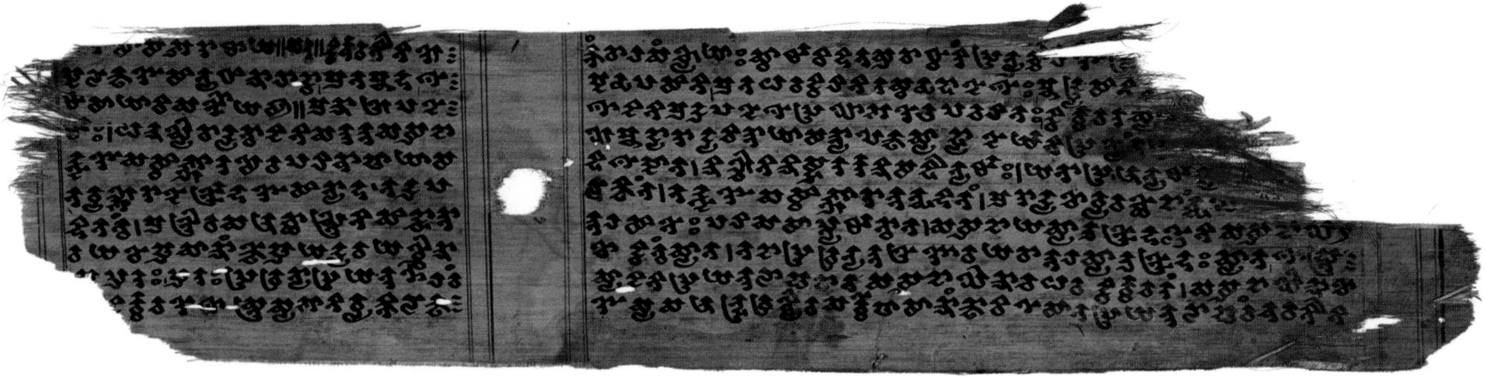

fol. 2IIa

fol. 2IIb

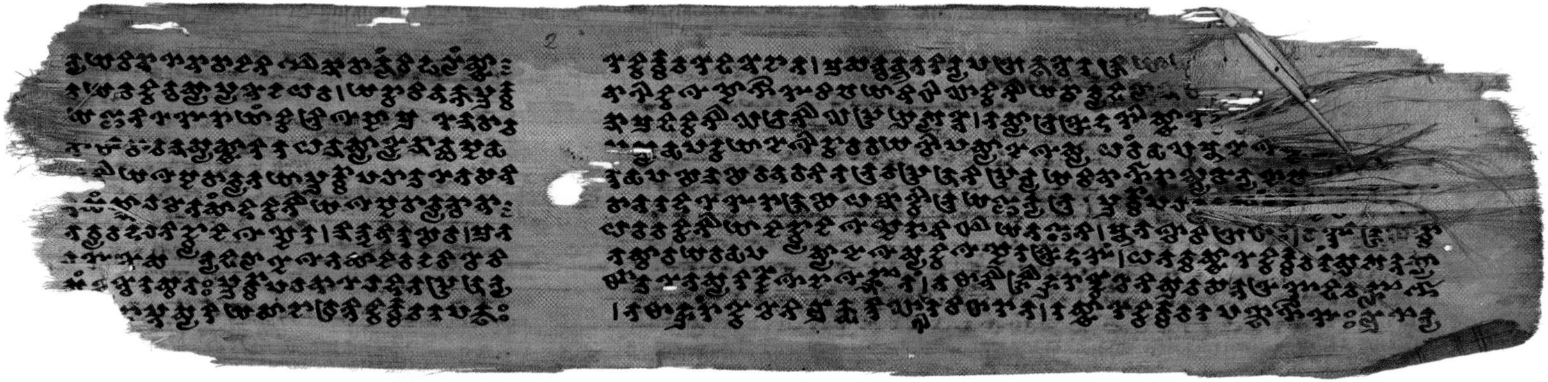

fol. 3IIa

fol. 3IIb

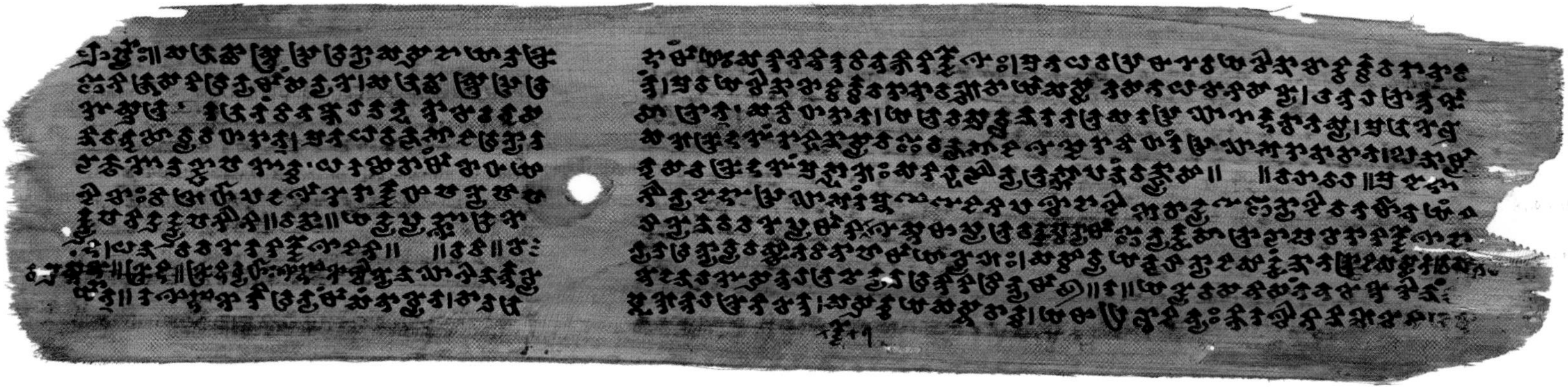

fol. 4IIa

fol. 4[II]b

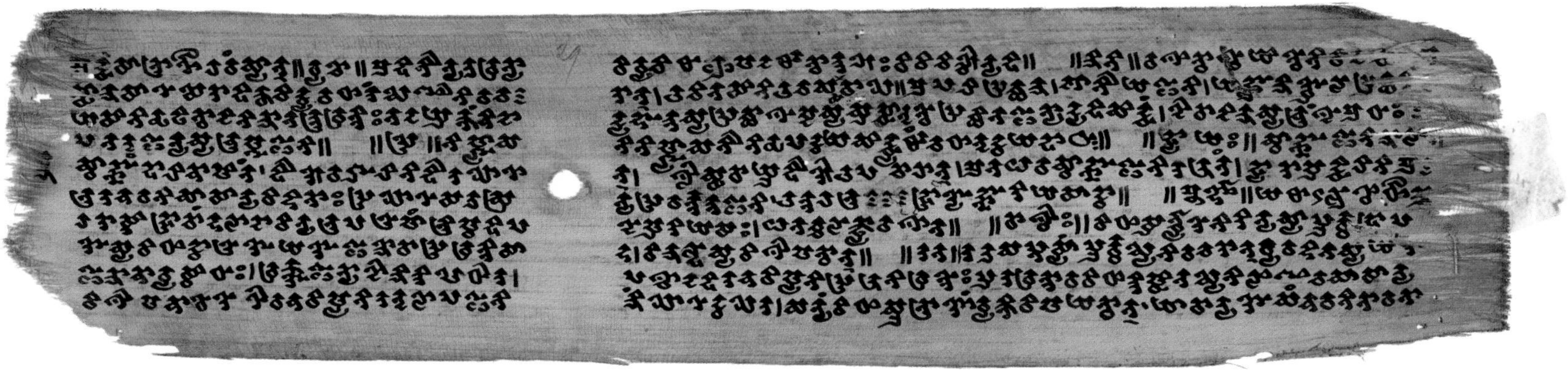

fol. 5[II]a

fol. 5$^{II}$b

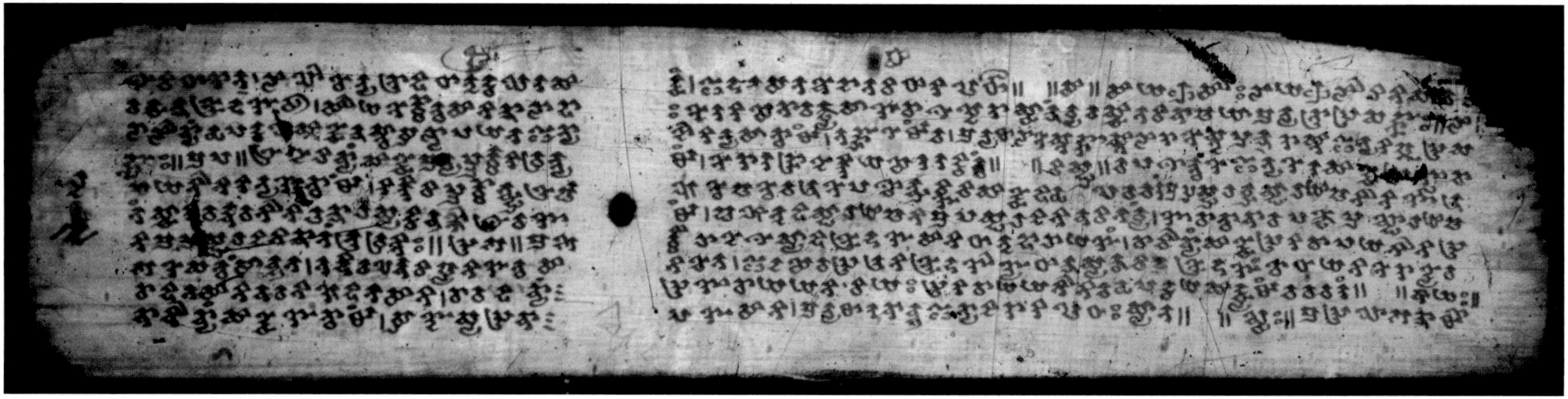

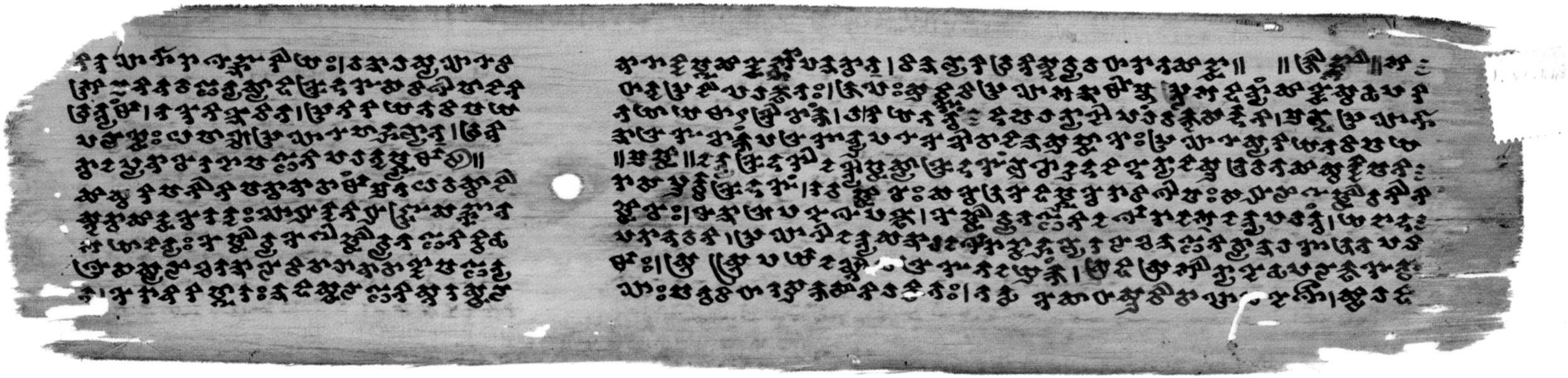

fol. 6$^{II}$a

fol. 6^II b

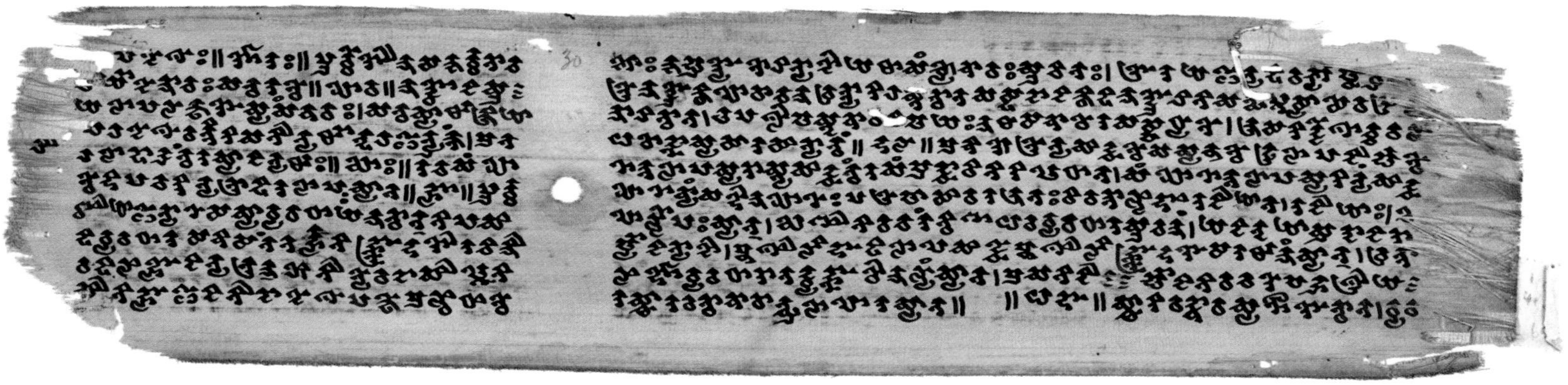

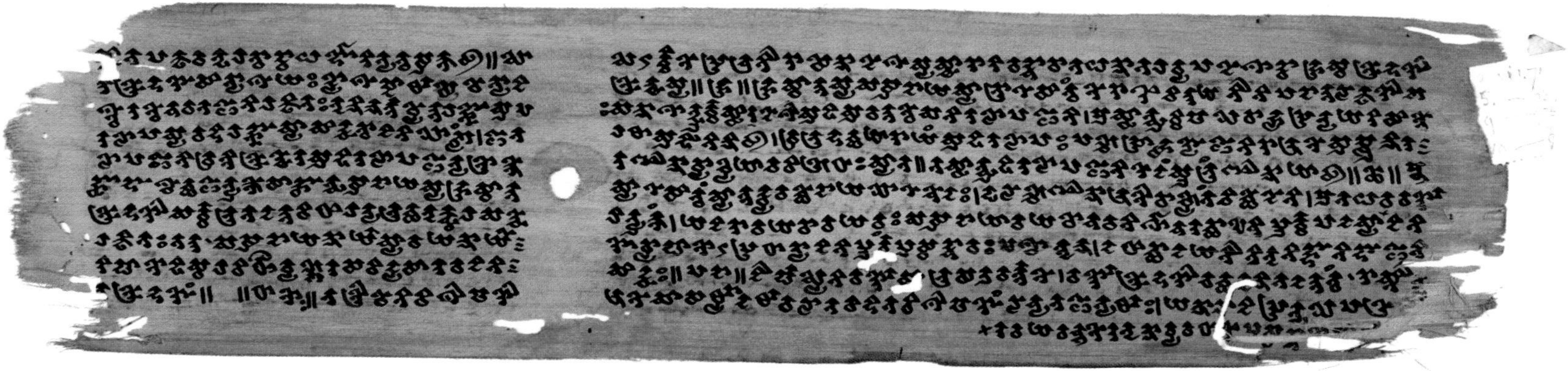

fol. 7^II a

fol. 7$^{II}$b

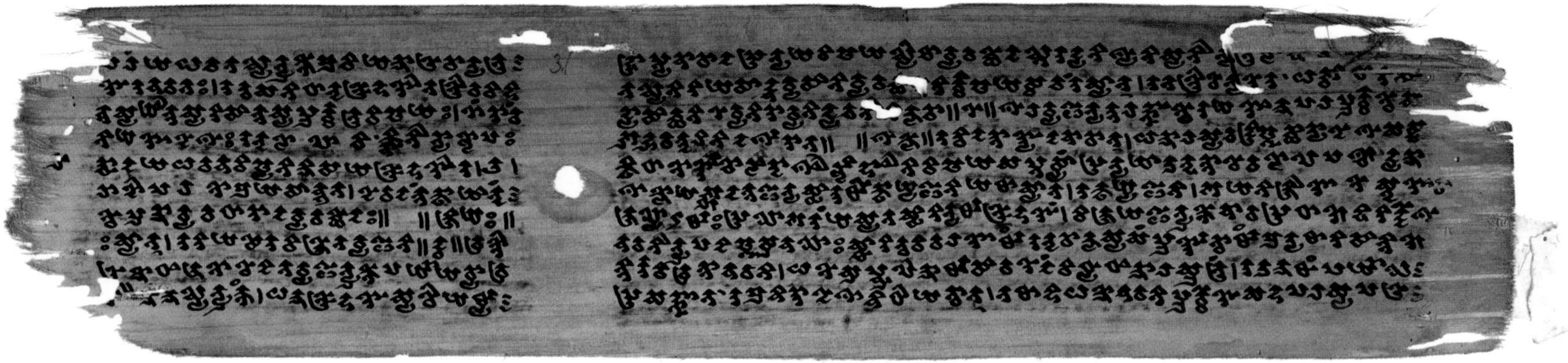

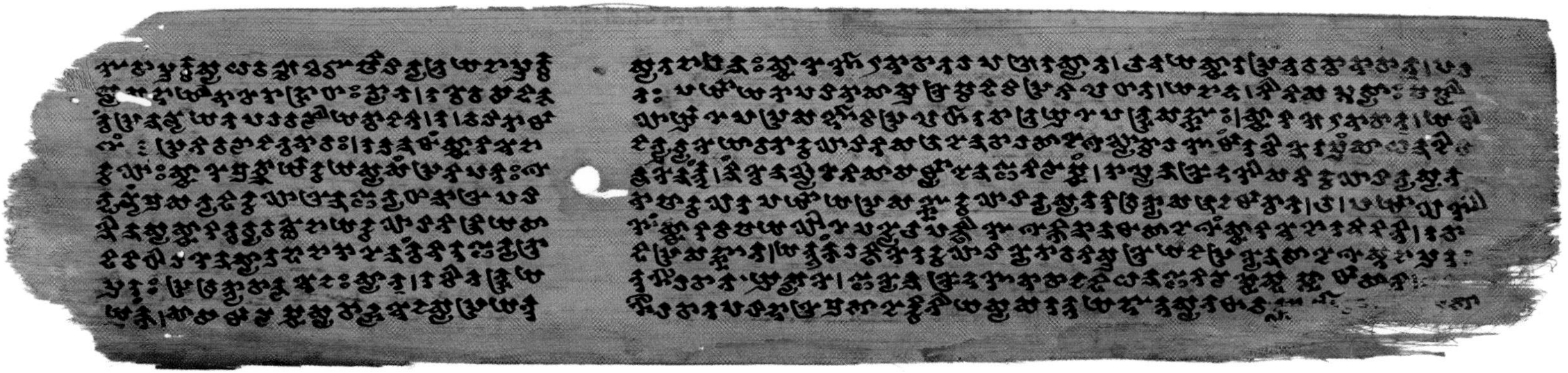

fol. 8$^{II}$a

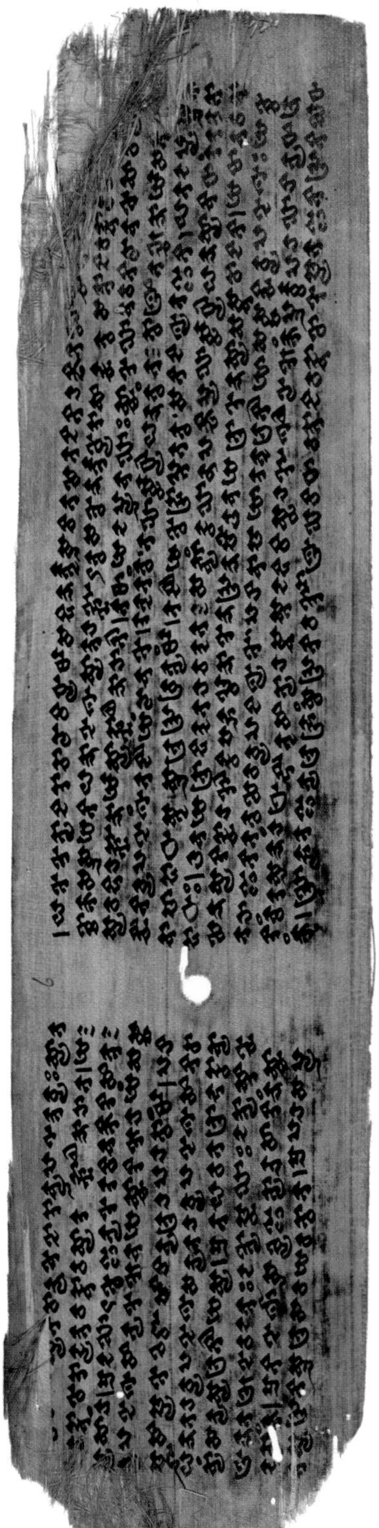

fol. $8^{\mathrm{II}}$b

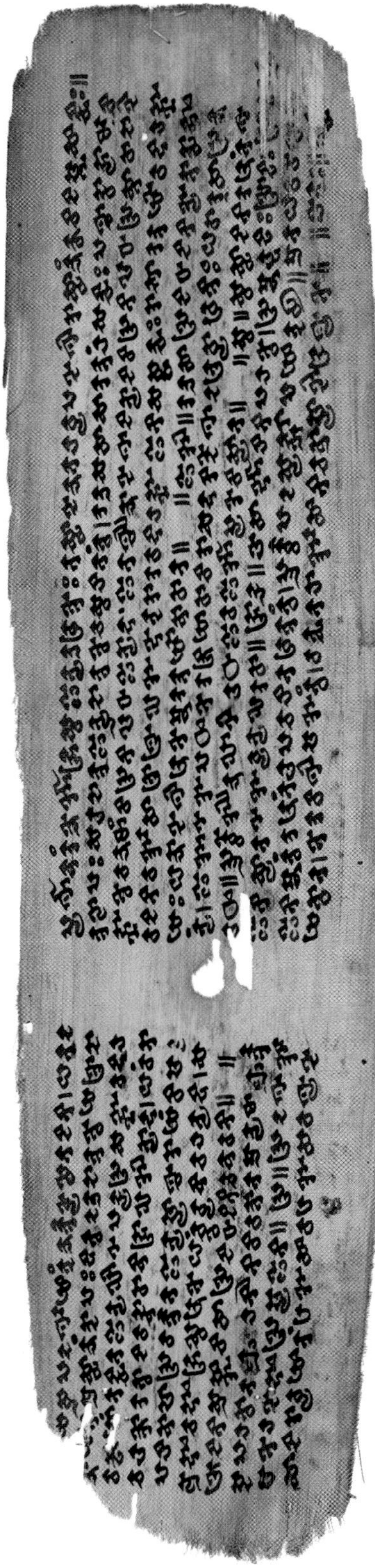

fol. $9^{\mathrm{II}}$a

fol. 9$^{II}$b

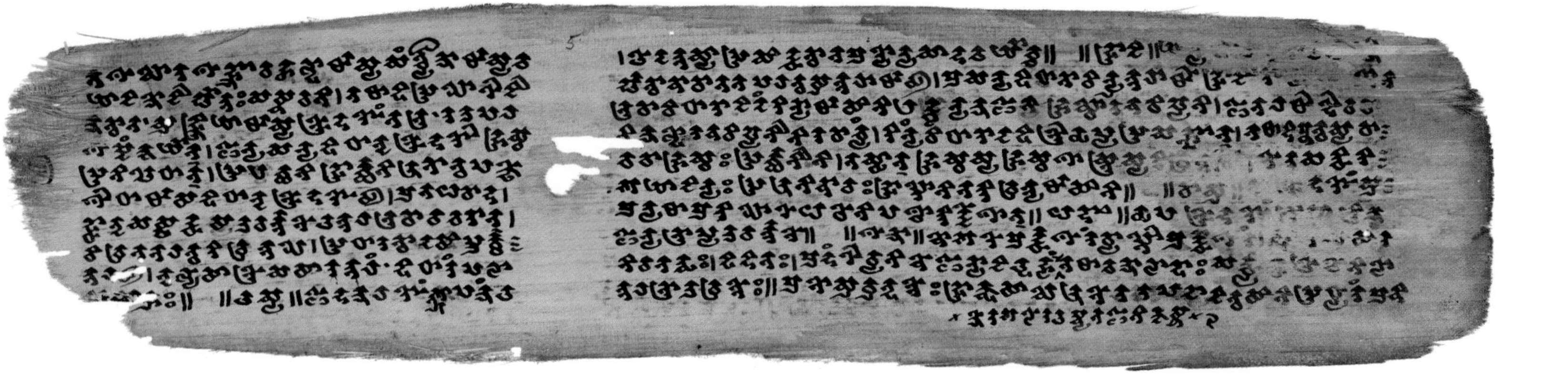

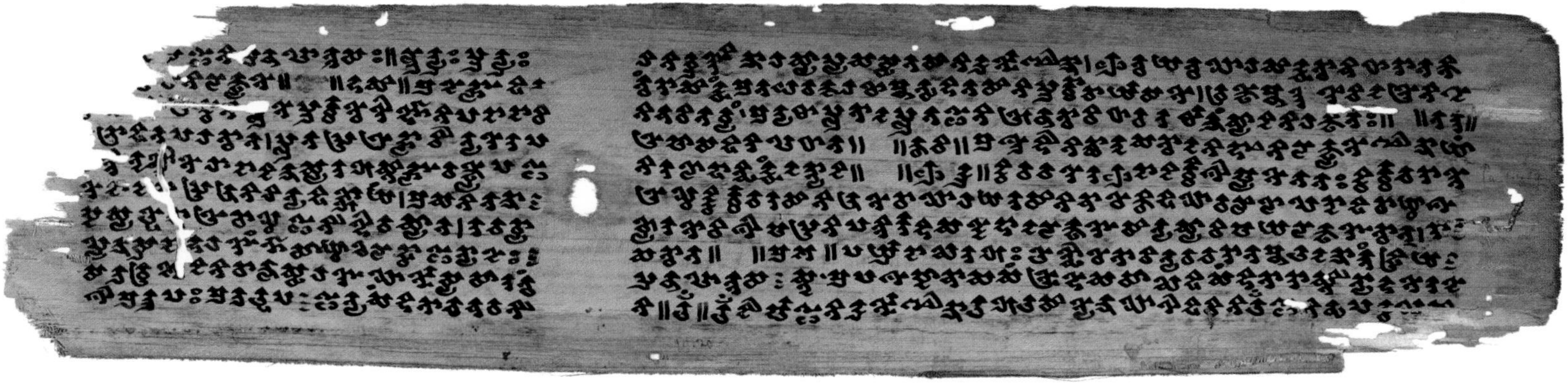

fol. 11$^{II}$a

fol. 11$^{II}$b

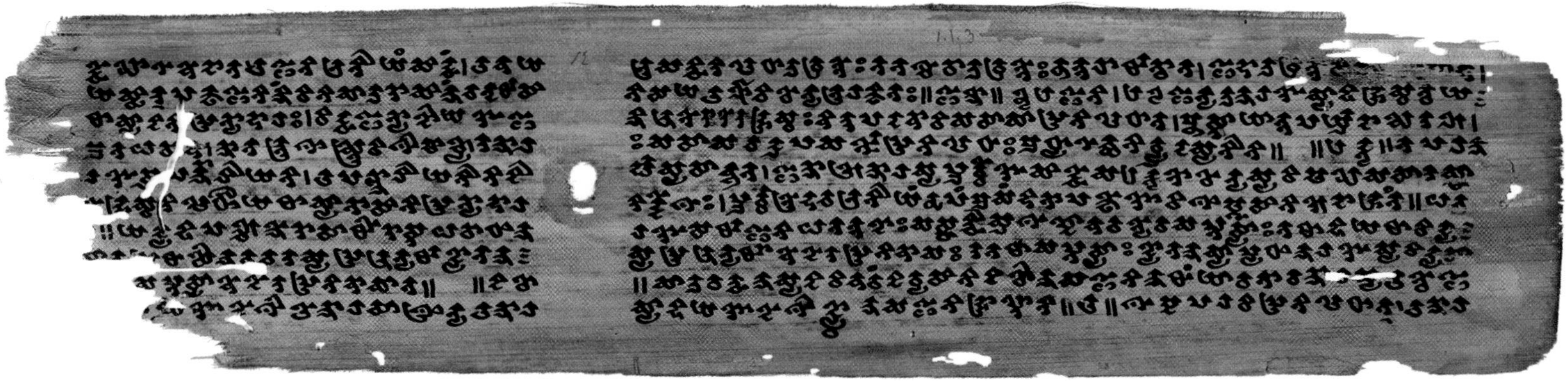

fol. 13$^{II}$a

fol. 13$^{II}$b

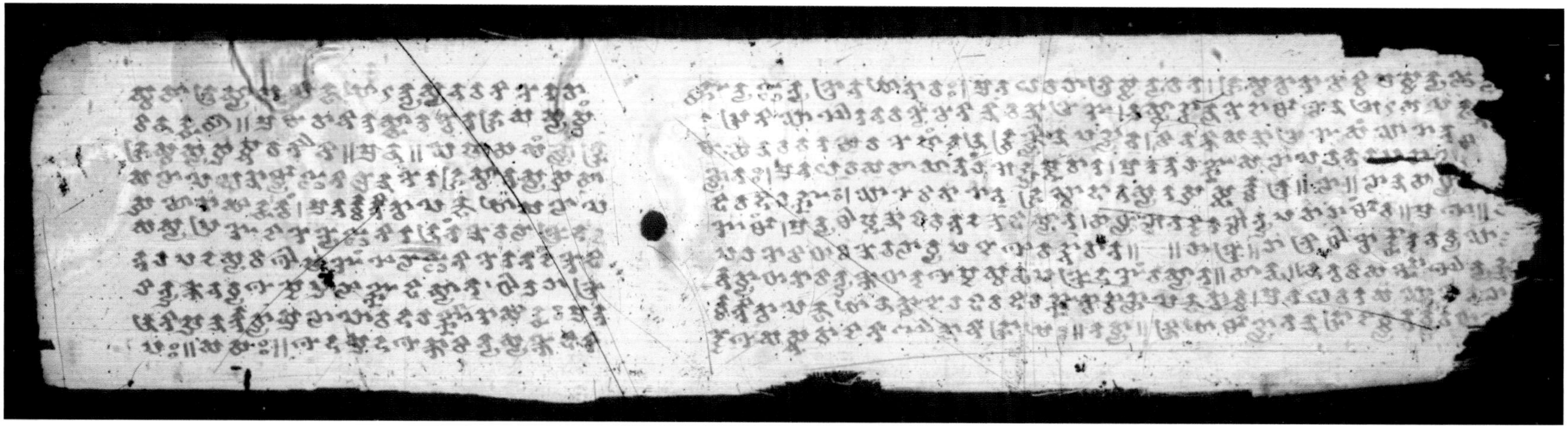

fol. 16$^{II}$a

fol. 16IIb

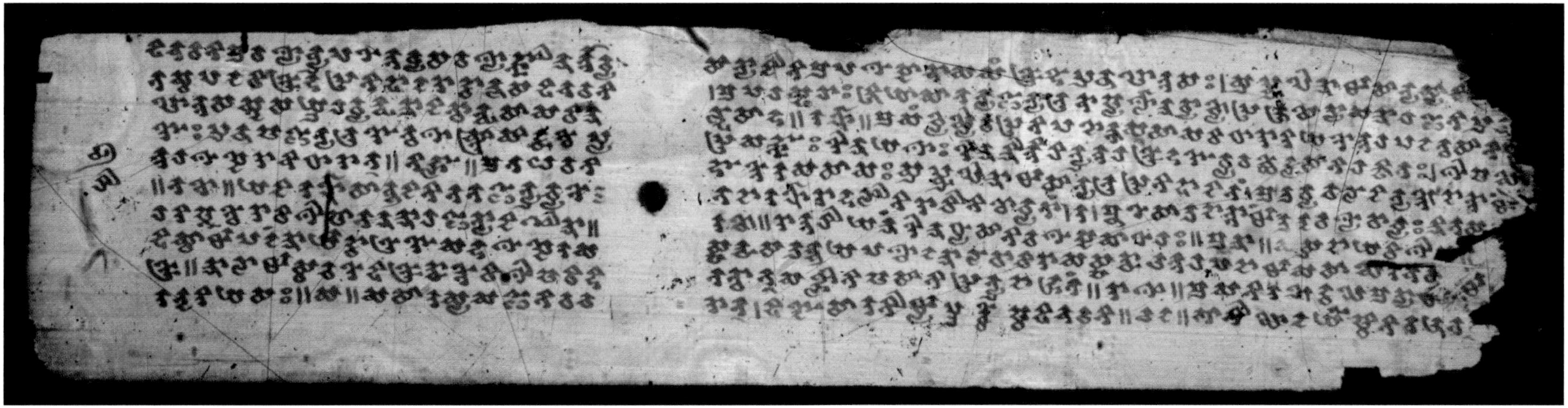

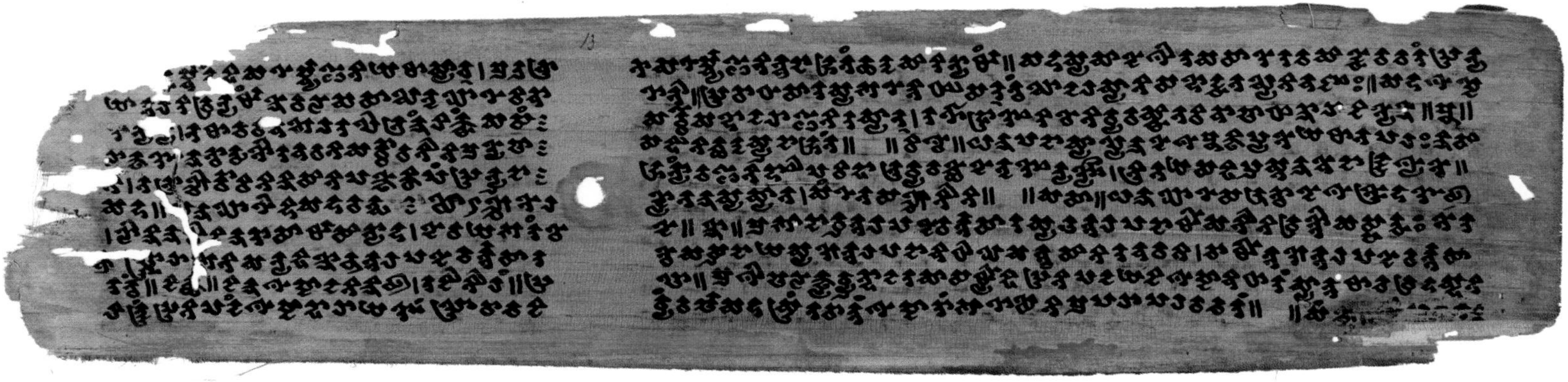

fol. 17IIa

fol. 17^II b

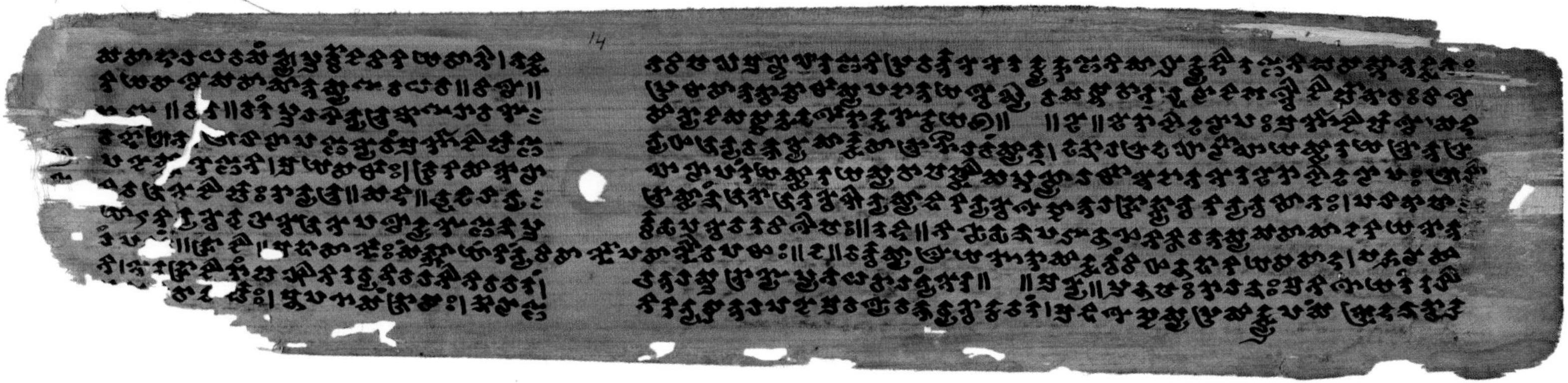

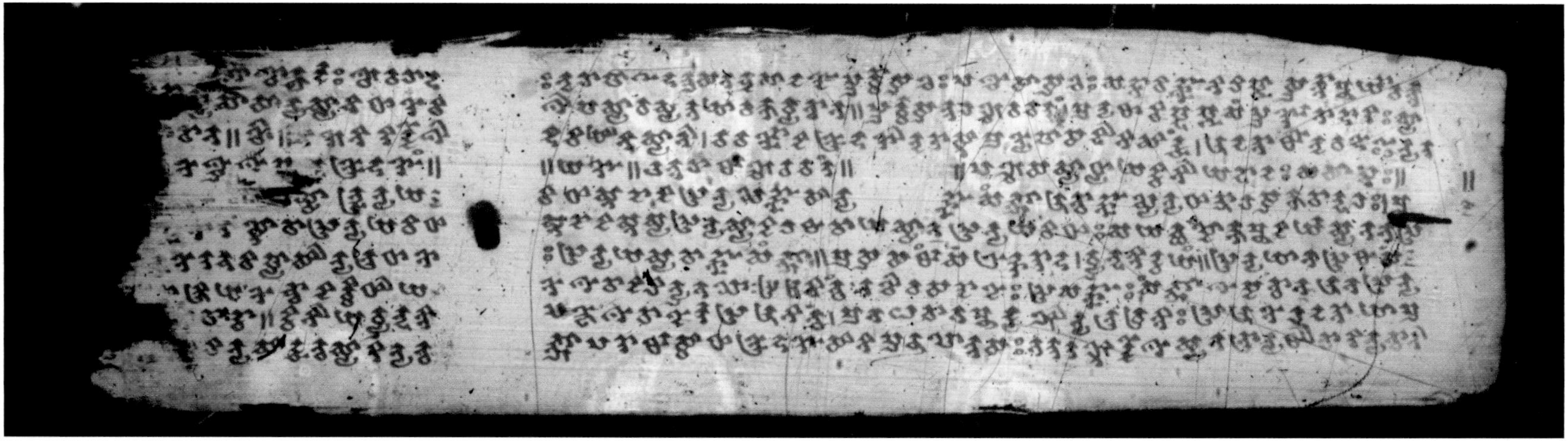

fol. 18^II a

fol. 18IIb

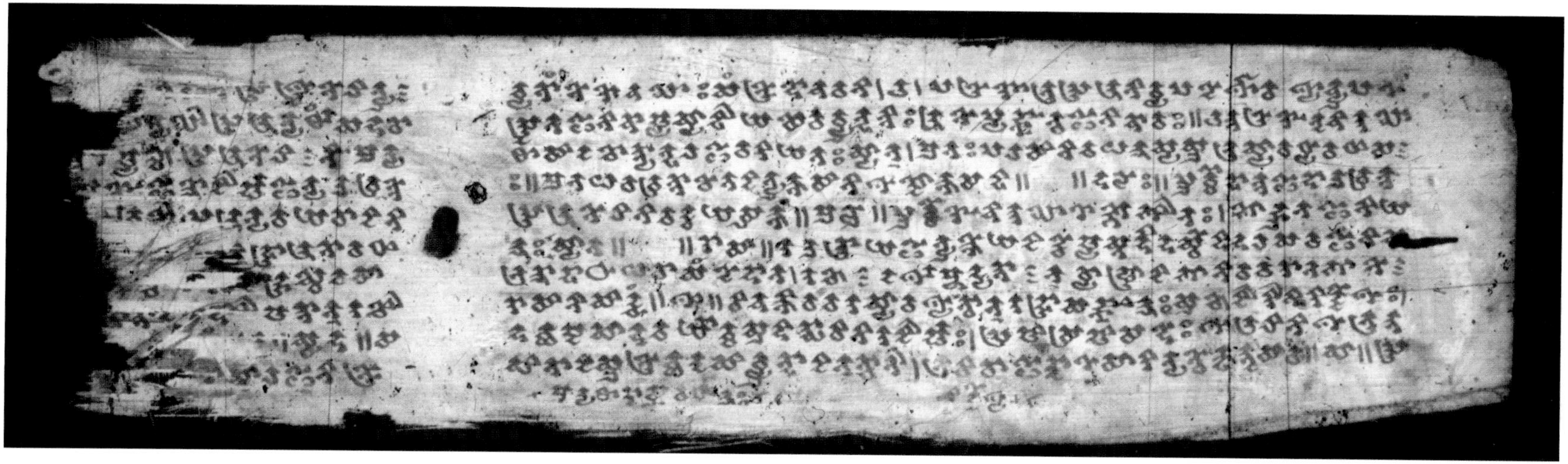

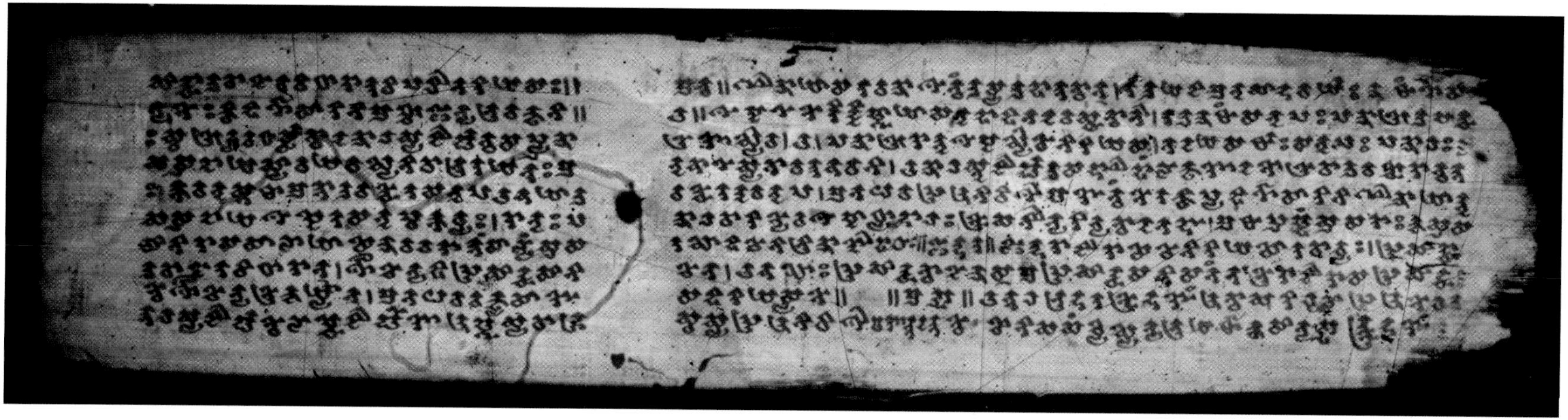

fol. 19IIa

fol. 19IIb

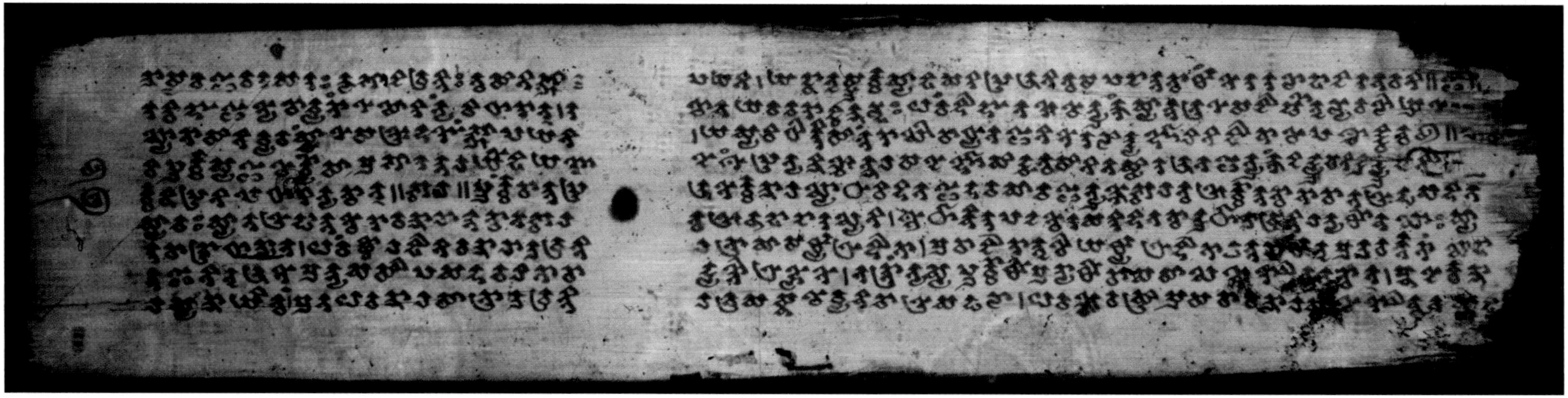

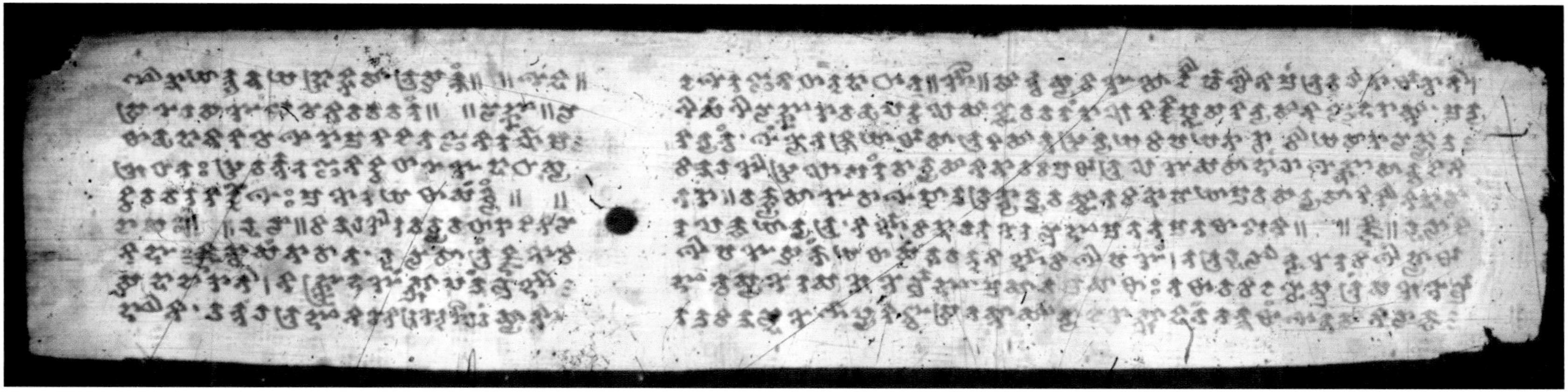

fol. 21IIa

fol. 21IIb

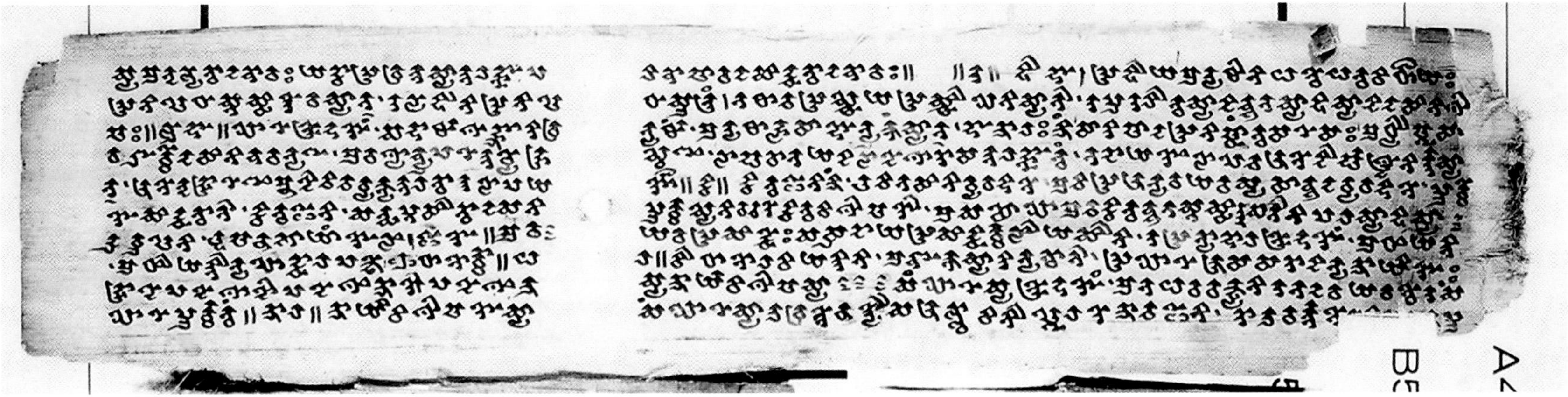

fol. 23IIa

fol. $23^{II}$b

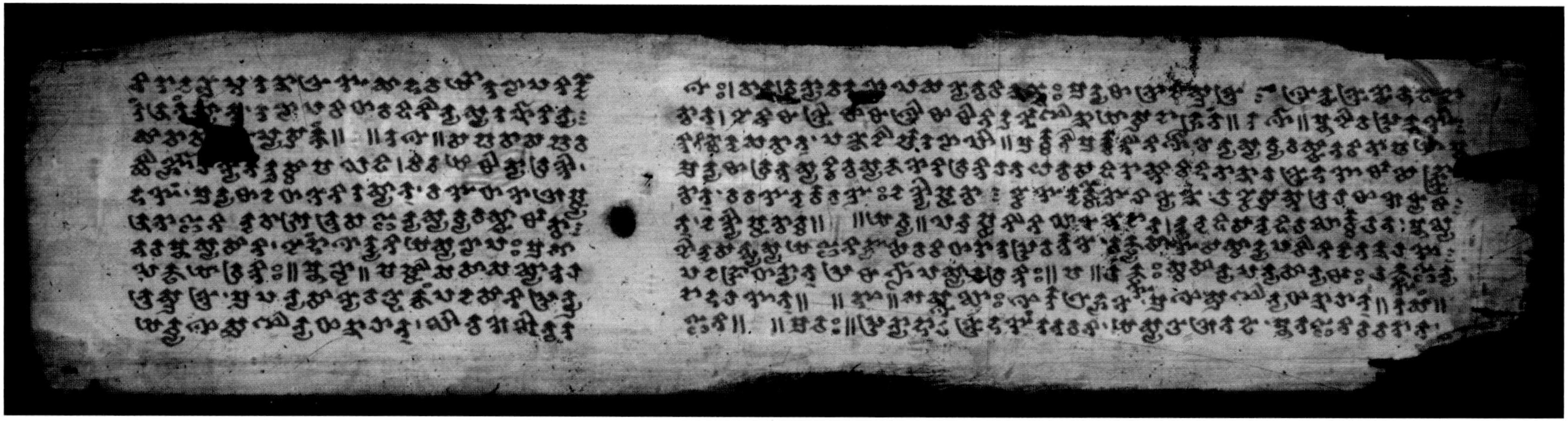

fol. $25^{II}$a

fol. 25IIb

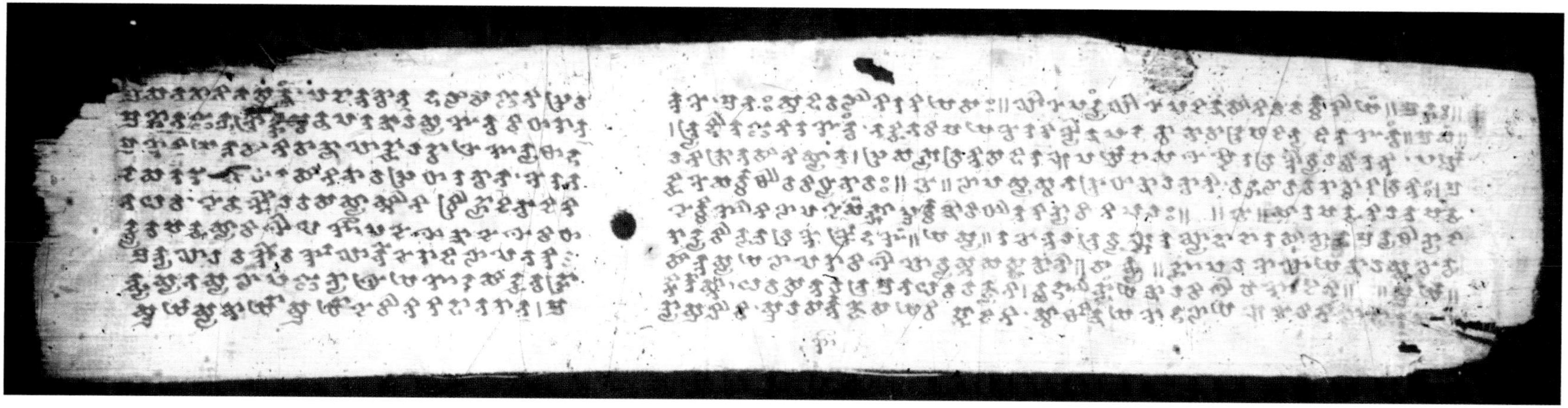

fol. 26IIa

fol. 26IIb

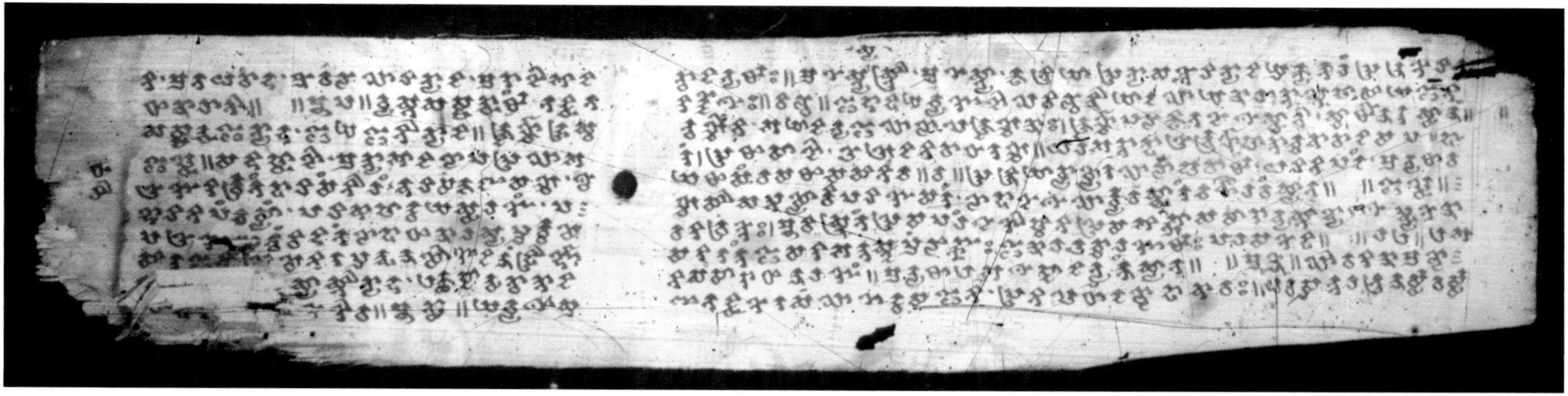

fol. 27IIa

fol. $27^{\mathrm{II}}$b

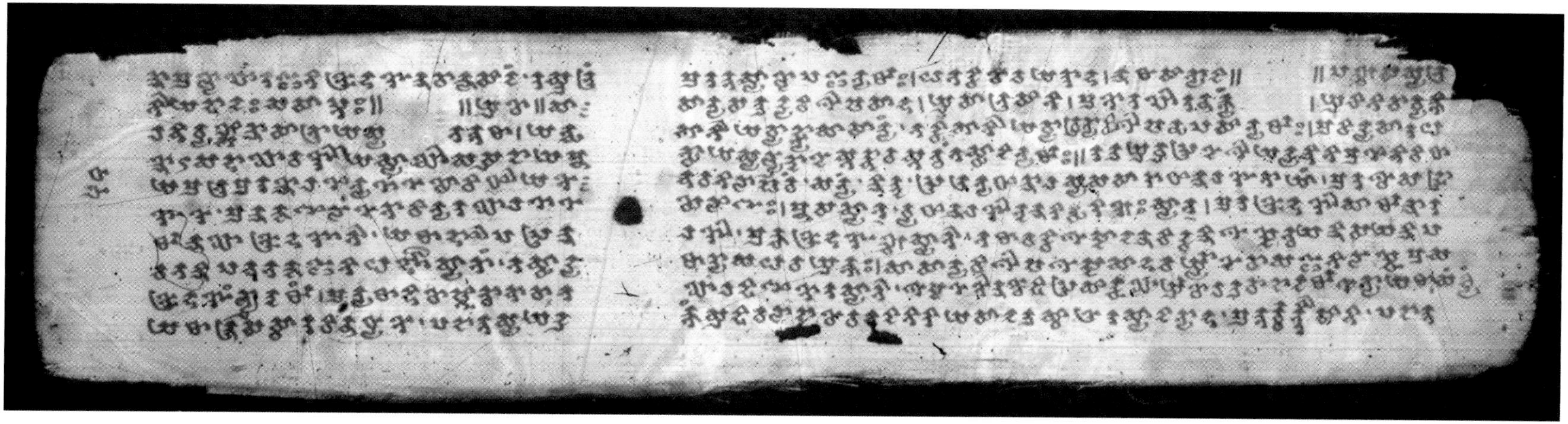

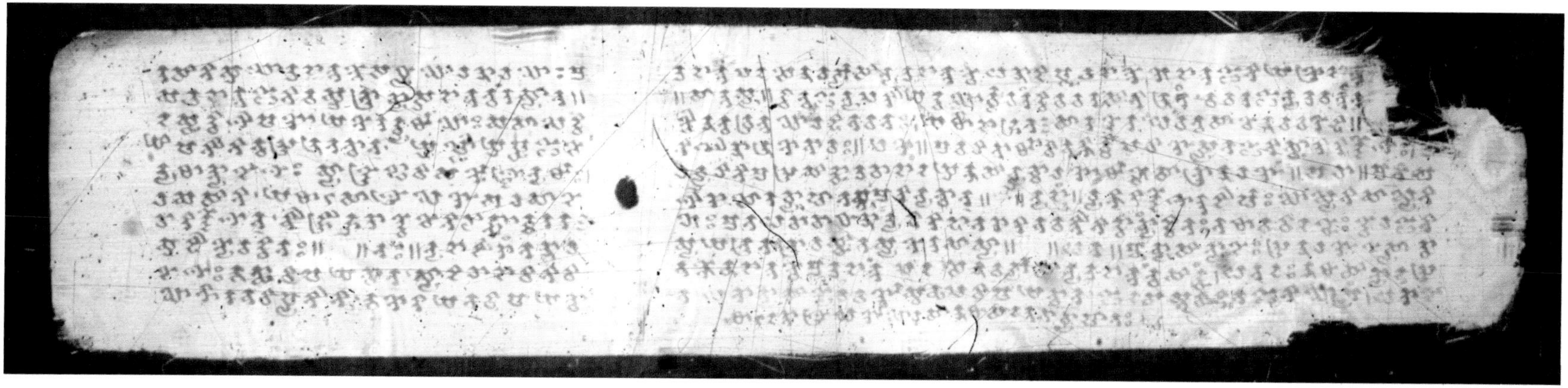

fol. $31^{\mathrm{II}}$a

fol. 31IIb

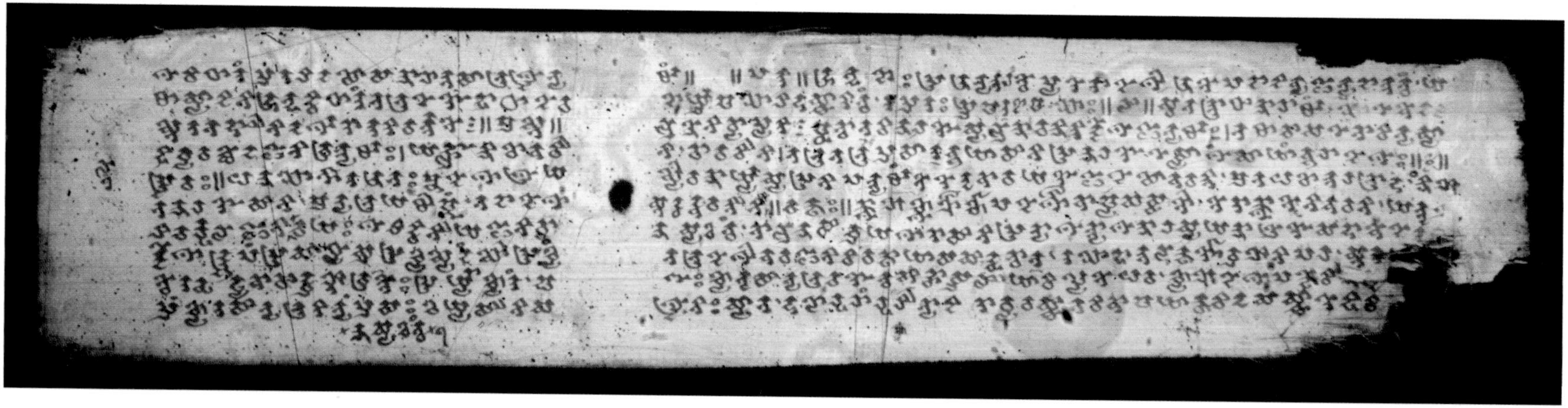

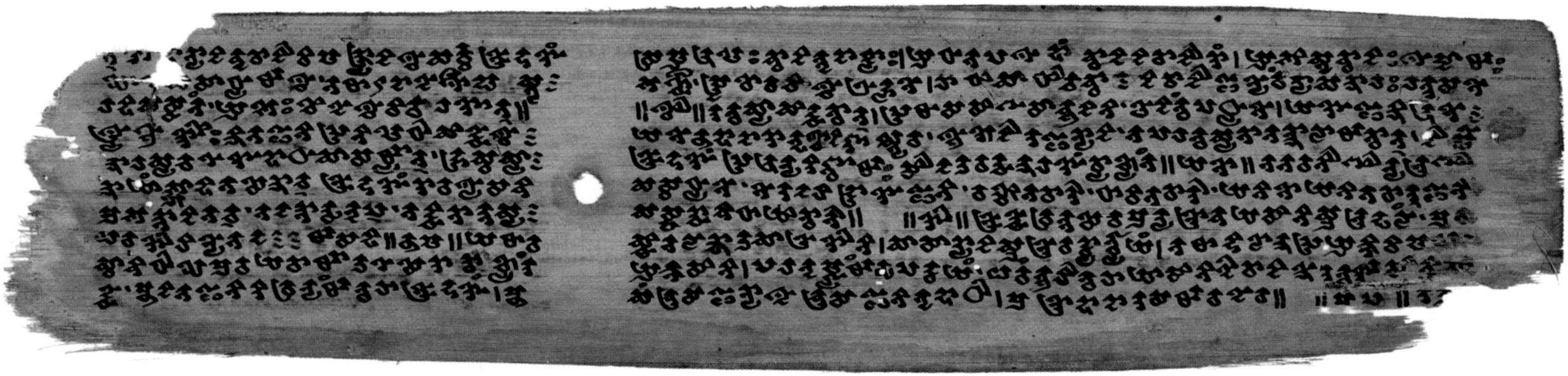

fol. 35IIa

fol. 35IIb

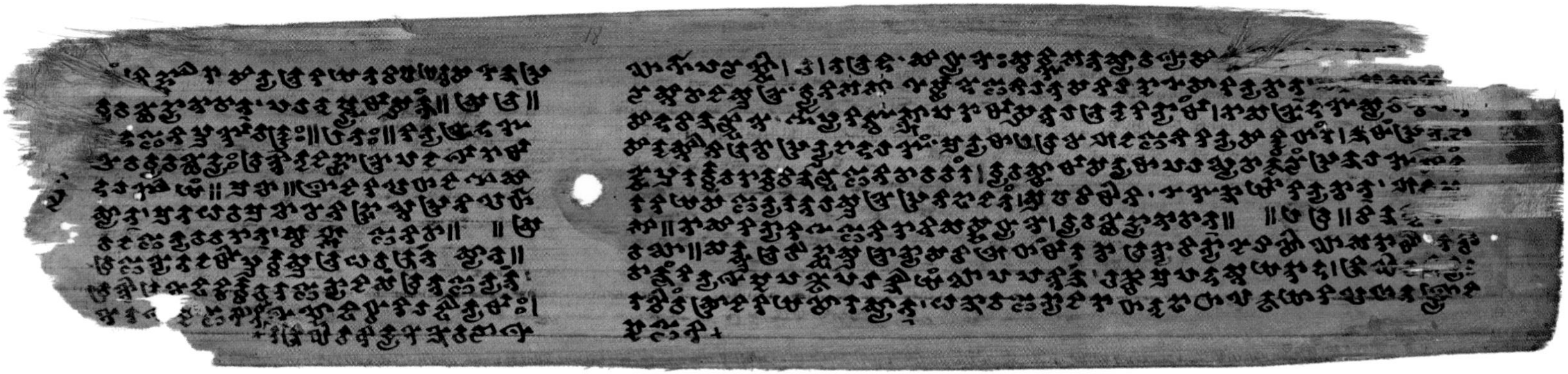

fol. 36IIa

fol. 36$^{II}$b

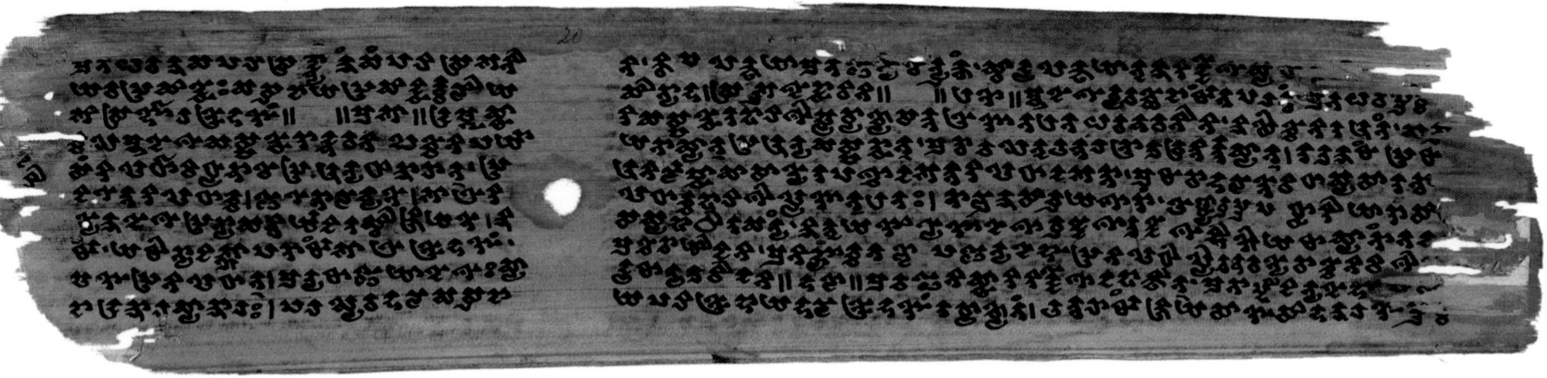

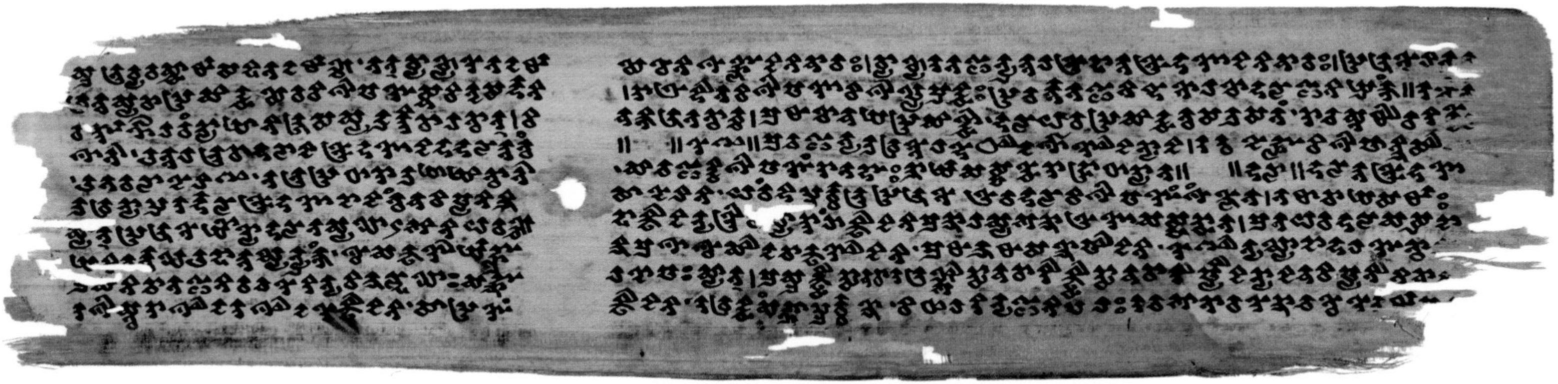

fol. 37$^{II}$a

fol. 45

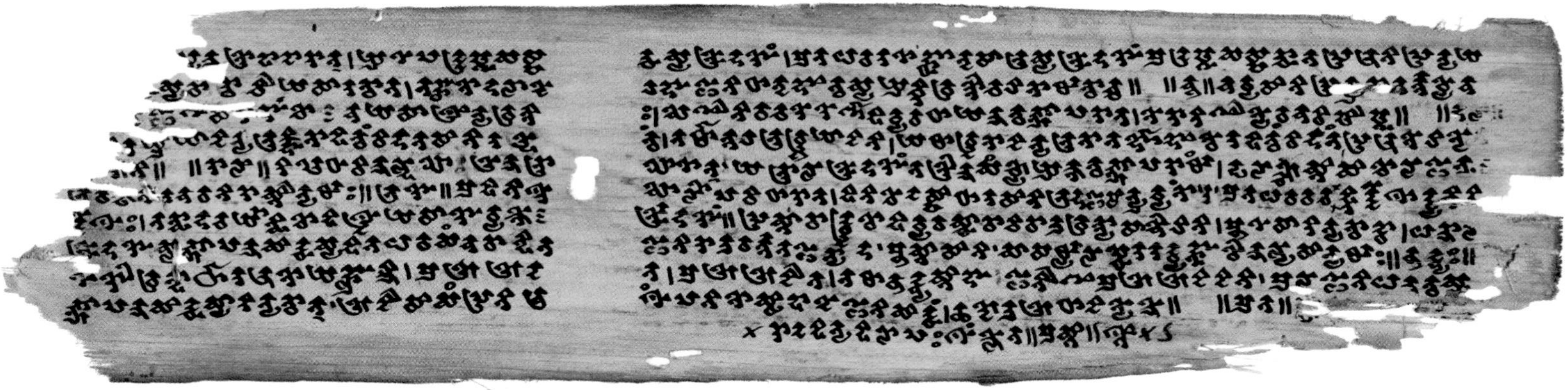

fol. 46$^{II}$a

fol. 46$^{\mathrm{II}}$b

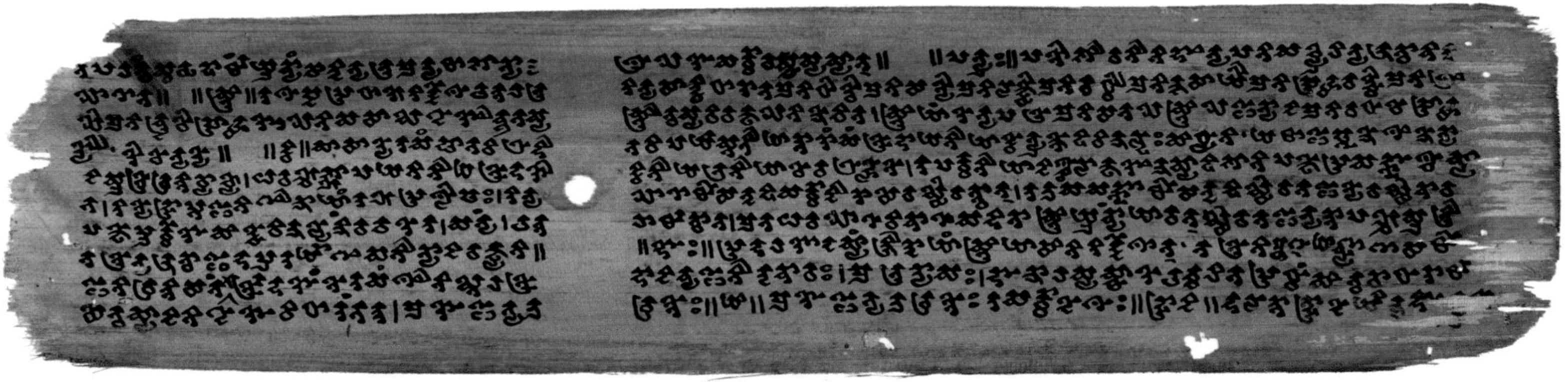

fol. 47$^{\mathrm{II}}$a

fol. 47IIb

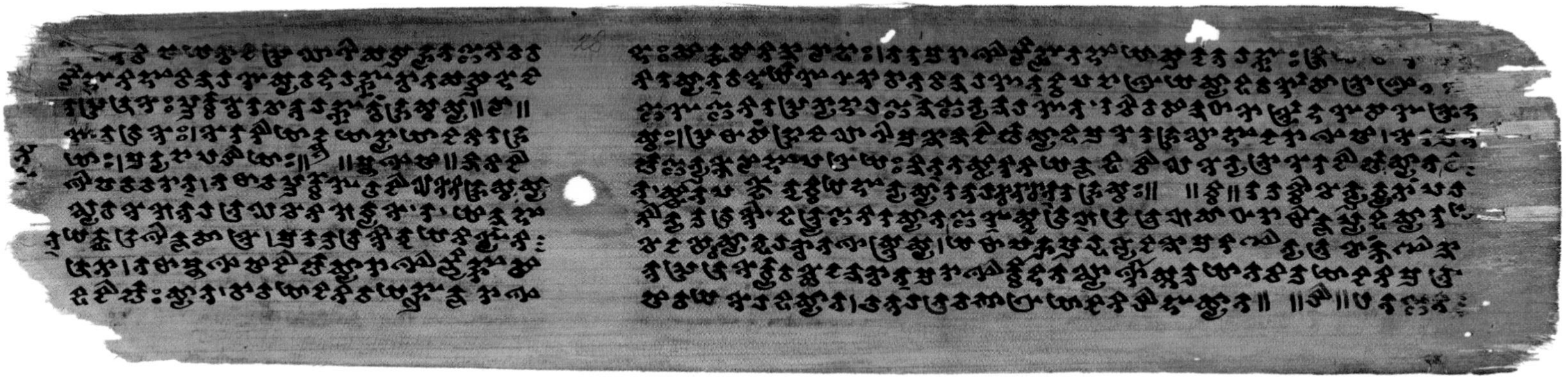

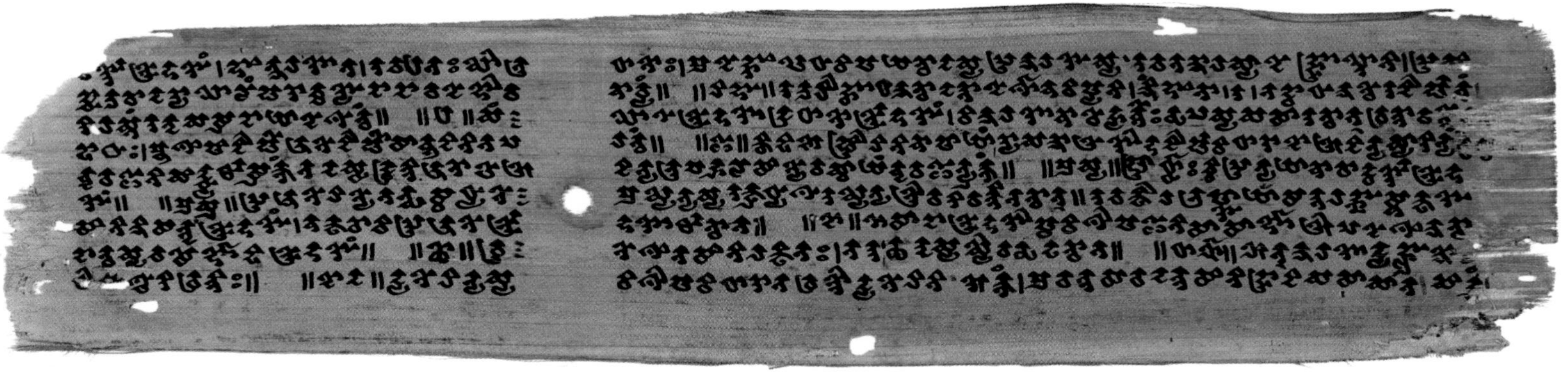

fol. 48IIa

fol. 48^II^b

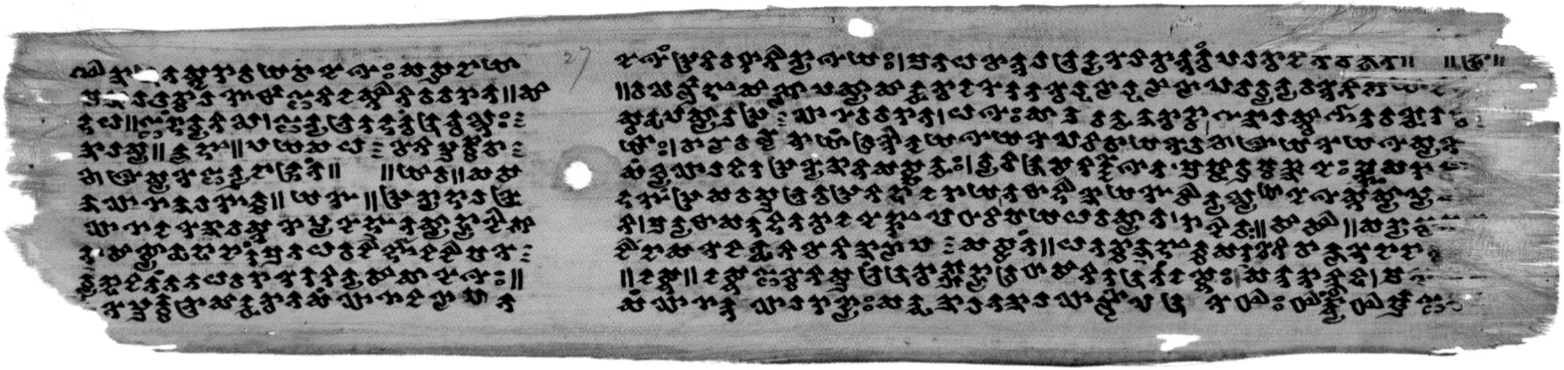

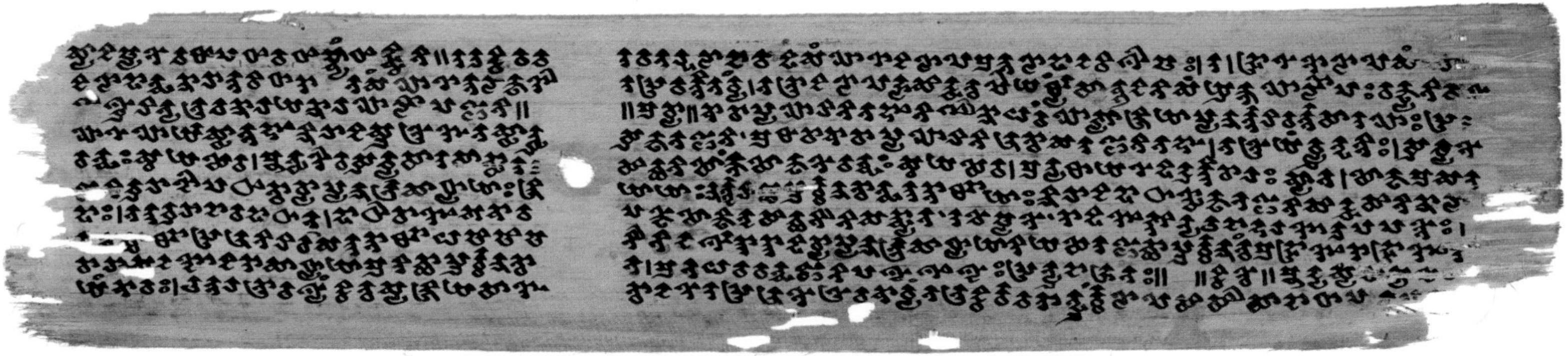

fol. 49^II^a

fol. 59$^{II}$b (?)

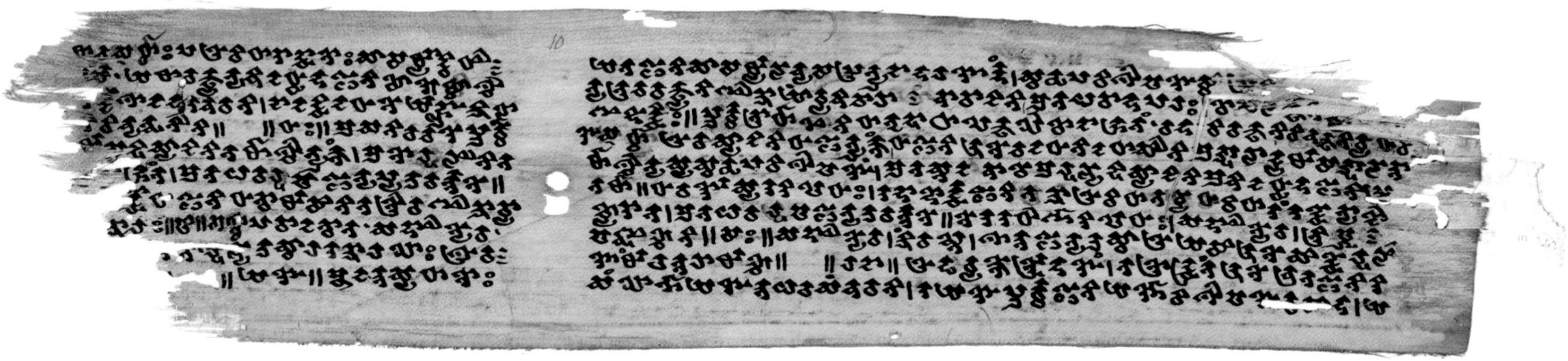

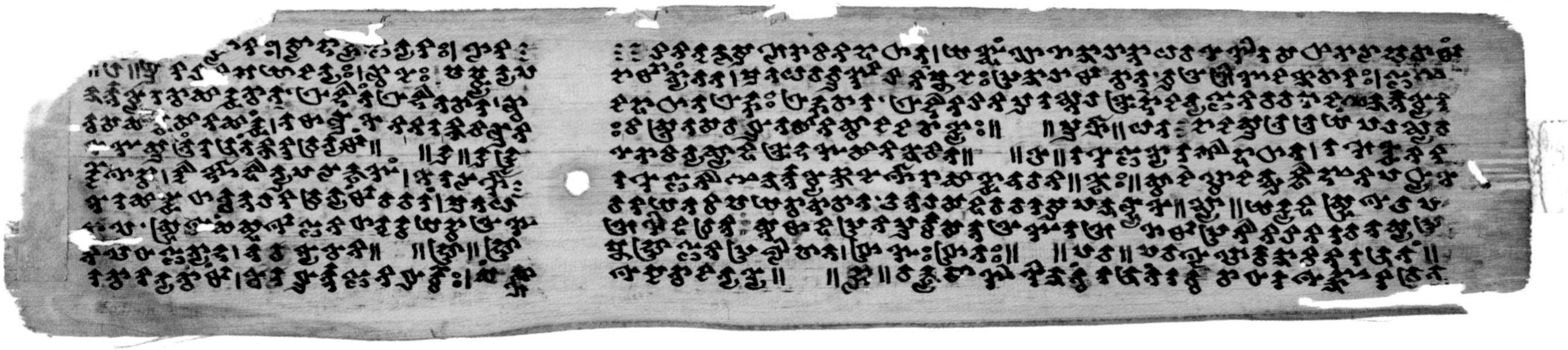

fol. 60$^{II}$a

fol. 60^II^b

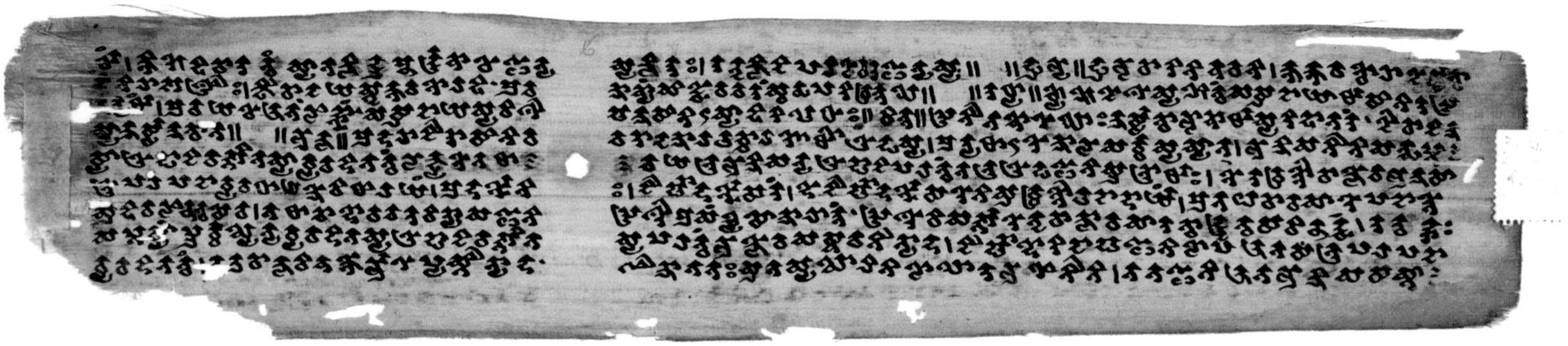

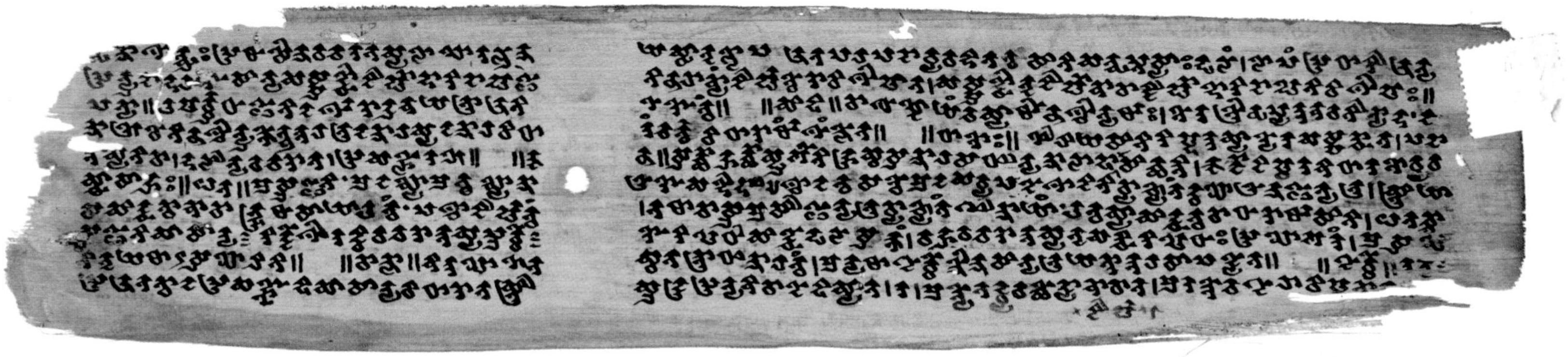

fol. 61^II^a

fol. 61[II]b

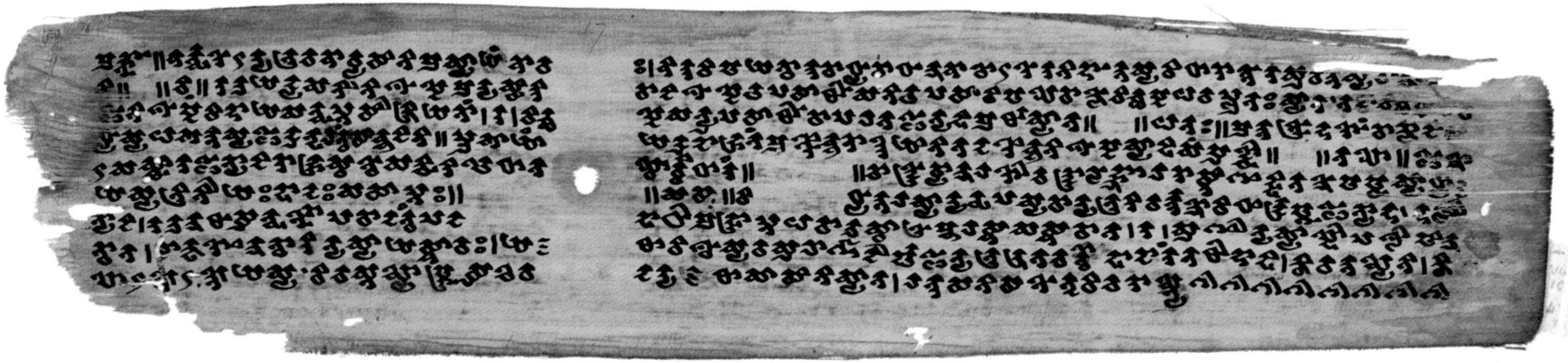

fol. 62[II]a

fol. 62IIb

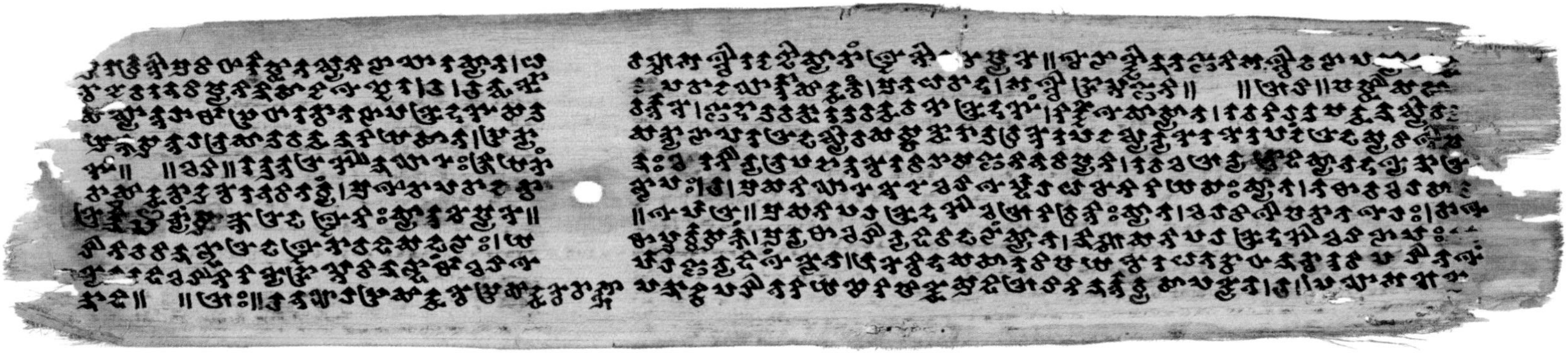

fol. 64IIa (?)

fol. 64$^{II}$b (?)

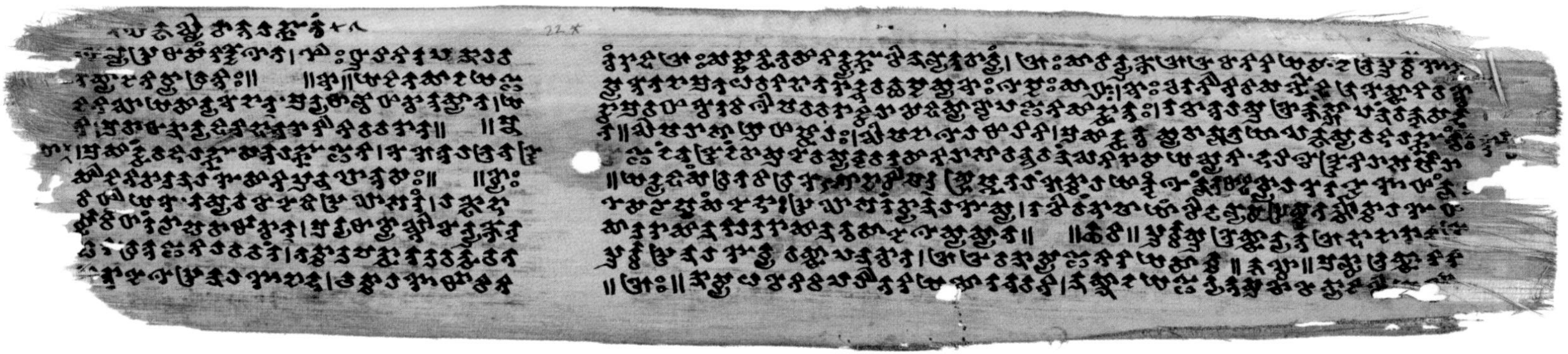

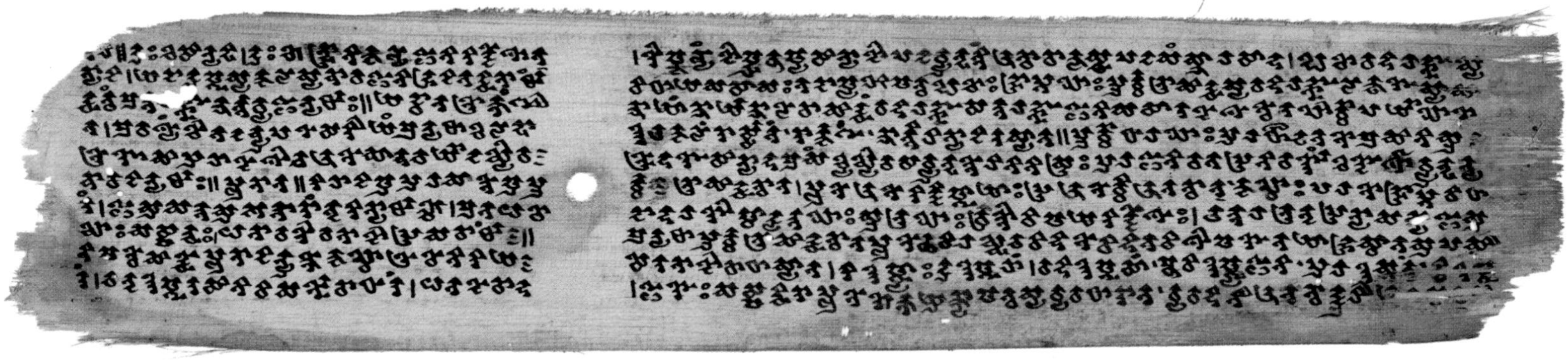

fol. 65$^{II}$a (?)

fol. 65$^{II}$b (?)

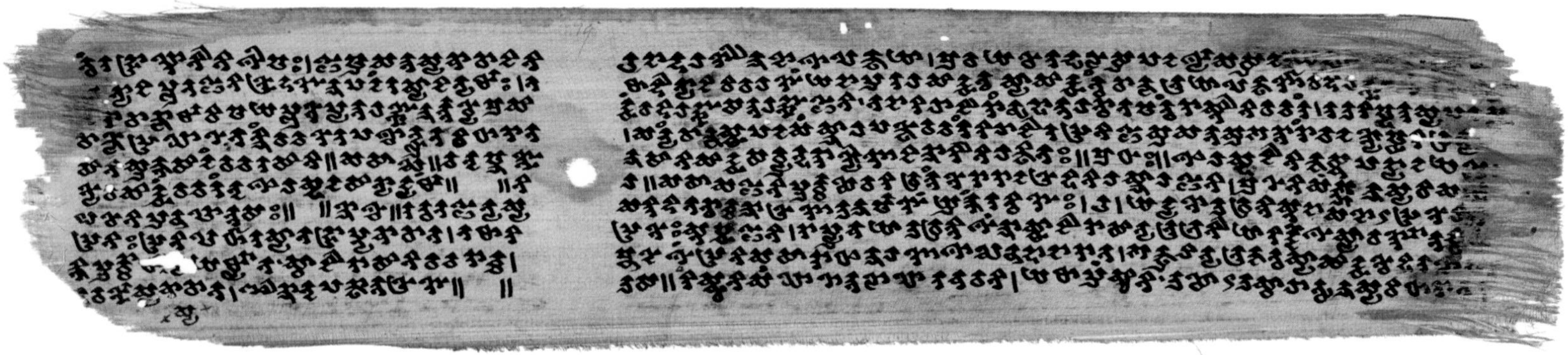

fol. 70$^{II}$a

fol. 70^{II}b

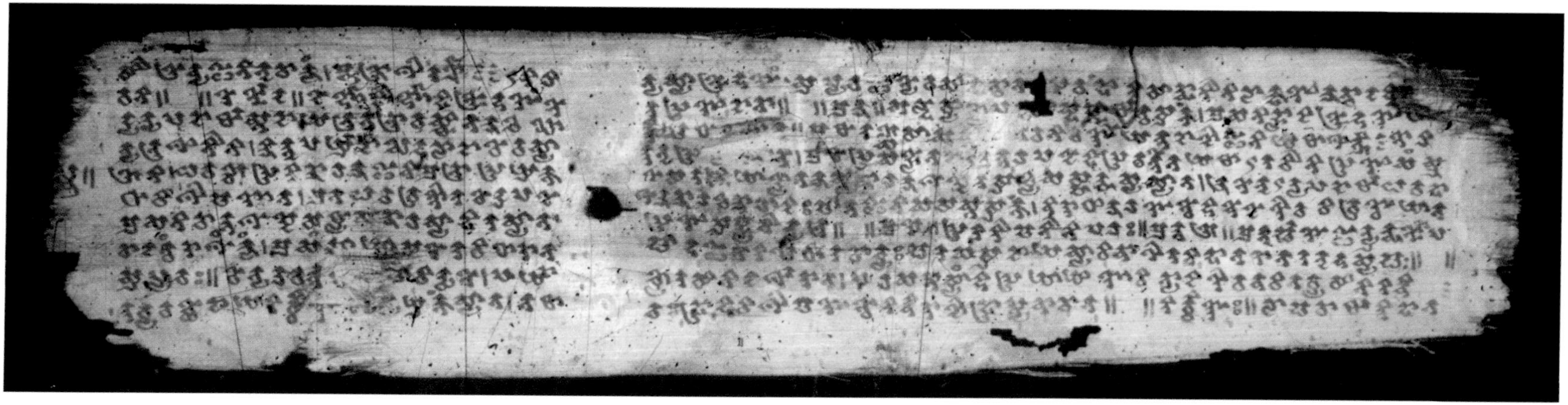

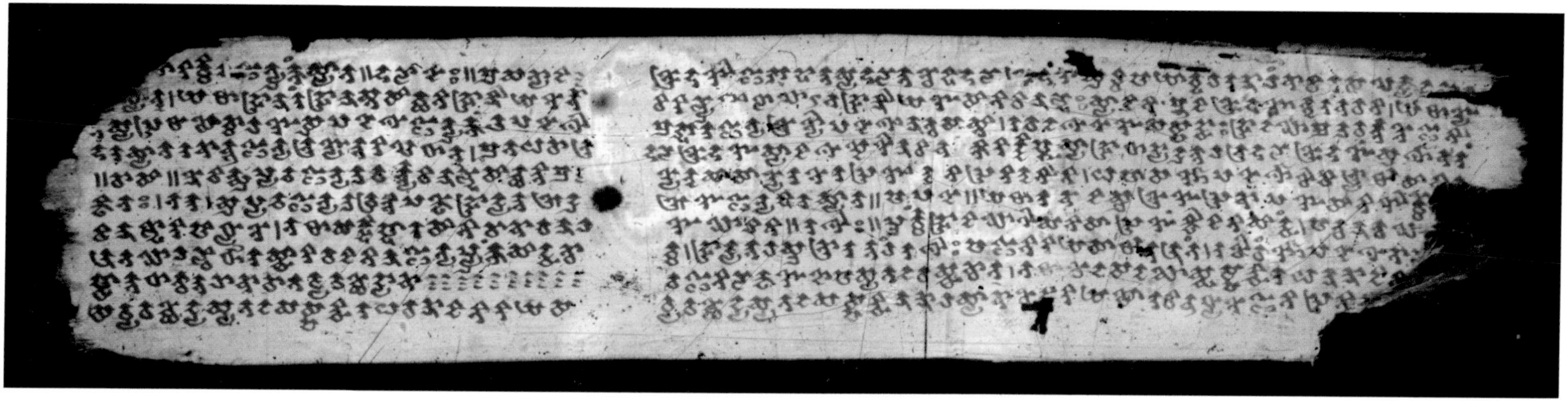

fol. 71^{II}a

fol. 71$^{II}$b

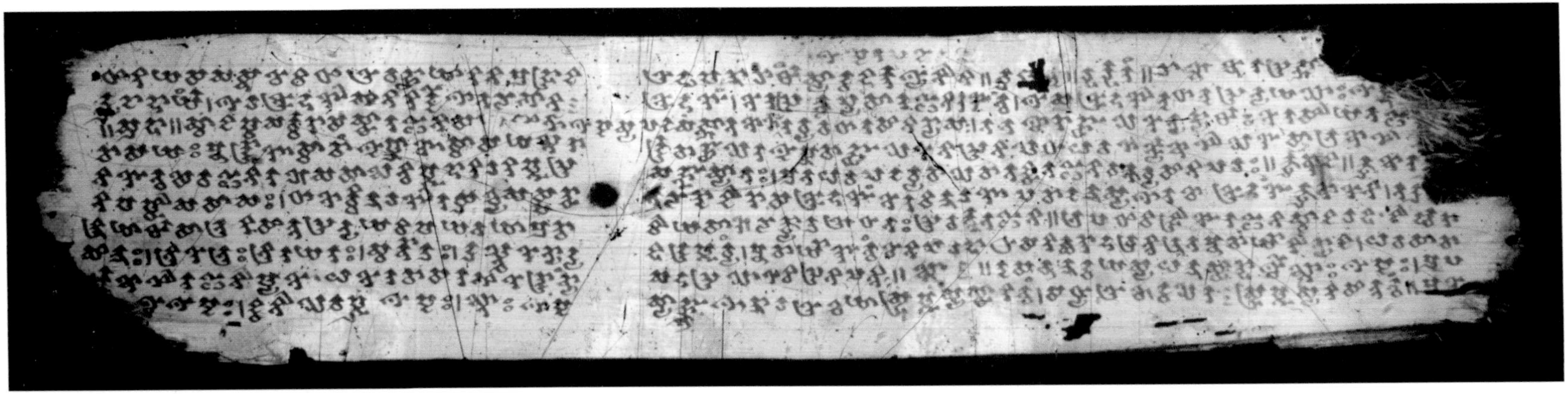

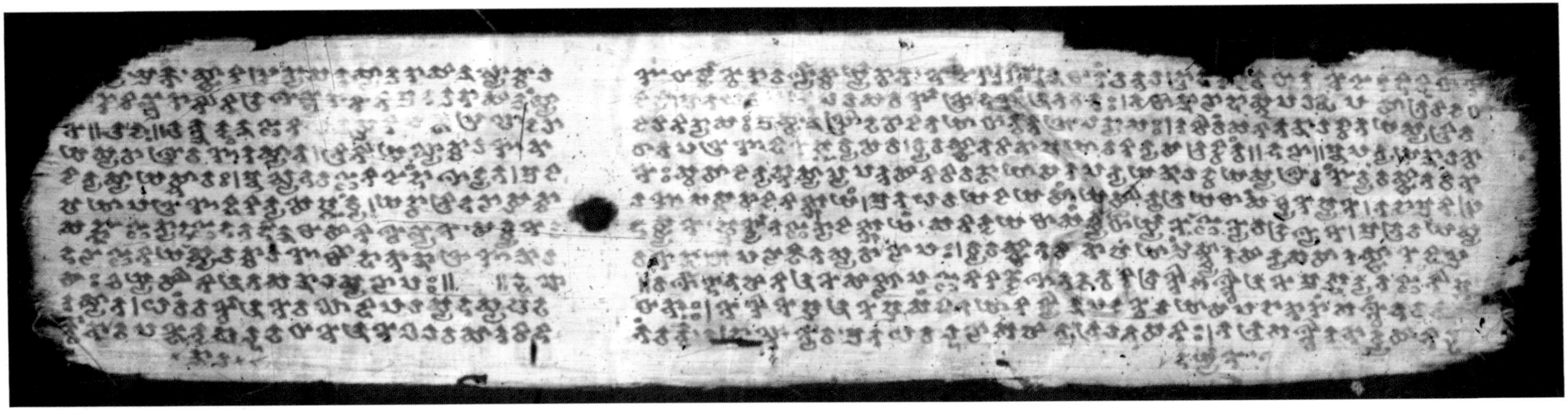

fol. 73$^{II}$a (?)

fol. $73^{II}$b (?)

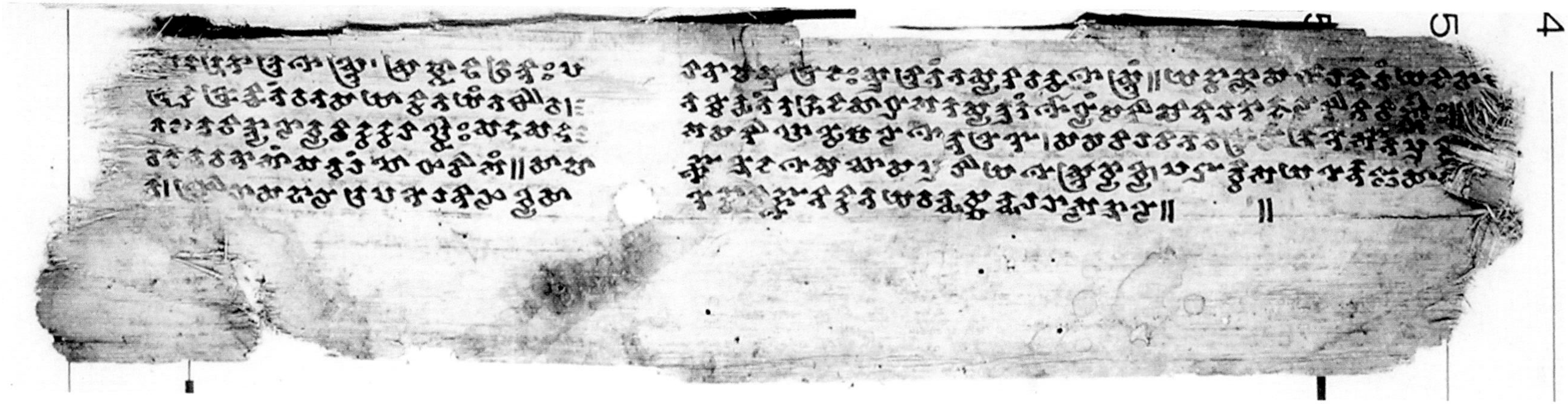

fol. $75^{II}$a (?)

fol. 75$^{II}$b (?)

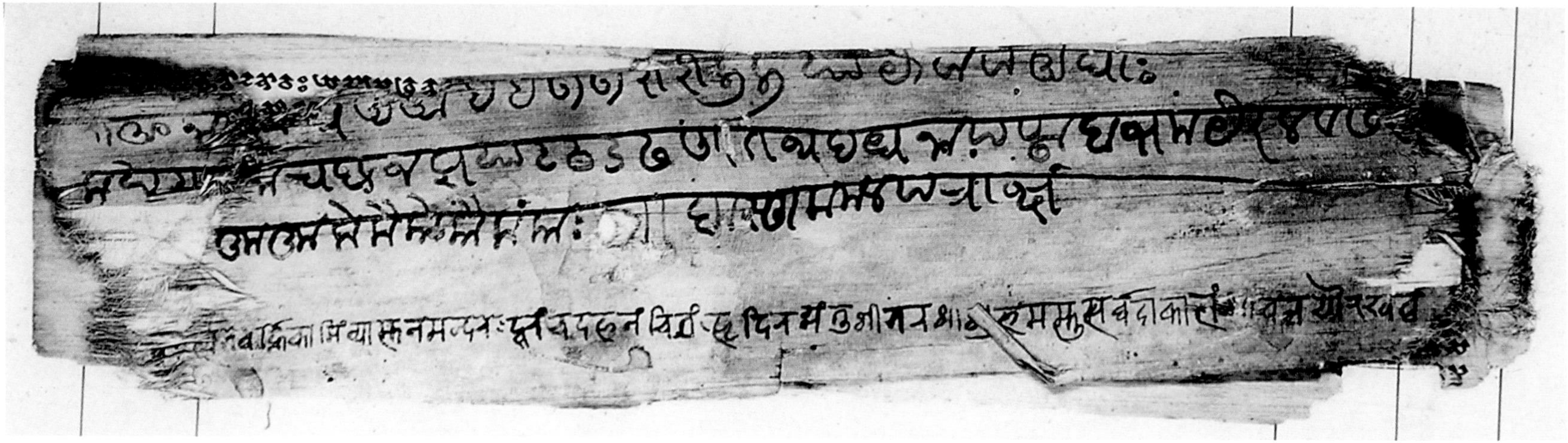

# BIBLIOGRAPHY


BANDURSKI, Frank

1994 "Übersicht über die Göttinger Sammlungen der von RĀHULA SAṄKṚTYĀYANA in Tibet aufgefundenen buddhistischen Sanskrit-Texte (Funde buddhistischer Sanskrit-Handschriften, III)", in: *Untersuchungen zur buddhistischen Literatur.* Bearbeitet von Frank Bandurski, Bhikkhu Pāsādika, Michael Schmidt, Bangwei Wang. Göttingen 1994. (Sanskrit-Wörterbuch der buddhistischen Texte aus den Turfan-Funden, Beiheft 5).

BANERJEE, Priyatosh

1969 "A Manuscript Dated in the Bengal Year 53 of Rāmapāla", in: *Indo-Asian Culture.* Vol. XVIII, No. 1. New Delhi 1969, pp. 61–63.

1975 "Some Inscriptions from Bihar", in: *Journal of Ancient Indian History.* Volume VII, Parts 1-2, 1973-74. Calcutta 1975, pp. 102–111.

BANERJI, Rakhal Das

1914 "Ekaṭi Buddhamūrtti", in: *Sāhitya Pariṣat Patrikā.* Volume. XX, Number 2. Calcutta 1914, pp. 153–156.

1933 *Eastern Indian School of Mediaeval Sculpture.* By R. D. Banerji. With ninety-six plates. Delhi 1933. (Archaeological Survey of India, New Imperial Series, Vol. XLVII). [Repr.: New Delhi 1981].

BECHERT, Heinz

1979 *Burmese Manuscripts.* Part I. Compiled by Heinz Bechert, Daw Khin Khin Su and Daw Tin Tin Myint. With 5 plates. Wiesbaden 1979. (Verzeichnis der orientalischen Handschriften in Deutschland, Band XXIII, 1).

1987 "Sanskrit-Grammatiken in singhalesischer Überlieferung", in: *Festschrift Wilhelm Rau zur Vollendung des 65. Lebensjahres* [...] Herausgegeben von Heidrun Brückner, Dieter George†, Claus Vogel und Albrecht Wezler. (= *Studien zur Indologie und Iranistik.* Heft 13/14). Reinbek 1987, pp. 5–16.

BENDALL, Cecil

1883 *Catalogue of the Buddhist Sanskrit Manuscripts in the University Library, Cambridge.* With Introductory Notices and Illustrations of the Palæography and Chronology of Nepal and Bengal. By Cecil Bendall. Cambridge 1883.

1886a *A Journey of Literary and Archaelogical Research in Nepal and Northern India, during the winter of 1884-5.* By Cecil Bendall. Cambridge 1886.

1886b "On a newly discovered form of Indian character", in: *Verhandlungen des VII. Internationalen Orientalisten-Congresses gehalten in Wien im Jahre 1886.* Arische Section. Mit zehn Tafeln. Vienna 1886, pp. 111–125. [Repr.: Nendeln/Lichtenstein 1968].

1890 "An inscription in a Buddhistic variety of nail-headed characters", in: *Indian Antiquary*, Vol. XIX. Bombay 1890, pp. 77–78, 1 table.

1895 "On Pali Inscriptions from Magadha (Behar)", in: *Actes du Dixième Congrès International des Orientalistes.* Session de Genève. 1894. Deuxième Partie. Sections I: Inde; I bis: Linguistique et langues Aryennes. Avec une planche. Leide 1895, pp. 153–156, 1 table.

BHIKKHU PĀSĀDIKA

2006 "The Development of Buddhist Religion and Literature in Cambodia and Vietnam", in: *India's Interaction with Southeast Asia.* Edited by G. C. Pande. New Delhi 2006. (History of Science, Philosophy and Culture in Indian Civilization, Volume I, Part 3), pp. 463–488.

BODE, Mabel

1896 "Index to the Gandhavaṁsa", in: *Journal of the Pali Text Society.* Volume IV. London 1896, pp. 53–86.

BÜHLER, Georg

1896 *Indische Palaeographie von circa 350 A. Chr. - circa 1300 P. Chr.* (mit 9 Tafeln.). Von G. Bühler. Straßburg 1896. (Grundriss der Indo-Arischen Philologie und Altertumskunde, I. Band, 11. Heft).

CHAKRAVARTI, N. P.

1938 "A Buddhist Inscription from Kara", in: *Epigraphia Indica.* Vol. XXII. 1933–34. Edited by N. P. Chakravarti. Delhi 1938, pp. 37–39, 1 plate.

CHATTOPADHYAYA, Alaka

1967 *Atīśa and Tibet. Life and Works of Dīpaṃkara Śrījñāna in relation to the History and Religion of Tibet.* With Tibetan Sources translated under Professor Lama Chimpa. [By] Alaka Chattopadhyaya. 1967. [Repr.: Delhi 1996].

CHIMPA, Lama / CHATTOPADHYAYA, Alaka

1970 *Tāranātha's History of Buddhism in India.* Translated from Tibetan by Lama Chimpa [and] Alaka Chattopadhyaya. Edited by Debiprasad Chattopadhyaya. Calcutta 1970. [Repr.: Delhi 1997].

CONZE, Edward

1962 *Buddhist Thought in India. Three Phases of Buddhist Philosophy.* By Edward Conze. London 1962.

CROSBY, Kate

2006 "Sāriputta's Three Works on the *Samantapāsādikā*", in: *Journal of the Pali Text Society.* Volume XXVIII. Lancaster 2006, pp. 49–59.

DALAL, Chimamlal D. / SHASTRY, R. Anantakrishna

1934 *Kāvyamimāmsā of Rājaśekhara.* Edited with introduction and notes by C. D. Dalal and R. A. Shastry. Revised and enlarged by K. S. Ramaswami Sastri Siromani. Third Edition. Baroda 1934. (Gaekwad's Oriental Series, No. I).

DAS, Asha

2000 *The Glimpses of Pali Literature (Gandhavaṃsa).* [By] Asha Das. Calcutta 2000.

DIKSHIT, Rao Bahadur K. N.

1938 "Excavations at Paharpur, Bengal", in: *Memoirs of the Archaelogical Survey of India.* No. 55. Delhi 1938, pp. i–vi, 1–99, plates I–LXVIII.

DIMITROV, Dragomir

2002 "Tables of the Old Bengali Script (on the basis of a Nepalese manuscript of Daṇḍin's *Kāvyādarśa*)", in: *Śikhisamuccaya. Indian and Tibetan Studies.* (Collectanea Marpurgensia Indologica et Tibetologica). Edited by Dragomir Dimitrov, Ulrike Roesler and Roland Steiner. Wien 2002, pp. 27–78. (Wiener Studien zur Tibetologie und Buddhismuskunde, Heft 53).

2010 *Śabdālaṃkāradoṣavibhāga* – Die Unterscheidung der Lautfiguren und der Fehler. Kritische Ausgabe des dritten Kapitels von Daṇḍins Poetik *Kāvyādarśa* und der tibetischen Übertragung *Sñan ṅag me loṅ* samt dem Sanskrit-Kommentar des Ratnaśrījñāna, dem tibetischen Kommentar des Dpaṅ Blo gros brtan pa und einer deutschen Übersetzung des Sanskrit-Grundtextes. Von Dragomir Dimitrov. 2010. [in print]

DIMITROV, Dragomir / TAMOT, Kashinath

2007 "Kaiser Shamsher, his Library and his Manuscript Collection", in: *Newsletter of the NGMCP*, Number 3, January-February 2007, pp. 26–36.

DUTT, Sukumar

1962 *Buddhist Monks and Monasteries of India. Their History and Their Contribution to Indian Culture.* By Sukumar Dutt. London 1962.

FLEET, John Faithfull

1888 "The Gupta Inscriptions: Text and Translations", in: *Corpus Inscriptionum Indicarum*. Vol. III: Inscriptions of the Early Gupta Kings and Their Successors. Calcutta 1888.

FOUCHER, Alfred

1900 *Étude sur l'iconographie Bouddhique de l'Inde.* D'après des documents nouveaux. Par A. Foucher. Paris 1900.

FRANKE, Otto

1902 *Geschichte und Kritik der einheimischen Pāli-Grammatik und -Lexicographie.* Von Otto Franke. Strassburg 1902.

FRASCH, Tilman

2002 "Anuradhapura – Angkor – Pagan. Versuch eines strukturgeschichtlichen Vergleichs.", in: *Die vormoderne Stadt. Asien und Europa im Vergleich.* [Herausgegeben von] Peter Feldbauer, Michael Mitterauer [und] Wolfgang Schwentker. München 2002, pp. 32–59. (Querschnitte, Band 10, Einführungstexte zur Sozial-, Wirtschafts- und Kulturgeschichte).

GEIGER, Wilhelm

1930 "The Trustworthiness of the Mahāvaṃsa", in: *The Indian Historical Quarterly*. Volume VI, Number 2. Calcutta 1930, pp. 205–228.

GEIGER, Wilhelm / RICKMERS, C. Mabel

1930 *Cūlavamsa Being the More Recent Part of the Mahāvamsa.* Translated by Wilhelm Geiger and from the German into English by C. Mabel Rickmers (née Duff). Part II. London 1930. [Repr.: Colombo 1953].

GEORGE, Christopher S.

1975 *Buddhist Sanskrit Manuscripts.* A Title List of the Microfilm Collection of the Institute for Advanced Studies of World Religions. New York 1975.

GOODALL, Dominic / ISAACSON, Harunaga

2003 *The Raghupañcikā of Vallabhadeva being the earliest commentary on the Raghuvaṃśa of Kālidāsa.* Critical Edition with Introduction and Notes by

Dominic Goodall & Harunaga Isaacson. Volume 1. Groningen 2003. (Groningen Oriental Studies, Volume XVII).

GUPTA, Chitrarekha

1985 "Inscriptions in the Bhaikṣukī-lipi and Associated Problems of Later Buddhism", in: *Buddhism. Early and Late Phases*. Edited by Kalyan Kumar Dasgupta. Calcutta 1985, pp. 108–118.

HAHN, Michael

2005 "Preliminary Remarks on Two Manuscripts Written in the So-called "Arrow-headed" Script", in: *Buddhism and Jainism*. Essays in Honour of Dr. Hojun Nagasaki on His Seventieth Birthday. Kyoto 2005, pp. 712–701, [119–130].

HANISCH, Albrecht

2006 "Progress in Deciphering the So-called "Arrow-head" Script Allowing Access to Sarvarakṣita's *Maṇicūḍajātaka*, a Text of the Buddhist Sāṃmitīya School", in: *Journal of Buddhist Studies*, Vol. IV. Colombo 2006, pp. 109–161.

2007 "The Contents of the Extant Portions of the *Candrālaṃkāra*, an Unknown Commentary on the *Cāndravyākaraṇa*, as Preserved in a Manuscript Fragment Written in the "Arrow-head" Script", in: *Saṃbhāṣā, Nagoya Studies in Indian Culture and Buddhism*. Volume 26. Nagoya 2007, pp. 127–161.

HIDAS, Gergely

2008 *Mahāpratisarā-Mahāvidyārājñī, The Great Amulet, Great Queen of Spells*. Introduction, Critical Editions and Annotated Translation. DPhil Thesis submitted by Gergely Hidas of Balliol College, Oxford for the degree of Doctor of Philosophy in Hilary Term 2008. Oxford 2008. [Unpublished PhD thesis]

HODGSON, Brian Houghton

1828 "Notices of the Languages, Literature, and Religion of the Bauddhas of Nepal and Bhot", in: *Asiatic Researches; or Transactions of the Society, Instituted in Bengal, for enquiring into the history and antiquities, the arts, and sciences, and literature of Asia*. Vol. XVI. Calcutta 1828, pp. 409–449.

HU-VON HINÜBER, Haiyan

2006 "Some Remarks on the Sanskrit Manuscript of the Mūlasarvāstivāda-Prātimokṣasūtra found in Tibet", in: *Jaina-Itihāsa-Ratna*. Festschrift für Gustav Roth zum 90. Geburtstag. Herausgegeben von Ute Hüsken,

Petra Kieffer-Pülz und Anne Peters. Marburg 2006. (Indica et Tibetica, Band 47), pp. 283–337.

HUNTINGTON, Susan L.

1984 *The "Pāla-Sena" Schools of Sculpture*. By Susan L. Huntington. Leiden 1984. (Studies in South Asian culture, 10).

KIPLING, Rudyard

1902 *Just so Stories for Little Children*. By Rudyard Kipling. New York 1902.

LAW, Bimala Charan

1925 *The Dāṭhāvaṁsa (A history of the Tooth=relic of the Buddha)*. Edited and Translated by Bimala Charan Law. Together with a Note on the Position of the Dāṭhāvaṁsa in the History of Pāli Literature by W. Stede. Lahore 1925. (The Punjab Sanskrit Series, No. 7).

1932 "Pali Chronicles", in: *Annals of the Bhandarkar Oriental Research Institute*. Volume XIII. Poona 1932, pp. 250–299.

LEUMANN, Ernst

1909 *Unvergessene, gestorben in den Jahren 1891-1908*. Lebensdaten, Bilder und Beileidbriefe. Von Ernst Leumann. Straßburg 1909.

LÉVI, Sylvain

1929 "Autour d'Aśvaghoṣa", in: *Journal Asiatique*. Tome CCXV. Paris 1929, pp. 255–285.

LIEBERMAN, Victor M.

1976 "A New Look at the Sāsanavaṃsa", in: *Bulletin of the School of Oriental and African Studies*. Volume 39, Number 1. London 1976, pp. 137–149.

LIEBICH, Bruno

1895 *Das Cāndra-Vyākaraṇa*. Von Bruno Liebich. [Göttingen] 1895. ([Sonderdruck a]us den Nachrichten der K. Gesellschaft der Wissenschaften zu Göttingen. Philologisch-historische Klasse. 1895. Heft 3).

1896a "The Chandra-Vyakarana", in: *The Indian Antiquary*. Vol. XXV. Bombay 1896, pp. 103–105.

1896b "Wenzel: Heinrich W.", in: *Allgemeine Deutsche Biographie*. Einundvierzigster Band. Walram – Werdmüller. Leipzig 1896, pp. 736–738.

1902 *Cāndra-vyākaraṇa. Die Grammatik des Candragomin. Sūtra, Uṇādi, Dhātupāṭha*. Herausgegeben von Bruno Liebich. Leipzig 1902. (Abhandlungen für die Kunde des Morgenlandes, XI. Band, No. 4).

1918 *Candra-Vṛtti.* Der Original-Kommentar Candragomin's zu seinem grammatischen Sūtra. Herausgegeben von Bruno Liebich. Leipzig 1918. (Abhandlungen für die Kunde des Morgenlandes. Vierzehnter Band).

LOKESH CHANDRA

1982 *Indian Scripts in Tibet.* Reproduced by Lokesh Chandra from the Collection of Prof. Raghuvira. New Delhi 1982. (Śatapiṭaka Series, Volume 297).

LUCE, Gordon Hannington

1969 *Old Burma - Early Pagán.* By Gordon H. Luce assisted by Bo-Hmu Ba Shin, U Tin Oo [*et al.*]. Volume One: Text. New York 1969. (Artibus Asiae. Supplementum, Vol. 25).

LUCE, Gordon Hannington / TIN HTWAY

1976 "A 15th Century Inscription and Library at Pagán, Burma", in: *Malalasekera Commemoration Volume.* Edited by O. H. de A. Wijesekera. Colombo 1976, pp. 203–256.

MAJUMDAR, Ramesh Chandra

1943 *The History of Bengal.* Volume I: Hindu Period. Edited by R. C. Majumdar. Dacca 1943.

1971 *History of Ancient Bengal.* By R. C. Majumdar. Calcutta 1971.

MALALASEKERA, Gunapala Piyasena

1937–38 *Dictionary of Pāli Proper Names.* By G. P. Malalasekera. Volume I: A–DH, Volume II: N–H. London 1937–38. (Indian Text Series).

1928 *The Pāli literature of Ceylon.* By G. P. Malalasekera. London 1928. [Repr.: Colombo 1958].

MINAYEFF, Ivan Pavlovič

1886 "Gandha-Vaṃsa", in: *Journal of the Pali Text Society.* Volume II. London 1886, pp. 54–80.

NAMIKAWA, Takayoshi

1993 "The Transmission of the New Material Dharmapada and the Sect to which it Belonged", in: *Buddhist Studies* (*Bukkyō Kenkyū*), Vol. XXII. Hamamatsu 1993, pp. 151–166.

NARASIMHASWAMI, H. K.

1960–61 "B.-Inscriptions on Stone and Other Materials, 1960-61", in: *Annual Report on Indian Epigraphy.* Edited by H. K. Narasimhaswami. Delhi 1964, pp. 52–115.

NORMAN, Kenneth Roy

1983 *Pāli Literature, Including the Canonical Literature in Prakrit and Sanskrit of All the Hīnayāna Schools of Buddhism.* [By] K. R. Norman. Wiesbaden 1983. (A History of Indian Literature, Volume VII, Fasc. 2).

OKANO, Kiyoshi

1998 *Sarvarakṣitas Mahāsaṃvartanīkathā.* Ein Sanskrit-Kāvya über die Kosmologie der Sāṃmitīya-Schule des Hīnayāna-Buddhismus. [Von] Kiyoshi Okano. Second revised edition. Sendai 1998. (Tohoku-Indo-Tibetto-Kenkyūsho-Kankokai Monograph Series I).

OL'DENBURG, Sergĕj Fjodorovič

1894 "Otryvki kašgarskich sanskritskich rukopisej iz sobranija N.Th. Petrovskago. I.", in: *Zapiski vostočnago otdĕlenija imperatorskago russkago archeologičeskago obščestva.* Tom vos'moj. 1893–1894. S.-Peterburg 1894, pp. 47–67.

PANDEY, Janardan

1997 *Bauddhalaghugrantha Samgraha* (A Collection of Minor Buddhist Texts). Editor: Janardan Pandey. Sarnath, Varanasi 1997. (Rare Buddhist Text Series, 14).

PECENKO, Primoz

1997 "Sāriputta and his works", in: *Journal of the Pali Text Society.* Volume XXIII. Oxford 1997, pp. 159–179.

2002 "Līnatthapakāsinī and Sāratthamañjūsā: The *Purāṇaṭīkās* and the *Ṭīkās* on the Four Nikāyas", in: *Journal of the Pali Text Society.* Volume XXVII. Oxford 2002, pp. 61–113.

2007 "The Theravāda Tradition and Modern Pāli Scholarship: A Case of "Lost" Manuscripts Mentioned in Old Pāli Bibliographical Sources", in: *Chung-Hwa Buddhist Journal,* Volume 20. Taipei 2007, pp. 349–378.

PENSA, Corrado

1964 "Indian Studies in Italy", in: *Indian Studies Abroad.* [Published by the] Indian Council for Cultural Relations. London 1964, pp. 41–48.

*Proceedings*

1900 *Proceedings of the Asiatic Society of Bengal.* Edited by the Honorary Secretary. January to December, 1899. Calcutta 1900.

RAPSON, Edward James

1906 "Obituary Notices: Cecil Bendall", in: *The Journal of the Royal Asiatic Society of Great Britain and Ireland for 1906.* London 1906, pp. 527–533.

RAY, Niharranjan

1936 *Sanskrit Buddhism in Burma*. By Nihar-Ranjan Ray. Calcutta 1936.

RHYS DAVIDS, Thomas William

1884a "Report of the Pâli Text Society for 1884", in: *Journal of the Pali Text Society*. Volume I. London 1884, pp. ix–xvi.

1884b "The Dāṭhāvaṃsa", in: *Journal of the Pali Text Society*. Volume I. London 1884, pp. 109–151.

1897 *Lectures on the Origin and Growth of Religion as Illustrated by Some Points in the History of Indian Buddhism*. By T. W. Rhys Davids. London 1897.

RIDDING, Caroline Mary

1931 "Professor Cowell and His Pupils", in: *Bulletin of the School of Oriental Studies*. Volume VI, Part 2: A Volume of Indian Studies Presented by His Friends and Pupils to Edward James Rapson, Professor of Sanskrit in the University of Cambridge, on His Seventieth Birthday, 12th May, 1931. London 1931, pp. 461–468.

ROHANADEERA, Mendis.

1985 "Mahāsāmi Sangha Rāja Institution in Sri Lanka. Its Origin, Development, Status, Duties and Functions.", in: *Vidyodaya Journal* (Arts, Sciences, & Letters). Volume 13, Number 1. Nugegoda 1985, pp. 27–43.

SACHAU, Edward Carl

1887–88 *Alberuni's India. An Account of the Religion, Philosophy, Literature, Geography, Chronology, Astronomy, Customs, Laws and Astrology of India about A.D. 1030*. An English Edition, with Notes and Indices. By Edward C. Sachau. In Two Volumes. London 1887–88.

SĀṄKṚTYĀYANA, Rāhula

1937 "Second Search of Sanskrit Palm-leaf MSS in Tibet", in: *Journal of the Bihar and Orissa Research Society*. Vol. XXIII, Part I. [Bankipore] 1937, pp. 1–57.

ŚĀSTRĪ, Haraprasāda

1931 *A Descriptive Catalogue of the Sanskrit Manuscripts in the Collections of the Asiatic Society of Bengal*. By Haraprasāda Shāstrī. Volume VI. Vyākaraṇa Manuscripts. Calcutta 1931.

SFERRA, Francesco

2000 "Sanskrit Manuscripts and Photos of Sanskrit Manuscripts in Giuseppe Tucci's Collection. A Preliminary Report.", in: *On the Understanding of Other Cultures*. Proceedings of the International Conference on Sanskrit and Related Studies to Commemorate the Centenary of the Birth of Stanislaw Schayer (1899-1941), Warsaw University, Poland, October 7-10, 1999. Edited by Piotr Balcerowicz & Marek Mejor. Warszawa 2000. (Studia Indologiczne, tom 7), pp. 397–447.

SHASTRI, Kali Charan

1972 *Bengal's Contribution to Sanskrit Grammar in the Pāṇinian and Cāndra Systems.* Part One: General Introduction. By Kali Charan Shastri. Calcutta 1972. (Calcutta Sanskrit College Research Series No. LXIII; Studies No. 44).

SIRCAR, Dinesh Chandra

1958 "Four Bhaikshuki Inscriptions", in: *Epigraphia Indica.* Vol. XXVIII. 1949–50. Edited by B. Ch. Chhabra and D. C. Sircar. Delhi 1958, pp. 220–226, 1 plate.

1966 "Bhaiksuki Inscriptions in Indian Museum", in: *Epigraphia Indica.* Vol. XXXV. 1963–1964. Edited by D. C. Sircar and G. S. Gai. Delhi 1966, pp. 79–84, 2 plates.

1976 "Indological Notes: No. 21 – *R.C. Majumdar's Chronology of the Pāla Kings*", in: *Journal of Ancient Indian History.* Volume IX, Parts 1-2, 1975-76, D. R. Bhandarkar Centenary Number. Calcutta 1976, pp. 200–210.

1977 "Indological Notes: No. 23 – *Bhaikṣukī Inscription on a Bronze Buddha Image from the Pagoda of Shin-ma-taung (Burma)*", in: *Journal of Ancient Indian History.* Volume X, 1976-77. Calcutta 1977, pp. 110–111.

SKILLING, Peter

1997 "On the School-affiliation of the "Patna *Dhammapada*"", in: *Journal of the Pali Text Society.* Volume XXIII. Oxford 1997, pp. 83–122.

SMYTH, Herbert Weir

1893 *Weber's Sacred Literature of the Jains.* Translated by Herbert Weir Smyth. Reprinted from the Indian Antiquary. Bombay 1893.

STEINKELLNER, Ernst

2004 "A Tale of Leaves. On Sanskrit Manuscripts in Tibet, their Past and their Future.", Eleventh Gonda lecture, held on 21 November 2003 on the premises of the Royal Netherlands Academy of Arts and Sciences. [By] Ernst Steinkellner. Amsterdam 2004.

TENNAKŌN, Rä.

1962 *Siri Rahal Pabaňda.* [Edited by] Rä. Tennakōn. Colombo 1962. [[1]1957].

THAN TUN, U

1998 "An original inscription dated 10 September 1223 that king Badon copied on 27 October 1785", in: *Études birmanes en hommage à Denise Bernot*. Réunies par Pierre Pichard et François Robinne avec le concours de Bénédicte Brac de la Perrière, Sylvie Pasquet et Catherine Raymond. Paris 1998, pp. 37–55. (Études Thématiques, 9).

THAW KAUNG, U

1998 "Bibliographies compiled in Myanmar", in: *Études birmanes en hommage à Denise Bernot*. Réunies par Pierre Pichard et François Robinne avec le concours de Bénédicte Brac de la Perrière, Sylvie Pasquet et Catherine Raymond. Paris 1998, pp. 403–414. (Études Thématiques, 9).

TISSA, Paññāmoli Toṭagamuve / TISSA, Valagedara Somāloka

1960 *Abhidhammattha Sangaha by Bhadantachariya Anuruddha Mahathera. With the Sinhalese Paraphrase by Teekachariya Sariputta Sangharaja Maha Swami.* Edited by T. Pannamoli Tissa. Revised by W. Somaloka Tissa. Fifth Edition. Colombo 1960.

TUCCI, Giuseppe

1956 *To Lhasa and Beyond. Diary of the Expedition to Tibet in the Year MCMXLVIII.* [By] Giuseppe Tucci. With an Appendix on Tibetan Medicine and Hygiene by R. Moise. Roma 1956.

VIMALASĀRA, Ācariya

1929 *The Sásanavansa dípo or The History of the Buddhist Church in Páli Verse, Compiled from Buddhist Holy Scriptures, Commentaries, Histories, &c., &c.* By Ácariya Vimalasára Thero. Colombo B. E. 2473 [AD 1929]. [1 1880].

VON HINÜBER, Oskar

2000 *A Handbook of Pāli Literature.* [By] Oskar von Hinüber. Berlin [etc.] 2000. [1 1996] (Indian Philology and South Asian Studies, Volume 2).

WADDELL, Lawrence Austin

1892 "Discovery of Buddhist Remains at Mount Uren in Mungir (Monghyr) district, and Identification of the site with a celebrated Hermitage of Buddha", in: *Journal of the Asiatic Society of Bengal*, Volume LVI, No. I. Calcutta 1892, pp. 1–24, 4 plates.

WARDER, Anthony Kennedy

1980 *Indian Buddhism.* [By] A. K. Warder. Second Revised Edition. Delhi 1980.

WEBER, Albrecht

1883 "Ueber die heiligen Schriften der Jaina", in: *Indische Studien*. Beiträge für die Kunde des indischen Alterthums. Sechszehnter Band. Leipzig 1883, pp. 211–479.

WIELIŃSKA-SOLTWEDEL, Małgorzata

2006 *The Bhāṣāvṛttivivaraṇapañjikā of Viśvarūpa, the first adhyāya and a detailed examination*. Dissertation zur Erlangung der Würde des Doktors der Philosophie der Universität Hamburg vorgelegt von Małgorzata Wielińska-Soltwedel aus Warschau. Hamburg 2006. (PhD thesis, *http://www.sub.uni-hamburg.de/opus/volltexte/2006/2884*)

WIJESEKERA, Oliver Hector de Alwis

1955 "Pali and Sanskrit in the Polonnaruva Period", in: *The Ceylon Historical Journal*. Volume IV. Special Number on the Polonnaruva Period issued in Commemoration of the 800th Anniversary of the accession of King Parākrama Bāhu the Great. 1153–1953. Edited by S. D. Saparamadu. Dehiwala 1955.

WINTERNITZ, Moriz / KEITH, Arthur Berriedale

1905 *Catalogue of Sanskrit Manuscripts in the Bodleian Library*. Vol. II. Begun by Moriz Winternitz, continued and completed by Arthur Berriedale Keith. With a Preface by E. W. B. Nicholson. Oxford 1905.

YAṂ, Ūḥ (also written Ūḥ Yam, Ūḥ Ran, U Yan)

1905 *Piṭakat samuiṅḥ cā tamḥ*. [By Ūḥ Yaṃ. Edited by] Ūḥ Bha Kyō [*et al.*]. Rankun 1267 [AD 1905].

# INDEX

*Abhidhammatthasaṅgaha*, 33
*Abhidharmārthasaṃgrahayasannaya*, 32, 41
*Abhidharmasamuccayakārikā*, 19–21, 48
Ajayagarbha, *44n124*
*Akṣaraviśvamātra*, 6, *7n12*
al-Bīrūnī (Alberuni), 4, *48n136*
Alderman Library of the University of Virginia, 121
Allahābād, 13
Anurādha(pura), 37
Anuṣṭubh, *63n160*
Arabic numbers, 61, 64
arrow-headed (character), 4, 6
Arrow-headed script, 5
ARROW-HEADED SCRIPT PROJECT, 21, 25
arrow-top character, 10
*Asiatic Researches*, 6
*Aṣṭasāhasrikāprajñāpāramitā*, *47n134*
Atiśa Dīpaṃkaraśrījñāna, 34, *44n124*
Avalokiteśvara Lokanātha, 13

B. R. Sen Museum, 13
Badhauli, 12
*Bālāvabodhana*, 33
BANDURSKI, Frank, *50n145*
BANERJI, Rakhal Das, *13n32*, *14n37*
Bangladesh, 43, 45
*Bauddhagrantha*, 16
BENDALL, Cecil, 3–6, 9–10, 13–15, *19n50*, 25–26, 28, 49, 58, 61, *62n158*, 73, 117
Bengal, 13, 32, 34, 45, 49, 57, 59
Bhāgalpur, 12
Bhaikṣukī inscriptions, 12–13, *14n37*
Bhaikṣukī letter-numerals, 50–61, 64
Bhaikṣukī manuscript(s), 9, 17, 20–22, 25–27, 31, 39, 40*n112*, 42, 46–48, 50, 51*n146*, 57, 62
Bhaikṣukī script, 3–4, 6, 8, 11, 14*n37*, 15, 19*n50*, 47, *48n136*, 50–51, 58–59, 61–62, 73ff.
*Bhāṣāvṛtti*, *32n80*
BHIKKHU PĀSĀDIKA, *45n125*
Bihar, 12–13, *21n55*, 47
Bihar Sharif, 58
BODE, Mabel, *35n95*
Bogra District, 45
Brāhmī script, 59
Buddha, 4, 12–13, 26, 34, 45, 64
Buddhadāsa, 37
Buddhanāga, 33
BÜHLER, Georg, 4, 11, *19n50*, 73
Burma, 12–13, 34–35, 37–38, 49

Calcutta Museum, 12, 13
Cambridge, 15, 17–19, 26–27, 58, 61, 64, 66, 74, 121
Cambridge University Library, 15, *18n48*, 49, 64, 121
Candragarbha, *44n124*
Candragomin, 9, 25–26, 33, 34, 40, 42, 44
*Candrakārikā*, *38n105*
*Candrālaṃkāra*, 4, 9–11, 15, 17, 19, 25–28, 31–32, 34–35, 38–40, 42–44, 46–52, 61–67, 73, 117, 119, 121
*Candrālaṃkṛti*, 41, *44n123*
*Candrapañcika*, 33
*Cāndravṛtti*, 25, 28, 34, 39

*Cāndravyākaraṇa*, 9, *17n44*, 18, 25, 26*n66*, 33–34, 38, *43n118*, *44n122*, 61–62, 64, 67
*Cāndravyākaraṇapañjikā*, 25, 27–28, 31, 34, *38n105*, 39*n107*, 40*n112*, 41, 50–53, 59*n153*, 60–61, 64
**Cāndravyākaraṇapañjikālaṃkāra*, 42
*Candrikāpañcikā*, 37
CHAKRAVARTI, N. P., *4n5*, *12n24*
Chandimau, 45
CONZE, Edward, 21
COWELL, Edward, 3
*Cūlavaṃsa*, 38, *46n133*
cuneiform headed character, *4n3*

Daṇḍin, 25
Daśabalagarbha, *44n124*
*Dāṭhāvaṃsa*, 34, 42
Devapāla, *43n120*
Dhammakitti, 33–35
Dharmadāsa, 25
Dharmapāla, 43
Dinajpur District, 45
Dīpaṃkaraśrījñāna, *see* Atiśa ~
Durgasiṃha, *27n68*
*Durghaṭavṛtti*, *32n80*

FLEET, John Faithfull, *12n24*
FRANKE, Otto, *36n97*

*Gandhavaṃsa*, 35–36, 42
GARGANO, Antonio, *20n53*
Gayā, 12*n24*, 14
Ghoshīkuṇḍī, 13
Gongkar (Goṅ dkar), 19–21, *48n139*
Göttingen, *17n44*, *38n105*, 121
Gurdih, 12

HAHN, Michael, 17, 21–22, 25, 73
Halle, *9n19*

HANISCH, Albrecht, *16n43*, 17*n45*, 18, 21–22, 25, *26n66*, *43n118*, *44n122*, *62n157*, *63n159*, 67, 73, *117n167*
HIDAS, Gergely, *46n130*
Hīnayāna, 8, 47
HODGSON, Brian Houghton, 6–8
Husainpur, 12

India, 12, 32, 45, 47–48
Indian Museum, 13
Institute for Advanced Studies of World Religions (IASWR), 15, 16*n42*, 17*n43*, 18*n48*, 49, 65, 121
Istituto Italiano per l'Africa e l'Oriente, 21

Jagaddala, 48
Jambhala, 13
Japan, 20
Jetavana, 33, 36, 46

Kaiser Library, 26
Kajra, 12–13
Kara, 13
*Kātantra*, *27n68*
Kathmandu, 14–19, 26–27, 49, 61, 65–66, 73–74, 121
*Kāvyādarśa*, 25, 31
*Kāvyamīmāṃsā*, *31n78*
Khotang (Khotāṅga, Khoṭāṅga), 16–17
KIELHORN, Franz, 9*n16*
KIPLING, Rudyard, 120
Kiul, 12–13

Lcan luṅ Paṇḍita Ṅag dbaṅ blo bzaṅ bstan pa'i rgyal mtshan, 7
Lhasa, *21n55*, 50
LIEBICH, Bruno, 9–11, 25–29, 61–63
LOKESH CHANDRA, 7*n12–13*
London, 9, 10, *28n70*